# Our Tribe

*A BASEBALL MEMOIR*

## TERRY PLUTO

*Simon & Schuster*

SIMON & SCHUSTER
Rockefeller Center
1230 Avenue of the Americas
New York, NY 10020

Copyright © 1999 by Terry Pluto
All rights reserved,
including the right of reproduction
in whole or in part in any form.
SIMON & SCHUSTER and colophon are
registered trademarks of Simon & Schuster, Inc.
Designed by Edith Fowler
Manufactured in the United States of America

10   9   8   7   6   5   4   3   2

Library of Congress Cataloging-in-Publication Data
is available.
ISBN 0-684-84505-9

PHOTO CREDITS

1, 2: Terry Pluto
3, 6, 20: Cleveland Indians
4, 13, 15, 16, 25: Cleveland State University/
    Cleveland Press Collection
5, 7, 8, 9, 10, 11, 12, 14, 18, 19, 21, 22, 23: Russell J.
    Schneider Collection
17, 24, 26, 27, 28, 29, 30, 31, 32, 33, 34: Ron Kuntz

To my father, Tom Pluto
A REAL TRIBE FAN

# Acknowledgments

No author could hope for a more thorough and caring researcher than Wally Mieskoski of Action Media in Cleveland. His ability to uncover wonderful nuggets from old newspapers and magazines is truly amazing.

This manuscript also was critiqued by Roberta Pluto and Sam Amico, who offered wise and helpful suggestions. Bill Becker of Cleveland State Library was also a big help, as were Russell Schneider and Ron Kuntz.

This book would not have existed without the support and vision of Simon & Schuster editor Jeff Neuman, who has been my guide for many years. The same for Faith Hamlin, who is the Rocky Colavito of agents.

# Contents

# CHAPTER 1

# One More Run

Iᴛ ɪѕ ᴀ Sunday night in late October, and the Cleveland Indians are in the World Series.

I'm still not used to this.

Neither is my father.

Nothing in our lives prepared us for the Indians in the World Series—and here they are in it for the second time in three years.

These were not his Indians.

These were not my Indians.

Our Tribe didn't go to the World Series. But this is the 1997 World Series, the seventh game, the Indians vs. the Florida Marlins. I sit in the press box at Miami's Pro Player Stadium, watching the Indians try to hold a 2–1 lead in the late innings, knowing they never will. They need another run. They always need another run. My heart beats a little faster. My throat is dry, even on this humid night. I am one of the lucky ones: I am a sportswriter. It is a blessing and a passion, watching these Indians and being paid to write about them. It still astonishes my father that his son goes to ballgames and a story appears in the newspaper the next day, a story about the Indians.

Our Indians.

And this is my job.

"I had to *work* for a living," my father often told me.

Sometimes that annoyed me. The implication was clear: He worked, I play. He paid the dues, I rode on his back to a better life.

I let it pass.

I always let it pass.

To his credit, he never elaborated. For us, it was easier to go to a baseball game and pour salt on popcorn rather than on old wounds. It was more fun (and safer) to talk about the Indians than ourselves. Some psychologists might have a problem with that; they'd say we needed to cut a vein and let it bleed. Spill our guts. Say what was really on our minds. I don't think so. In those moments when we did really talk, I got a pretty good idea what was on my father's mind. He worked at a job he hated for most of his life, because it was the right thing to do. He supported his wife and two kids. He played by the rules and in the end, he thought he didn't get much out of it.

Meanwhile, I caught a break. I never have to punch in or punch out. I don't have set office hours. I go to games and go to lunch with men whose names are in the newspapers. I can write in the morning or in the evening, and no boss is looking over my shoulder. What my father would have given to have that life. But nothing I could do would ever give him that life. Nothing I could say would ever change what happened to him. He grew up during the Depression; I grew up in the 1960s. He lost four years to the Army during World War II; I spent four years in college. He was the first in his family to graduate from high school; it was a given that I'd have a chance at higher education. For him, the dream was a steady job, a good family, and a house in the suburbs. It was the dream of millions from his generation, men and women who knew only the Depression and the world at war during their youth. They sacrificed for us to go to college, to find work that was more than a job, to be happy. My father wanted all that for me, he really did—but a part of him wished he could have had it for himself, and a part of him couldn't help but be envious when he saw his son at ballgames, or when he saw his son's name and picture in the newspaper. That's because part of him knows he worked harder to give me that chance than I did to get it. I can't disagree with that. He never really said this, but I knew . . . just as I knew talking about it would do little good. So we talked about the Indians. And yes, he still threw in his line about having to work for a living, but I refused to bite. Sometimes I was annoyed—but I was always silent.

Only now, I wish he'd tell me how he had to WORK for a living—just once more.

Only now, I wish he'd say just about anything.

On this night in October, with the Indians in the seventh game of the 1997 World Series, my father is alive, but he no longer really speaks.

One word.

MAN.

Over and over, he says Man . . . MAN . . . MAN!

And reading: He can't read.

My father used to love to read my stories. I found this out—not from him, but from others. He'd tell them. He'd show them my stories and my books. But he didn't talk about them with me. Sometimes, he'd even say, "I heard the Indians were about to do this . . ."

I'd say, "Dad, I know. I wrote that story."

Talk about being put in your place. Here, my own father didn't even remember what his son wrote. Now I just wish he'd say that one more time, that he'd heard something about the Indians—something I'd written. Instead, he looks at my picture in the newspaper over my columns. He recognizes me. He shows the picture to the few people who still come to see him. But he can't read the story under the picture.

Can't talk. Can't read.

Now, I wish he could tell me about his job—those long hours in a dark grocery warehouse making sure that the right trucks took the right products to the right supermarkets. That was his life. All he heard was when something went wrong. The wrong truck went to the wrong place. The right truck had the wrong products. The truck was late, or the truck didn't get there at all. As I sit in the press box on the night of October 26, 1997, waiting to see if the Indians will actually win a World Series, I think of my father.

I am not with him, but I can see him.

He sits in his special recliner chair. His right hand is in his lap, nestled softly on a pillow. The right arm is paralyzed, and he keeps the arm in front of him so he doesn't forget about it.

There have been times when he's lost track of that right arm, then sat on it—then screamed. The arm is paralyzed, but not dead. By keeping the arm on a pillow in his lap, he knows where it is and can keep it out of trouble. Sometimes, I think about that—about having to worry about sitting on your arm or getting your fingers caught in the spokes of a wheelchair.

He sits in that chair wearing Depends under his Nike sweatpants, because he can't always make it to the bathroom in time. He sits in that chair with pain shooting down his right arm, an electric bolt that varies in intensity but never really stops. His right arm can't move, but it sure can hurt. He sits in that chair at the age of seventy-seven watching the Indians and the Florida Marlins in the seventh game of the 1997 World Series, and knowing I am at the game.

How do I know?

Because he occasionally points to the screen, trying to tell something to his caregiver, an angel of a woman named Karen Cochran.

"Man . . . MAN . . . MAN!" he says.

"Terry's at the game?" asks his caregiver.

"Yes," he says.

It's strange. Once in a while, he'll come out with another word—a Yes or No. When he does, he'll sometimes mean No when he says Yes. And sometimes he'll get it right. My father suffered a stroke in 1993. It was a major one, the kind that killed Richard Nixon. The difference was that Nixon had a series of strokes and mercifully passed away. My father just had the Big One. It wasn't big enough to take away his life—just the life that he once knew. It sentenced him to a life few of us would consider worth living. But on this night, my father isn't thinking about his stroke. He's thinking the same thing I am, even though we're 300 miles apart: In his Sarasota living room, he is thinking the Indians need another run. I'm thinking the same thing in the Miami press box.

He raised me with the Indians. We both have so much history with this team. We went to about 500 games together at the old Stadium, and watched another 500 on TV. My father taught me that the Indians will never hold a 2–0 lead—especially not in the seventh game of the World Series. Not with young Jaret Wright tiring, and Jose Mesa warming up in the bullpen.

When it is 2–1 in the eighth inning, my father and I are still thinking about one more run. Because this is a Sunday night game and my deadlines are tight, I am writing a story about the Indians winning the World Series. I am writing it, not believing a word because I know the Indians will never make the lead hold up. But I have to write it just in case, so I can send it to the newspaper office as soon as the game is over. They want the story RIGHT NOW—right after the last out. So I write the story about a World Series winner in Cleveland while watching the Indians blow their 2–0 lead . . . their 2–1 lead . . . and finally lose, 3–2, in the 12th inning.

When it happened, I was not surprised.

The Indians needed one more run, and they didn't get it. What else is new?

The day after the World Series, I was at my father's home in Sarasota. We were watching ESPN, and Peter Gammons was talking about the seventh game.

As Gammons spoke, my father held up one finger. I asked a couple of questions, trying to figure out what he meant with the one finger. "One more run?" I finally asked.

"Yes!" he roared.

"They needed one more run?" I asked.

"Man . . . MAN . . . MAN!"

"I know," I said. "I was thinking the same thing. They were never going to make that 2–0 lead hold up."

He shook his head and waved at the TV set.

"I knew they'd blow it, too," I said.

He laughed. We both laughed. We have history with this team. I was born in 1955, the year after the Indians won 111 games. It was an American League record for the most victories until the 1998 Yankees came along.

In 1954, that team with the greatest pitching staff ever assembled, according to my father—well, that team was swept in the World Series. Four & Out. One of the biggest flops by one of the best regular-season teams in World Series history, a team with tremendous pitching that should have ensured a long, competitive World Series.

Instead, it was Four & Out.

That was our Tribe.

I was born on June 12, 1955. That means that I was conceived toward the end of the 1954 regular season. I like to think it happened during the World Series. I'm not sure when it happened, and this was not the sort of thing I ever imagined of discussing with my parents—but it would have been appropriate, my parents first giving me life as the Indians were falling flat on their faces in the World Series. My father and I both took a masochistic Tribe fan's delight in talking about how I had to wait forty years for the Indians to go back to the World Series. My father was born in 1920, the year the Indians won their first World Series. Of course, he was only six months old when they won, so he has no memories of it—and it really doesn't count, as I liked to tell him.

He waited twenty-eight years for his Indians to go to the World Series.

That was in 1948.

The Indians actually won the 1948 World Series. He saw it. He liked to talk about it. I eventually got tired of hearing about it. Now, I wish he'd tell me about Bill Veeck, Gene Bearden, and Lou Boudreau one more time—and if he could talk, he probably would. He'd talk about those Indians and these Indians, about 1948 and the Tribe of the middle 1990s. Even with his body ravaged by a stroke, he'd rather talk about baseball than anything else.

Our family is small. My mother died of a heart attack in 1984. I have an older brother, Tom, but because my brother is ten years older, we both felt like only children. For my father and me, the Indians have been like a second family—a more interesting family. When I was growing up, he talked to me of players from the 1920s through the 1950s. Starting in the 1960s, we were on common baseball ground.

Since the stroke-enforced silence built a wall around his life, the Indians have been one of the few ways to penetrate it. I can talk to him about this team, or the teams of his youth. I can look at pictures of the players, and suddenly I realize that it's like a family album.

That was what I thought on the day after the Indians lost the 1997 World Series as I sat in his living room, looking at this man in a recliner with his right arm nestled on that pillow.

This man who is my father.

# CHAPTER 2

# The Stroke

WHEN MY FATHER had his stroke, I ran.

It's not something I've ever talked about, except to my wife. She was with me in the Black Hills of South Dakota, where we'd arrived to start a vacation in September of 1993. On our second day, there was a message on my answering machine back in Ohio. It was from my aunt Pat—my father's sister, who lived in Cleveland. My father had spent the summer of 1993 with her; I had seen him only a week before. Then he drove to his home in Sarasota, Florida.

The day after his arrival, he was playing cards with a friend when he keeled over. It was a stroke; that's all my aunt knew.

I called my brother, who lives in Sarasota. He had already been to see my father. He said it was a stroke, but no one knew the severity. No one in our family knew much of anything about strokes. I thought it was like a heart attack, which had killed my mother in 1984. I knew a stroke could paralyze you, but that was it. I figured, "Well, he may end up walking with a limp or something."

My brother said there was paralysis on the right side, but the doctors weren't sure if it was permanent.

"He also can't speak," my brother said.

"Can't speak?" I asked.

"That sometimes happens when you have a stroke," he said.

I had no idea that a stroke could take away your ability to talk.

"The doctors said it could be temporary," my brother said.

At this point, we should have driven home to Ohio, and I should have caught a plane to Sarasota. Or I could have flown from Rapid City to Sarasota, as my wife suggested, and she'd drive back to Ohio in our vehicle. That is what you do in a crisis. Instead, I asked my brother if I should cut my vacation short. He said he wasn't sure. He said he didn't know what I could do. He didn't see any reason for me to rush to Florida.

I drove to the Badlands of North Dakota. My wife thought I had lost my mind, but she went along with me. We had planned to go there—and I was going! So what if my father had a stroke? I thought, "Let my brother handle this."

I thought of how I had last seen my father only a week earlier. We'd gone bowling one morning, and the next day he went with me to a Cleveland Browns practice at their complex in Berea. The Browns had just signed Vinny Testaverde, and my father liked the new quarterback's arm. My father was fine, I told myself. I tried to convince myself that he couldn't really be seriously ill.

I went to North Dakota.

I also kept calling Florida. I kept hearing there wasn't much change. I kept denying that anything was wrong.

"He'll be in the hospital for a week, then he'll be fine," I thought to myself.

But I knew better. I knew something was wrong, very

wrong. I remembered how my mother died in 1984; at the time, I was working in Savannah, Georgia. I was at the newspaper office. It was a late Friday night, and I was taking the results of a girls basketball game on the telephone when I got another call.

It was my father.

He was crying.

My mother was in the hospital. She'd had a heart attack. Supposedly, she was stable, but . . .

But I did the right thing. I told my boss that my mother had suffered a heart attack. I stopped at home just long enough to throw some clothes in a suitcase, then I drove all night and through the morning from Savannah to Cleveland. I spent three days visiting my mother in the hospital. She seemed fine. The crisis seemed to have passed. I drove home to Savannah. I wasn't in the house for an hour when the phone rang again.

It was my father.

He was crying.

My mother was dead, another heart attack.

I repacked my bags, and my wife and I drove back to Cleveland for the funeral. I was grateful for those three days with my mother before she passed away. I was proud of myself for those all-night drives, because I knew it was exactly what my father would do in that situation—something he had trained me to do.

But when his stroke came, I froze—then ran.

As we drove to North Dakota, I thought of my father. I thought about how I didn't consider him a great father, how I thought he seemed to work all the time—and then came home and shoveled supper down while reading the newspaper. His next stop would be the sofa, where he'd watch a game on TV for about forty-five minutes, then he'd fall asleep.

My father worked long hours. My mother also worked long hours. My brother was older and out of the house.

In my self-absorbed world, I felt alone.

But I really wasn't. Driving to North Dakota, I thought about how my father would skip out of work in the afternoons to watch me play ball. I thought of how he'd come home from work, and I'd convince him to take me to an Indians game; he'd come home, change his clothes—and we'd be in the car, on the way to the Stadium. He could not have been home for more than fifteen minutes. He had to be exhausted. He could have said, "Let's listen to the game on the radio, I'm tired." Instead, he took me to the games. We listened to Herb Score and Pete Franklin on the radio, finishing up their pregame radio shows. Score would interview the Indians manager, and Franklin would supply a commentary on his *Clubhouse Confidential* show. My father owned a deep purple Chrysler 300, a nice big car he'd bought cheap because it looked like the world's largest violet on four tires. I remember sitting next to him, on the blindingly white front seats. In his purple and white car, it was as if every day were Easter Sunday.

I remember him smoking Newport cigarettes.

I remember him never saying a word about the job he hated.

I remember listening to those Indians pregame shows, talking with my dad about what was being said on the radio.

I remember my heart beating a little faster as we drove into the Stadium lot, and we could see the ballpark looming right in front of us—all 80,000 seats worth.

I remember the huge Chief Wahoo neon sign above it all, the Chief holding a bat and standing on one foot as he if were preparing to hit the ball into Lake Erie; and I remember those walks from the car to the Stadium, my little hand in his big paw, my hand lost in his—and feeling more secure than I ever did in my young life.

My father would buy tickets from a scalper, a guy in a fe-dora who always had his leg in a cast and used a cane. The guy wore what he thought was a dapper sports jacket, but it was one of those Checkerboard Square jobs that made him look like a bookie. I remember my father buying tickets from this man—box seats for half their cover price. For five bucks, we usually sat fifteen rows up, right behind home plate. That was the Indians in the 1960s, where the real bargains could be found with the scalpers. They picked up tickets from fans who didn't want to go to games, bought them for a buck each—and sold the tickets for what they could. With 80,000 seats, the Indians of my youth should have had this motto: GOOD SEATS ALWAYS AVAILABLE.

I remember those drives home, my father sitting across from me, his cigarette glowing in the dark. We'd listen to Pete Franklin's postgame show, and usually Franklin and the callers had a wonderful time second-guessing the manager.

I don't remember a word my father said to me at those games or during those drives, but I remember him just being there, being with his son. I thought of all this while I spent the night in North Dakota. I asked myself, what was wrong with me? Had I forgotten how to be a son? Had I forgotten what my father had meant to me? Was my vacation so important that I couldn't be at my father's side when his life was in the balance?

The next day, we started the long drive back to Cleveland.

Meanwhile, I kept calling Florida, checking with my brother. My father was the same, whatever that meant. He couldn't move his right arm or leg. He really couldn't talk, except for a few words. His heart was okay.

Otherwise, he was supposed to be fine.

I heard this from my brother as I spoke into a pay phone at the Burns Brothers Truck Stop outside Mitchell, South Dakota. He was in my father's room, and he handed the phone to my father.

"Dad, this is Terry," I said.

"Man," he said.

"Dad, how are you?" I asked.

"Man . . . MAN . . . MAN!" he said.

My brother had told me about this, about my father being stuck on the word MAN.

But to hear it, over and over . . .

"Dad," I said. "I'll be there as soon as I can."

He started to cry.

"I'm praying for you," I said. "I'll be there soon."

Through his tears, I heard the word MAN again—several times.

I hung up the phone.

In that small truck stop in eastern South Dakota, I looked out at the windshield wipers and fan belts hanging on the wall. I looked at the plastic jugs of oil. I looked at the CB radios and tape players in a glass case, and I looked at the nice display of floor mats. It was in Burns Brothers Truck Stop that I had to ask myself, what kind of son did I plan to be?

I took a deep breath and I went outside.

I remember blinding sun.

I remember pumping gas.

I remember knowing that my life would never be the same.

For the next four and a half years, I went to Florida every month to visit my father. I went to Florida to learn how to be a real son, and I went to Florida to learn something about love, about duty, about doing things as my father did them for his family.

My father could be silent, brooding, and sarcastic. I still cringe when I remember him calling me "Half-a-job Terry." His hugs were usually stiff and forced, at least until he had his stroke.

But my father was always *there*.

That's what I thought about on those long flights from Cleveland to Sarasota, and during those hours waiting to change planes in Charlotte.

Good mood, rotten mood, mad at me, mad at my mother—my father was always there. He was there to tell me that I did a lousy job cutting the lawn or dusting the house, and he was there to play catch with me in the driveway. I will always treasure those games of catch. He'd come home from work, exhausted, bone-tired, and more than a little angry. He'd plop down on the sofa, turn on the TV, lean back—and I swear, his entire body would just moan. The sound didn't just come from his mouth, it bellowed from all of the pores of his skin.

Then I'd say, "Dad, do you want to play catch?"

Now I know that he'd rather have swallowed a power saw than play catch. To him, playing catch must have felt like one more boulder someone had tossed on his already slumping shoulders. Work twelve hours, listen to idiots in the warehouse . . . and all he wanted to do was sit on the sofa and watch the news . . . and his kid wanted to play catch.

Most of the time, he'd moan again.

Most of the time, he'd then take a deep breath, somehow pull himself out of the sofa and stand up.

Most of the time, we'd head out to the driveway. He still had his pencil pouch holding several different pens and pencils in his pocket. My father was in his middle forties, about the age I am today. He had a potbelly. He had aching, arthritic knees. He'd beg me not to throw the ball low so he wouldn't have to bend down.

But we'd play catch.

I'd pretend I was Bob Feller. I had never seen Bob Feller, but he was my father's favorite pitcher. I had a strange windup with a high leg kick and a motion where I brought the ball behind my back—something my father said Feller had once done. Only I threw the ball like Terry Pluto, future rag-armed sportswriter. My pitches didn't POP when they hit his glove, it was more like a soft, embarrassed belch.

But we played catch. He'd lean over a bit in his work clothes. He'd have a cigarette in his mouth. The darkness would fall. The brightest light would be from his cigarette. If nothing else, I learned control; seldom did I throw anything he couldn't reach. I wanted to please him. I loved the moments when we were done, when he'd put his arm around me as we walked into the house. He seldom said a word. But I can still see the genuine smile on his face. I can see the beads of perspiration on his bald head. I can smell his clothes, smoky and sweaty. That was my father at his best. That was the father I wanted to serve.

So every month, it was a trip to Florida. I usually flew down on a Thursday night, arriving near midnight. I left the first thing on Monday morning.

When I was an infant, I had colic. Nights were nightmares, because I couldn't sleep. I just cried and cried and cried.

"We walked miles carrying you around the house," he said. "Then we'd put you down, and five minutes later you were bawling your head off again."

I thought about that during some of the nights when my father couldn't sleep, when he had fluid in his lungs. He'd cough and cough and cough until I swore he was about to gag up a lung. I'd spend many of those nights at the side of his bed, helping him drink water, cough syrup, tea with honey—anything I'd ever heard used to drown a cough.

Most of the time, nothing worked.

Okay, I might find fifteen or twenty minutes of peace, but just as I was about to fall back asleep in the next room, he'd begin to gag and gag again. I had never heard such coughing. I had never seen anyone cough until they were blue in the face—not until my father.

I never felt so helpless . . . and I never felt so like my father must have felt when he held me in his arms and all I could do was cry.

I don't remember a time in my life when someone had to dress me, but I know it happened. I also know I never dreamed there'd be a time when I had to dress my father, starting with diapers. I don't have children, so I don't recall ever touching a diaper until my father's Depends. Then I learned more about diapers than anyone should: Which ones worked well at night, which ones were best for the day. Which ones were the most comfortable, which ones were the most absorbent. And I also was subject to my father's whim, as he'd suddenly grow tired of one style and want another—for no reason that I could ever discern.

So I studied diapers. I learned how to change his bed every morning. I learned about rubber pads, extra sheets, and towels placed in strategic areas to keep the bed as dry as possible. I learned how to hug my father when we didn't make it to the bathroom in time, and his tears would flow as I went to change him. I learned a lot of bathroom and fart jokes, because he loved those—especially in these tough moments.

I learned how not to be embarrassed when we went out to eat and food dropped from his mouth. The right side of his mouth had also suffered some paralysis from the stroke, and food would pouch in that cheek, and sometimes drop out onto the bib I had tied around him.

I learned to rub his feet and his back and his bottom with cream to keep the skin from drying up.

I learned about dozens of prescription medicines. I learned how the Medicare system works. I learned about his health insurance. I even learned the name of the guy who came to my father's home every month to spray for bugs. My father used to do bowling averages in his head for his league. He kept an immaculate checkbook. His financial records were always in perfect order. But after the stroke, he couldn't do the most basic bookkeeping—and I learned to be my father's financial keeper.

I never thought I'd see that day . . .

I learned that minor league ballgames in Sarasota were great for people in a wheelchair—wide aisles, small crowds, and a friendly staff. I learned that a bingo parlor (one of my father's favorite haunts) could be the coldest, most depressing place to take someone with a disability, someone who can't quite keep up with the numbers. The closest I've ever come to getting into a physical fight in my adult life was with the manager of a bingo hall who told me, "The people around you are complaining because you're talking too loud."

"They said *what?*" I asked.

"YOU . . . ARE . . . TALKING . . . TOO . . . LOUD," he said.

"See that guy in the wheelchair?" I said. "He's had a stroke. He was a regular customer here for years. All I'm doing is repeating the numbers so he can play his card."

"Well . . ." he said.

I felt my hands turning to fists. I also felt tears in my eyes.

"Do you want to throw him out?" I asked. "Is that how you operate?"

A compromise was reached. We were sent to the back of the hall, a table by ourselves, where my repeating the numbers wouldn't send a bunch of blue-haired old ladies into a collective hissy fit.

We never went to a bingo parlor again.

After his stroke, my father spent nine months in a rest home, working with various therapists. While he made a lot of progress, he still had major disabilities. His doctor didn't think my father was capable of living at home. My brother and I thought he'd earned the right to go home. My father wanted to live in his own home. At several crucial moments in my father's care, my brother stepped in and found the right doctor to help us. He agreed to release my father to his home. We set up a rest home situation at his condo. One woman worked four days a week, another worked three. When I came down every month for the three days, the ladies would take that time off. My brother lived in Sarasota and dropped in to keep an eye on everyone. Even before his stroke, my father was a little like Dustin Hoffman in *Rain Man* when it came to his home, everything had its place, and it seemed as if Western Civilization was about to crumble if anything ended up in the wrong spot. After the stroke, he was even more rigid, more attached to his home. It was his sanctuary, his comfort zone. Rather than move him closer to me, I realized I had to go to him—even if it meant countless flights to Florida.

After a while, I became like my father in that place. His routines were my routines. I'd line up his dentures, his denture powder, his denture cleaner—all in their appropriate spots in the bathroom. No matter where he sat, he had to have a small box of tissues within arm's reach. His diapers had to be stacked in a special way on a certain shelf.

Thank God for sports events on TV, especially baseball. We'd sit and watch the games, any games. He'd point at the screen and I knew what he was saying. It always sounded like, "Man . . . MAN . . . MAN!" but we had been to so many games together, it wasn't hard to guess what was on his mind.

Baseball filled those long, lonely nights when there was just the two of us, and when we really had little to say to each other. Baseball was a medicine when his legs hurt, his chest ached, and depression was gnawing away at the edges of his heart. For the four-plus years after my father's stroke, baseball helped hold us together.

# CHAPTER 3

# The Spiders

To THIS DAY, the best memories of my father revolve around the Indians. After he had his stroke, baseball still was a savior to us. It gave me something to talk about, something that would keep his attention.

I spoke with NBC broadcaster Bob Costas about my father and our connection to baseball, and he responded in kind, recalling how he and his father played catch in the driveway.

"I don't care if some people consider it to be sloppy sentimentalism," Costas said. "It's very real to those of us who have that kind of relationship."

Costas likes the topic, the meaning of baseball and how it can be a glue that helps hold some families together.

"Some people can try to discount it," he said. "They can say they thought the Ken Burns' [baseball] series went overboard, or that all of this is just a cliché. But would they say that if a family had a connection through opera? Or music? Or art? What about the families who go to theater together? Is that more socially acceptable than baseball? To me, I see no difference."

Because there is none. Baseball is not art, it's not classical music—but when it glues a family together, it's special and it's important.

A fan named Mark Sumner wrote me a letter about what baseball meant to his family: "Like your dad, my father grew up during the Depression, served in the military, and had to pinch pennies and sacrifice his own enjoyments to take care of his family. He was an excellent ballplayer, but gave up playing in his leagues when his kids started playing ball so he could devote time coaching and teaching us. My mom also sacrificed. She was the only mom I knew who would shag balls while my dad threw batting practice to my brother and me. . . . My father had two heart attacks that interrupted some of the plans we made to go to Indians games at Fenway Park and Yankee Stadium. . . . Finally, we made it to both places. . . . Those trips remind me of the good times with my father."

Sumner also wrote that they nearly canceled one of their trips to New York when they heard the Indians were going to start a minor league lefty named Jason Jacome, known to Tribe fans as Jason How-Come-Me? Naturally, they went anyway. When it came to Indians baseball, the team had far more pitchers like Jason How-Come-Me? than Jaret Wright or Bartolo Colon. There is a certain comfort for Tribe fans when their team reverts back to the Indians of old, such as in Game 5 of the American League Championship Series in 1998 when the lineup included rookies Einar Diaz, Enrique Wilson, and Richie Sexson, with injury-prone veteran Chad Ogea on the mound. Those guys were supposed to beat the Yankees in the biggest game of the season?

Fat chance.

The Indians lost. The three rookies went 1-for-3. Ogea didn't survive the second inning. When it was over, Tribe fans had yet another memory—one that will seem more humorous than painful as the years pass, one that will be talked about between fathers and sons, Tribe fans from many generations.

Tribe fans always think they know the worst of it. They understand the Curse of Rocky Colavito. A fan who came to the Tribe in the 1960s, the 1970s, or the 1980s will remember Sam McDowell playing second base, Chris Chambliss being traded for four guys, or the 1987 Indians being picked to win the pennant by *Sports Illustrated*—and then losing 101 games.

Remember Ten Cent Beer Night? The evening the Indians had Bozo the Clown throw out the first ball? That June evening in 1997 when Manny Ramirez stole second base, then immediately ran back to first and was tagged out?

If those are some of your favorite moments, then the Cleveland Spiders are for you. If you are a true Indians fan with a sense of history, these guys are your founding fathers.

The 1899 Cleveland Spiders are the great-grandfathers of your current Indians. The 1899 Cleveland Spiders were 20-game winners—and 134-game losers. You knew they were in trouble right from the start when they held spring training in—of all places—Terre Haute, Indiana—make that in a high school gym in Terre Haute, Indiana, with only eight guys showing up for the first day of camp. The *Cleveland Press* called them "a shameful travesty," and added, "they're a handful of half-frozen has-beens." When they did win their first game, the Cleveland *Plain Dealer* reported, "it was due more to accident than good playing," and added, "they won, but it was through no fault of their own."

The *Cleveland Press* just called them "The Misfits."

Picky, picky.

This was a group of baseball gladiators who would be close to the heart of any real Tribe fan. How could you resist Harry Colliflower, known as "The Pitching Vegetable"? The Spiders found him working at a racetrack. He told them that he once pitched professionally for a team in Washington. He didn't tell them that when he faced the Washington Senators, he gave up 20 hits ... and walked nine ... and plunked six hitters with pitches ... and threw three wild pitches ... and was charged with 20 runs in a 31–4 loss. With the Spiders, he had a 1-11 record and 8.17 ERA. Cynics began to call him "pickled Colliflower." If nothing else, the Pitching Vegetable was enthusiastic: If he couldn't pitch, he'd play the field. Or at least he'd stand in the field and pray no one would hit the ball to him. They tried him in center field; he made three errors in a game. They tried him at first base; he made three errors in one game. They kept playing him and he kept making errors. But he did have a .303 batting average. After his stellar pro career was over, he became a minor league umpire and an after-dinner speaker who supposedly wowed the folks with his rousing rendition of "Casey at the Bat."

Or how about Still Bill Hill? In his first game for the Spiders, sportswriters noticed that there was nothing still about Bill's belly; it jiggled every time he walked. It kept him from seeing his shoes—or even the pitcher's mound. In his debut, Still Bill plunked two batters, uncorked a wild pitch, gave up too many hits to count. Final tally: one inning, seven runs. But he was known as a fine gentleman and a very good polo player.

There was James Ulysses Hughey. His nickname was "Cold Water Jim." According to sportswriters, James Ulysses Hughey had about as much ambition as a ball of lint. During one of his many difficult days on the mound, he simply sat down in the mud for a few minutes, just to catch his breath. To his credit, Cold Water Jim always took the ball. And the batters always hit it. He was 4-14 at midseason—and then went into a slump, losing his last 16 decisions.

Final record? How does 4-30 sound? But Cold Water Jim did tie for the team lead in victories with a fellow named Charlie Knepper.

Charlie Knepper was the tallest guy on the team ("well over 6-foot," according to sportwriters), and maybe the bravest.

In his first start for the Spiders, his teammates supported him with seven errors. And that led to nine unearned runs. Poor Charlie lost that game, 10–6. But he kept coming back for more. And Charlie believed in finishing what he started. When the season was over, Charlie Knepper had a 4-22 record—and had completed all 26 of his starts!

The catcher was Ossee Schreckengost, who was best known as baseball's pie-eating champion, although he ate mostly crow with those 1899 Spiders. In one stretch, he caught 18 games in 11 days for the worst baseball team ever to take the field. The other catcher was Joe Sugden, whose nickname was "Peanut Hands," because his gnarled fingers looked like peanuts. One fan said to him, "You must have caught a lot of balls with those hands." Honest Peanut Hands answered, "No, they show I missed a lot of baseballs."

The shortstop was Harry Lochhead. He made 81 errors, but then again, he batted only .238. The center fielder was Thomas Jefferson Dowd. For some reason, several Spiders were named after presidents. Anyway, Thomas Jefferson Dowd went by the nickname of "Buttermilk." He was bald, probably from all the losing. He played big league baseball for eight years, and his teams' best record was 57-75. Three of those eight teams finished in 11th place. Writers said he wore "anarchistic neckties." It's amazing he didn't use one to hang himself.

The Spiders were doomed because of something called Syndicate Baseball. It was an era when the same man could own more than one baseball team in the same league. A fellow named Frank DeHaas Robison owned the Cleveland Spiders from 1889 to 1898. Before the 1899 season, he also bought the St. Louis Browns, a 12th-place team. He liked St. Louis better than Cleveland; he'd had some beefs with the local politicians (who had banned Sunday baseball) and the newspapers (for being critical). He also thought the St. Louis fans would be better behaved and more supportive of his team than the dirty-nailed, blue-collar, unsavory European immigrants who were the backbone of the Cleveland crowds. Robison didn't exactly endear himself to the Cleveland fans when he hired scabs to operate his streetcar company, which caused some unions to boycott his baseball team. His revenge was to load his St. Louis team with his best players and stick Cleveland with the leftovers. If you saw what Florida Marlins owner Wayne Huizenga did after his team won the 1997 World Series—beating You Know Who, then dismantling his roster to bring the payroll in line—you have a taste of how the Spiders did business back in 1899. His team pretty much went from first to worst in the National League.

The 1899 Spiders opened their season before a throng of "about 500 fans," at League Park. And the Spiders won, 5–4, in 14 innings. Their April roster consisted of twelve players. They won only nine home games all year—but, they'd pretty much stopped playing at home by July. The crowds were lousy (wonder why?), so most of the Spiders' games were transferred to the road. The team traveled from city to city on rickety old trains; most of the players sat in their underwear, playing cards and swilling gin as they endured what seemed like baseball's version of *Groundhog Day*—another town, another game, another loss. Another newspaper story reading, "How can a team make seven errors, being of the simple kind that make both players and spectators laugh?" as the *Plain Dealer* asked.

As if that wasn't bad enough, the Spiders weren't even being paid their salaries—just a pittance of meal money. They were told they'd receive their checks as soon as they returned home, but ownership kept canceling the games in Cleveland and sending the team to yet another city to take a horrible beating. At one point, they were six weeks behind on their salaries.

Mike Ferraro would know the feeling.

He managed the Indians for half of the 1983 season. In what was yet another road trip from hell, Ferraro sat in front of his desk after a loss in Kansas City. It was a game where his

Tribe team had run off the field with two outs in an inning. They were led by first baseman Mike Hargrove, the same man who was supposed to be Ferraro's smartest player, and who later became the manager of the 1995 pennant-winning Tribe. Ferraro sat there almost in a trance, flipping down one card after another and saying, "We aren't a baseball team, we're the traveling circus. Winning? Losing? It doesn't matter. We just go from one town to another. We're entertainment for the other team."

Ferraro was mercifully fired at midseason.

Unfortunately, the Spiders made their manager, Joe Quinn, finish the schedule. And it was some finish, as they lost 40 of their last 41 games. In an October 1 defeat in St. Louis, the *Globe-Democrat* reported, "The contest was closely waged throughout, and was only settled after the third inning." One sportswriter insisted the Spider pitchers "were turning senile."

The final game of the season was started by Eddie Kolb, a nineteen-year-old who worked at a cigar stand in the Cincinnati hotel where the Spiders stayed. He was friends with Quinn, and when he heard Quinn moaning that his regular starting pitcher was sick, Kolb offered to take the mound. Quinn handed him the ball. He lost, 19–3. The *Cincinnati Enquirer* reported that Kolb "had the underpinning of a Kansas grasshopper and the complexion of a yellow fever convalescent."

Say this much for Kolb, he went the distance, allowing 18 hits and 19 runs in eight innings. Because his team lost—what a surprise!—Kolb mercifully didn't have to pitch the ninth.

As was the custom, the Spiders traveled from the ballpark to the hotel by horse-drawn wagons. After that game (and 134 others), the team was pelted by rotting fruit from fans. They finished 84 games out of first place and drew a total of only 6,000 fans at home.

This had a profound effect on some Spiders. After his baseball life, Manager Joe Quinn became an undertaker. But, amazingly, pro baseball in Cleveland did not require Quinn's subsequent services. The reason is that a man named Davis Hawley was a baseball fan; he was also president of the Cuyahoga Savings and Loan Association, and he served as secretary for the old Spiders. While the Spiders were indeed dead, Hawley set out to bring another team to Cleveland. He made calls. He found a few guys with money. He met with a fellow named Ban Johnson, president of something called the Western League.

Ban Johnson was desperate to bring anyone in who had any sort of baseball acumen and was from any sizable city.

"Mr. Hawley," said Johnson, "we are forming something called the American League, and we'd like Cleveland to be in it. We're sure there's room for another major league, and Cleveland should be a part of it."

With that, the team we know as the Indians was born. One of Hawley's investors, a fellow named Charley Somers who made a million in the coal business, became the offical owner— and Cleveland was back in the baseball business.

# CHAPTER 4

# The Name Game

You probably think the Indians were named to honor Louis Sockalexis, the Penobscot Indian who played for Cleveland from 1897 to 1899. The 1998 Cleveland Indians media guide states, "A Cleveland newspaper held a contest to rename the team. The winning entry in the contest was 'Indians.' The fan that sent it in explained it would be a testament to the game's first American Indian player."

Don't bet on it.

The team was renamed after the 1914 season. While Sockalexis was a colorful character with a cannon arm and a potent bat, he only played 94 games for the team. That's right, 94 games. And the last of those games was in 1899, which was fifteen years before the team was renamed. There was no great outcry of support for Sockalexis fifteen years after he last played for the Indians; this would be like the 1995 Indians changing their name to the Super Joes, after Super Joe Charboneau, who was the 1980 American League Rookie of the

Year. Sure, some Tribe fans still remember Charboneau. The hard-core fans tell stories of his drinking beer through a straw—and the straw was in his nose . . . or him opening bottles with his eye socket . . . or him pulling his own teeth with a set of pliers.

All great stories.

But Charboneau had one big year with the Tribe, and that was 1980. His last season in Cleveland was 1982, as injuries ended his career. Sockalexis played 66 games in 1897, batting .338. He played 21 games in 1898, hitting a rip-roaring .224. In 1899, he came back for seven games. That's it, 94 games over three years. A grand total of three home runs. And while it's not politically correct to say this, the man was a drunk. The 1998 U.S. Olympic hockey team could have taken lessons from Sockalexis when it came to getting a snootful and tossing furniture out a window, which was one of his favorite pastimes. He had a major drinking problem long before he played for Cleveland, which dispels another fairy tale: Supposedly, Sockalexis had never touched a drop of Old Panther Juice until he came under the spell of evil professional ballplayers. Legend has it that after he won a game with a grand slam, his teammates supposedly carried him on their shoulders to a local tavern, where they poured booze down his reluctant throat. After that incident, there was no turning back: This man who wouldn't even touch a cup of coffee was transformed overnight into an alcoholic.

Don't believe a word of it.

Truth is, he attended the College of Holy Cross in 1894, but was disciplined for "imbibing alcohol." He either quit or left Holy Cross shortly thereafter, heading to Notre Dame. His friend, Doc Powers, was a Holy Cross catcher who also transferred to Notre Dame, and Sockalexis supposedly followed. Sounds like a package deal by some recruiter who was well ahead of his time.

At Notre Dame, Sockalexis and one of his buddies busted up a South Bend watering hole called Pop Corn Jenie. They were drinking Old Oscar McGroggins, which apparently was strong enough to remove two coats of paint from a boiler. It also got Sockalexis's blood boiling as he began to break chairs over his knee, throwing the sticks of wood out the window. A couple of police arrived, and Sockalexis belted both of them in the jaw. He was carted off to the pokey, where the *South Bend Tribune* found out that Notre Dame's star player was behind bars for assaulting policemen and other indiscretions. Sockalexis was immediately expelled by the Good Fathers at Notre Dame, but his buddy, Doc Powers, had friends with the Cleveland Spiders. He told them of Sockalexis's wondrous athletic abilities, and mentioned that he was looking to begin a professional career because of some unfortunate circumstances with the South Bend police.

So the Cleveland team bailed him out of jail and signed him for $1,500. That was in 1897. Another legend is that the Cleveland team wanted to sign him, but Sockalexis had promised to stay at Notre Dame—so Manager Patsy Tebeau took him out, filled him with some other derivation of Old Panther Juice, then took his steady hand and helped Socklaxis sign a contract.

Don't believe a word of that, either.

This brings us to how teams received their nicknames around the turn of the century. There were no trademarked, researched, or carefully thought-out nicknames like today. It was very casual, often coming from how sportswriters wrote about the teams in their stories. The St. Louis Browns were called the Browns because—you guessed it, they had brown in their uniforms. Guess what color were the socks of the Cincinnati Red Legs? The Chicago White Sox? The Boston Red Sox? The Chicago Cubs were called the Cubs after a number of their veteran players jumped to the Chicago White Stockings of the American League, leaving the Chicago franchise in the National League with a bunch of young players: a bunch of cubs, said a sportswriter—and it stuck.

After signing with Cleveland, Sockalexis received tremendous press. Some sportswriters called him "The Great Sockalexis" even before his first game, just as Charboneau was tagged "Super Joe" while he was still in his first big league spring training camp. Some reporters started to call the team "Patsy Tebeau's Indians." The March 27, 1897, edition of *The Sporting Life* headlined, "They're Indians Now," in its story about Sockalexis coming to the big leagues.

So you can say, "See, there's the connection."

But consider that this was 1897, eighteen years before the team supposedly was named after him. In his first game as a "Cleveland Indian," he batted cleanup and played right field. He went 0-for-4. A week later in St. Louis, he hit his first home run, a blast to center field that supposedly was the longest ball ever hit in that part of the park. A few days later, he played in Cleveland in front of a wildly supportive crowd and crushed a towering drive that carried over the right field fence and through the window of a store across the street from the ballpark. He was a very big man for his era, 5-foot-11 and 185 pounds—nearly all of it muscle. That's why stories of him hitting balls 600 feet or more were believed by some naive writers and fans, as he looked strong enough to do it. Sockalexis had two home runs in his first month with Cleveland—and he hit only one more for the rest of his career. His flamethrower arm received as much attention as his bat. He continually impressed crowds and other players with his heaves from right field.

On the road, Sockalexis was subjected to the usual knuckleheads screaming "Scalp 'em," and doing rain dances and other stupid fan tricks. *The Sporting News* reported, "In many cases, these demonstrations bordered on extreme rudeness." That means they must have been really ugly, because *The Sporting News* at the turn of the century was not exactly a bleeding-heart liberal rag. Even fifty years later it had to be dragged by the scruff of the neck into baseball's age of integration, so it's hard to imagine there being much sympathy for Sockalexis in the paper's St. Louis headquarters.

By July 3 of his rookie year, Sockalexis was a .328 hitter with 16 stolen bases. He was on a hot streak, with 11 hits in his previous 21 at bats. He appeared to be a rising star. He also was receiving plenty of free drinks, and he considered it a sin to turn any of them down. On July 4, he was in a bar-brothel. He was drunk. He was running down a hallway on the second floor. He either ran through a window, not seeing it, or was so drunk he just decided to jump out. One newspaper reported he had a "tryst with a pale-faced maiden and a dalliance with the grape."

Either way, the result was a severely sprained (or broken) ankle and other injuries. Manager Tebeau reported that Sockalexis's foot was put in a cast, but the next night, the ballplayer limped out of his room, down some stairs, and walked a city block to a bar, where he resumed his drinking. Three days later, he ripped the cast off and tried to play. No luck. As he sat on the bench, he brooded. He drank even more. There were whispers (probably racist in nature) that he couldn't handle pain, which was why he didn't play on the injured foot.

He came back on July 13 to play again. The Cleveland *Plain Dealer* called him "A Wooden Indian" and stated, "Sockalexis acted as if he had disposed of too many mint juleps previous to the game."

For all practical purposes, his career was over.

By the end of the 1897 season, the *Plain Dealer* called him "a broken idol." In 1900, he served thirty days in jail on drunkenness and vagrancy charges. He died in 1913 at a logging camp near Bangor, Maine. Supposedly, it was a heart attack, which was technically true—but he had been drinking outrageously for years and that's what really killed him. He was forty-one years old.

Why would the Indians name their team as a way of honoring this fellow? Remember, this was 1915, not exactly an enlightened age when it came to America's view of its native people and their problems.

From 1903 to 1914, the Indians were called the Naps, after star second baseman Napoleon Lajoie. Interestingly, Lajoie was seldom called by his given first name of Napoleon; he was known to teammates, fans, and the newspapers as "Larry." It was a nickname he received long before coming to Cleveland, from a teammate who couldn't pronounce Lajoie, and just started calling him Larry. In the newspapers, the team was called the Naps, but Lajoie was simply known as Larry.

Lajoie was a great player, a true superstar. He was the kind of guy who would have a team named after him. He also had been a heckuva cab driver—only this was at the turn of the century, and Lajoie's cab was a sleek stagecoach. In his home town of Woonsocket, Rhode Island, he supposedly had the record for the fastest time between the railroad depot and the Grand Hotel. According to *The Sporting News*, "He was as good at the task of making the trains and time and money as he was at meeting the ball on the nose of the bat." When he signed his first pro contract, his father bellowed that Lajoie would "live to regret it," and that "ballplayers were a bunch of bums."

The quick version of how he came to Cleveland sounds a little like the old player wars between the National Basketball Association and the American Basketball Association in the 1970s. He began his career with the Philadelphia Phillies of the National League in 1897. He batted .329 but his team finished a whopping 32 games out of first place. He stayed with the Phillies through 1900. He was a terrific player, but could earn no more than $2,400. In the upstart American League, the money was bigger. Lajoie was supposedly still under contract to the Phillies, but he jumped to the new Philadephia Athletics of the American League for a four-year, $24,000 contract. Lawsuits flew. Injunctions were granted. Lajoie batted .422 for the Athletics in 1901, but the lawsuits over his services raged on. To escape the legal web in Philadelphia, he was traded to Cleveland in 1902.

In his first two seasons with Cleveland, he had to stay out

of Philadelphia when Cleveland played there because an injunction prevented him from playing pro ball in Pennsylvania. So what did he do while his teammates were in Philadelphia? Lajoie went to nearby Atlantic City and hung out at the beach. Then he rejoined the team on the train as it made its way to the next city on the schedule.

Lajoie gave Cleveland a big-time second baseman. A very *big* second baseman. He was 6-foot-1, 200 pounds. That would be like someone 6-foot-6 and 240 pounds playing the position today. Current Tribe general manager John Hart would have loved Lajoie, because the man could hit. Hart would have been very comfortable running a team at the turn of the century because second base was considered primarily an offensive position (much as Hart views it today). Because of all the bunting and stealing in the dead ball era, the double play wasn't a major factor, and a good glove at third was considered more important than at second. Lajoie was a right-handed hitter who held his hands a few inches apart on the bat. He was known for "smoting" (as they called it back then) fierce line drives down the third base line. One of his line drives supposedly killed two sparrows. That sounds a little suspicious, like a baseball version of killing two birds with one stone. A more believable story is that one of his line drives to center field imbedded itself in the fence and the outfielder could not pull the ball free.

When Larry came to Cleveland, the team was known as the Blues, because they wore blue uniforms. But when they lost, the writers referred to the fallen gladiators as the Bluebirds, which sounded wimpy to the players. So the team had a vote, and the players decided to call themselves the Broncos for the 1902 season—more macho, even if there wasn't a bucking bronc within 1,000 miles of Cleveland. And yes, the team changed its name simply on the vote of the players.

By 1903, the team clearly was Lajoie's. The fans were asked to vote, and several suggested Naps, honoring their great player. So they became the Cleveland Naps, with a star better known as Larry. He won three batting titles. He played a great second base. And according to *The Sporting News*, "The Big Frenchman made everything look so ridiculously simple that you got the impression he wasn't even trying."

He would not read while on trains or watch moving pictures because he thought they'd hurt his eyes and take seconds off his batting stroke. He was a quiet man who liked to play cards with his friends, who were mostly newspapermen and high school football coaches. But he once had an argument with teammate Elmer Flick. They were fighting over ownership of a bat. Larry got mad and threw a punch at Flick. For one of the few times in his life, Larry swung and missed. At least he missed Flick, but his fist squarely hit against a brick wall. Broken right hand. Imagine the headlines an incident like that would create today?

Lajoie became player-manager of the team from the middle of 1904 through 1909. One day, a player named George Stovall didn't like where Larry had placed him in the batting order. Stovall complained. Larry pleaded a form of baseball executive privilege. His point was, "I'm the manager, you're not. You'll bat where I tell you." Stovall picked up a chair and tried to break it over Larry's head.

Talk about headlines!

Well, think about this: Larry didn't even suspend Stovall. No fracture, no fine apparently was the rule of the day. Twenty years later, Larry characterized manager-player relationships of his day, recalling, "Many players hated their managers and didn't attempt to conceal their enmity, but they didn't rush to complain. They were told to settle the differences with the manager or get off the team. It wasn't uncommon to have a player threaten to crown a waiter with a chair if a steak was too tough or if he had to wait too long to be served."

Maybe Lajoie's father was right when he predicted his son would soon be keeping company with bums and other unsavory characters. Lajoie would later say that being player-manager "was the biggest mistake of my career."

Who could blame him for thinking that?

As Lajoie loved to tell people, baseball was a rough game in his day.

It also could be crooked.

In 1910, a car company said it would award its new Chalmers 30 automobile to the winner of the American League batting title. As the season came down to the final few games, the contenders were Ty Cobb and Lajoie. Even by 1910 standards, Cobb was a miserable SOB who made others very nervous just by being in the same room. No one wanted him to win the car. With two games left, Cobb had a six-point lead over Lajoie. Cobb has always been characterized as a burning competitor, but he didn't exactly show it here, not with a car at stake: He didn't play the last two games, sitting on his six-point lead.

Lajoie heard about this and fumed. So did nearly everyone else in baseball. Lajoie's team ended the season with a doubleheader against the St. Louis Browns. In his first at bat, Lajoie ripped a triple. Then Browns manager Jack "Peach Pie" O'Connor decided to stick it to Cobb, who was known as the Georgia Peach. O'Connor ordered his rookie third baseman to play so deep, he seemed to be a sign on the left field wall.

Lajoie recorded hits in his next six at bats. All bunts. All down the third base line, where the third baseman was nowhere to be found.

In his last at bat, Lajoie hit a ground ball to shortstop Bobby Wallace. The throw was high and Lajoie was safe.

Clearly an error.

But clearly the official scorer saw Cobb the way everyone else did: He gave Lajoie a hit. At the end of the doubleheader, Lajoie was 8-for-8, giving him a one-point lead over Cobb. Angered by the Browns' decision to let Lajoie bunt at will for hits, Chicago sportswriter Hugh Fullerton changed one of his decisions on a ball hit by Cobb earlier in the season, deciding it wasn't an error but a hit. Cobb won the batting title, .385 to .384. The company finally decided to give both men a Chalmers

30 before they tried any other tricks. Seventy years later, some baseball historians would check the records and discover that Cobb had received another "extra" hit, and Lajoie really should have won the batting title.

Either way, this whole thing stunk.

The good news is that Lajoie was known for his kindness with fans. While he was a shy man, he forced himself to shake hands, sign autographs, and do the right thing for the customers. There is a story of his team being stranded in rural Kentucky while heading to a game in Louisville. It was late and only one restaurant was open. Actually, it was a little diner, run by an elderly couple who nearly passed out in fear when they saw twenty-some hungry ballplayers at their door. Lajoie immediately sensed a problem. He told the owners not to worry, they'd prepare their own meals. Just show him where he'd find the bacon, eggs, and toast. Lajoie knew that pitcher Vean Gregg was a fine cook, so he was assigned to the kitchen. Catcher Steve O'Neill made the coffee. Other players cut and buttered bread. Lajoie made sure the operation went smoothly and the boys remained polite.

Certainly, today's players with their nearly $80 a day meal money would respond the same way, right?

Lajoie was considered the greatest Cleveland player ever. He recorded his 3,000th hit in his last at bat for the Cleveland franchise. The team had several days honoring him, attracting healthy crowds.

"I believe I'm the happiest man in Cuyahoga County," Lajoie told reporters after what became his final game with Cleveland in 1914.

Many years later, the Indians had a so-so lefty named Dennis Cook. In 1992, he came to the Tribe and found himself quoting Lajoie without even knowing it when he proclaimed, "I'm the happiest man in Cuyahoga County." Only he pronounced it, "Cal-A-Who-Ga."

At the end of the 1914 season, the owner of the Cleveland Naps was broke. Charles Somers had several businesses that turned sour and was $1.7 million in debt, which would be about $100 million today. In the tradition of many of today's owners, he slashed the payroll by dumping stars and their high salaries. Lajoie was shipped to the Philadelphia A's—just given away so Somers would not have to pay his $9,000 contract, one of the most expensive in the game.

Now that *does* sound like the baseball we know.

The deal created a problem: Should the team still be called the Naps, since Napoleon Lajoie was gone?

Somers didn't think so. He went to several newspapermen and asked them to run a contest to name the team. This was not to be an election; the newspapermen were simply to solicit names from the fans, then they'd go into a back room with Somers. Cigars would be lit. Gin would be swilled. Smoke would hang heavy. Finally, a name would be picked.

The *Cleveland News* reported it had received "hundreds" of suggestions, and the paper favored "Hustlers" or "Grays." Hustlers for the obvious reason, hoping it would match the team's style of play. Grays was to give the team an identity, as it would wear its gray traveling uniforms at home and on the road. The *Cleveland Press* reported, "Many Fans Favor Old Nickname," and still wanted the team named Naps after the beloved Larry Lajoie. "Other names suggested are Foresters, Some Runners, Tornadoes, Commodores, Rangers, Sixers, Speeders and Harmonics."

The *Plain Dealer* reported it had received "57 varieties of nicknames." It listed the seven most popular, and none were the Indians.

One fan suggested, "Why not call them the Napless Naps?"

Among the three local newspapers, thirty different nicknames were printed as suggestions. One fan said the team should keep the Naps name, "because it slept through the season," finishing 51-102.

Not one suggestion published was the Indians.

So there was no election, no public outcry in support of naming the team after Sockalexis—or even naming it the Indians—when the boys went into a room to make the decision.

Remember, this was after the 1914 season. The biggest baseball story of 1914 was the Miracle Boston Braves, a team that was in last place on July 4, but came back to win the pennant—and then swept the Philadelphia A's in the World Series. It was the most remarkable baseball story of its era, a team that caught the attention of fans everywhere who found themselves rooting for the guys who went from worst to first.

That's right, the Boston *Braves*.

Think about that.

The *Braves*.

The boys in the back room sure did. They couldn't call the team the Cleveland Braves, but why not the Cleveland Indians? A couple of sportswriters remembered the 1897 season when Sockalexis was on the team and it was briefly called the Indians.

So it would be the Cleveland Indians.

Why?

The Cleveland *Plain Dealer* reported, "It having been one of the names applied to the old National League club of Cleveland many years ago. The nickname is but temporarily bestowed."

The *Cleveland News* reported, "Indians is a popular name. One Cleveland fan, James Thayer, thinks the Indians may emulate the example of the National League counterparts, the Boston Braves, and show just as much reversal of form as the Braves did in 1914."

*The Sporting News* reported, "While there is no particular reason why the name Indians should be adopted, the same name was worn by the Cleveland National League team prior to the entrance of Charles Somers to the National Pastime."

Every newspaper reported the name was "temporary."

Nowhere on the sports pages was there a mention of Sockalexis.

In the January 18, 1915, edition of the *Plain Dealer*, an editorial mentioned that Sockalexis played for the team in the late 1890s and caused some brief excitement. The nickname can honor him and refer back to a time when Cleveland had a very good baseball team. But this editorial seemed more like an after-the-fact analysis, a pipe-smoking writer musing on the new name and old times. Given the nature of sportswriters, they probably were more taken with the heroics of the 1914 Boston Braves than with honoring a guy from the previous century who didn't even play 100 games for the team.

The *Cleveland Press* added, "The Cleveland ballclub was anxious to get a nickname that couldn't be converted into a joke. 'They won't be able to poke fun at the Indians,' said team vice president 'Barney' Barnard."

Guess again.

"Wait until they start to lose," added the *Cleveland Press*. "We'll see how soon the fans will dub them the squaws."

For whatever reason, the nickname stuck. And it was not immune to cheap shots, as the Tribe has been called "the beloved featherheads" and the "featherbrains" during some of its down decades.

As I write about the team's nickname, I think of how my father loved his Chief Wahoo cap and jacket. He never said a word about where the nickname came from, or if there was anything wrong with Chief Wahoo as a logo. I remember him telling me that Lajoie was a great ballplayer; he heard this from his father, an ironworker and baseball fan. He also heard this from his mother, a maid who loved baseball more than anyone in the family—and the only parent who could read English. They both had come from what is now Slovakia. Slovak was the language spoken most of the time in my father's home. Following baseball, especially the Indians, was a way for the Pluto family to feel like a part of America as it roared into the 1920s.

# CHAPTER 5

# Manny Ramirez and Joe Jackson

IF YOU HAVE someone in your family who is a longtime base-ball fan, you've probably played the game of comparing players from your era to those from when they first started watching baseball. Is Omar Vizquel the greatest Tribe defensive shortstop ever—as veteran Cleveland sportswriter Hal Lebovitz claims—or is it Lou Boudreau? My father always said the best Indians pitcher he ever saw was Bob Feller, "but I wasn't around when Cy Young pitched."

For us, it was always easier to talk about baseball than other things. My father was angry because he didn't stay in Santa Barbara, California, where he had been stationed in the final year of World War II. He loved it out there. He sensed California was the future. He wanted to be a part of it. But his family and my mother's family were in Cleveland, so he came home and went to work in the warehouse of a company called Fisher Foods. Manual labor. There were times when he mentioned this, when he dreamed those California dreams only to see them turn into bitter regrets. He'd start to tell me about them, wanting to blame someone for his not staying on the West Coast, but not finding a suitable scapegoat. He'd stop the story right there, remembering I was a kid. How could I understand? I liked Cleveland. I didn't want to move to California, which is what I thought he wanted to do every time he brought it up. Of course, that would never happen; Cleveland was his home, too, for better or worse. But when he started talking about Santa Barbara and the fun he'd had there while he was in the Army and how it was a mistake to come home to Cleveland, I wasn't interested. I'd change the subject. I'd ask him about baseball. I could deal with baseball. I knew the Indians' history from my father and the reading I'd done. I couldn't comprehend what it must have been like for my father to have visions of California palm trees dancing in his head while he worked in a dark, cold warehouse on a gray Cleveland February day. I was too young to know about regrets, about missed chances, and about the soul of a young man after World War II.

So I'd ask him about baseball, the Indians of the 1960s— my team—and the earlier Indians teams. Those conversations would brighten him up.

It's a game I still play, often in my head. I do it while watching Manny Ramirez, wondering if the Indians ever had a player quite like him.

Then it came to me: Joe Jackson.

One is from the Dominican Republic by way of New York City, the other from rural South Carolina.

One didn't finish high school, the other didn't make it through the fourth grade.

One trained by tying a rope around his chest and attaching it to a tire—then running five miles through the streets of upper Manhattan. The other would sit in a dark room with only a single candle lit; he'd cover one eye and stare at the candle with the other eye until it nearly blinded him. Then he'd cover the first eye, and stare again at the candle. He thought this strengthened his eyes.

One has the most natural swing from the right side of the plate in the history of the Indians franchise. The other owned the most beautiful left-handed swing that Tribe fans have ever seen.

One's name is Manny Ramirez.

The other is Joe Jackson.

Both played for Cleveland, Jackson playing for the team from 1910 to 1915, Ramirez being a mainstay with the Tribe in the 1990s.

Both were born to hit, and for both the other aspects of life could be as baffling to them as a curveball was to Gus Gil.

To know Manny Ramirez, you have to go to a place called Washington Heights, which is on the northern tip of Manhattan. You have to remind yourself this is still New York City, still the United States, because all you hear is Spanish on the streets and in the stores. From the cars cruising Amsterdam Avenue, it's the relentless beat of merengue music; from the brownstone tenements, you smell rice and beans simmering on the stoves.

As you walk these streets, you suddenly begin to feel the way Ramirez must in Northern Ohio: a stranger in a strange land.

You see a man selling gold watches and necklaces out of a trash bag.

You see stores called bodegas, not Dairy Marts.

You see storefront churches, and all the signs are in Spanish.

It is to these streets that Aristides and Onlecidad Ramirez brought their family in 1985. Aristides was a cab driver, Onlecidad a seamstress in the garment district. They had five children, Manny and four older daughters. They lived in a three-bedroom apartment with no phone. Manny was thirteen when they came to America, but this was Washington Heights; to Manny, it was pretty much the same as the Dominican Republic. As you walk the streets of Manny's neighborhood, you see teenagers hanging out on the corners. This is a school day. You wonder why they are out here. You try not to think the worst, but you can't help it. Washington Heights is not just New York's version of the Dominican Republic, it's one of the city's most notorious drug areas. "Going to Washington Heights?" said a policeman. "Well, they'll figure a white guy up there is either an undercover [cop] or out to make a drug buy."

Or maybe a baseball scout.

That is the other story of Washington Heights: It is home to thousands of kids who want to be Manny Ramirez, kids who can barely speak English but who understand the summer game perfectly. Baseball is all that matters here, or at least that is what so many people tell you. In the daytime, you feel safe in Washington Heights. People smile at you as they pass on the sidewalk, a rarity in New York. They try to help you with directions, even if their English is terrible and your Spanish is far worse. Yes, there are a lot of drug dealers here; you know it from the gang graffiti on the walls, from the hollow eyes of some of the wasted souls nodding on street corners. But there are people working two, even three jobs, trying to pay the bills, to make a life in this country. You ask a stranger where to find George Washington High, and she takes you there. Leads you to the door. She reminds you that there are a lot of good people here, too.

At the school, there is a guard named Lou. He checks your identification. Everyone has a picture ID card—teachers, students, administrators.

You can't walk the halls by yourself; a teacher escorts you. Want to use the bathroom? The teacher opens it with a key, then stands outside, waiting.

This huge, stately school was built in 1923, and it looks

like an old opera house with its marble floors, high ceilings, and chandeliers. Its alumni include Henry Kissinger, Senator Jacob Javits, and broadcaster Edwin Newman—and also Hall of Famer Rod Carew and Manny Ramirez.

On the windows, there are bars. On some spots of the roof, there is barbed wire. In the halls are fifteen policemen in uniform, others undercover. You walk out to the baseball diamond (it's artificial turf, believe it or not), and a plainclothes security man approaches you; he wants to see some identification, even though you're wearing a big red sticker proclaiming, "VISITOR."

"No disrepect," he says. "But a lot of stuff goes on out here. We try to keep everything cool."

Say this much for those running George Washington High, they are determined to make it a safe place—and the 3,000 students and teachers appreciate it.

To find Joe Jackson, you have to go deep into the past. You have to go to a place called Brandon Mill, South Carolina—not far from Greenville. But going there today doesn't tell you much. You need to know Brandon Mill in the late 1890s, Brandon Mill when it was just that—a town built around a textile mill.

You need to understand a culture where the mill supplied the job, the house, the grocery store. The mill was your present, your future. The mill was everything.

It was here that Jackson grew up. It was in the mill that Jackson went to work when he was eleven. It was in the mill that he worked twelve-hour shifts, first as a "linthead," because he was supposed to sweep the lint off the floors. He was also called "linthead," because he didn't seem very smart, not even by mill town standards.

Your paycheck was barely enough to survive, and not nearly enough to leave town. You always owed a little more than you made—to the mill for rent on your boxlike house, to the mill for groceries from the store, to the mill for your family's clothes. This was just another form of slavery, much like tenant farming. In this culture, there was no emphasis on education. Why? You learned all you needed at the mill. High school was for city kids with rich parents. College? You gotta be dreaming.

But the mill also was something else—baseball.

Baseball was to the people of Brandon Mill at the turn of the twentieth century what it is to the people in Washington Heights today.


You find Steve Mandl in the gym.

He was Manny Ramirez's high school coach. He is still the baseball coach and a good one. His teams commonly have records such as 44-2 and are ranked among the best in New York City. On the day you visit Mandl, he has about sixty kids in his gym class. All are sitting in assigned spots on the floor as attendance is taken. No one talks. Everyone knows the drill.

His baseball teams are coached the same way.

In a world where so much seems like chaos, Mandl not only wins, he brings order.

"It used to bother me when people talked about Manny's lack of fundamentals and his mistakes," Mandl says. "People wanted to know if he was coached. But he's been playing pro ball since 1991."

While he has been showing real improvement, there are still a few games when Manny is picked off base. There are still games when Manny throws to the wrong base, when he loafs after balls in the outfield or when he just doesn't seem interested.

There have been games when Manny thought he had struck out—and the count was only two strikes. And games when he began to walk to first base—and it was only ball three. There was the evening in 1997 when he stole second base, then got up and walked back to first. He thought Jim Thome had fouled off a pitch. Actually, Thome didn't even swing; Ramirez was just not paying attention. He was tagged out on a play that confounded even veteran baseball watchers.

Why did he do that?

"I don't know," Ramirez invariably responds.

Maybe it's because of what happened when he did try to answer a question.

As a rookie in September of 1993, Ramirez pulled himself out of the lineup. Why? "Because I have a sore throat," he said.

The front office and coaching staff were steamed. His teammates rolled their eyes and shook their heads. Ramirez knew he'd made a mistake, that you don't pull yourself out of a major league game because your throat hurts.

"I really believe Manny has a learning disability, an attention deficit syndrome," says Mandl, his high school coach. "I've seen other kids with it. That's the source of some of Manny's problems."

The Indians are aware that Ramirez has some problems. They just say they are trying to work with him.

"When we drafted Manny, we were aware of his situation," says Tribe GM John Hart. "But we also know Manny is a good kid. He is street-smart. He's from a tough neighborhood and has had few academic advantages. Believe me, we do all we can for Manny."

Ramirez did not graduate from high school, something all too common for kids at George Washington High. Books in English were impossible to read, and what he heard from his teachers had little relevance to his life.

"Manny is misunderstood," Mandl says. "People don't know him like we do. He was obsessed, absolutely obsessed with baseball. He had great talent, but his work ethic was tremendous."

Ramirez would awaken at 5:00 A.M. He'd tie a rope around his waist and attach the other end to a tire. Then he ran up and down Amsterdam Avenue—for miles, rain or shine— dragging that tire behind him.

"If I told Manny to be there for a game at 1:00 P.M., he was there two hours early," said Mandl. "If I said the team picture was at 1:00 P.M., he'd forget and not show up. Baseball is really all he cares about."

When Joe Jackson was thirteen years old, the mill became something else to him.

It became baseball. It made him a hero. Like Ramirez, he had a gift—the ability to swing a bat. The gift came from above and he wasn't sure why it was given to him; he couldn't explain why he hit the ball so hard, he just began calling his line drives "blue darters."

When he said that, people laughed.

Suddenly, he wasn't a linthead anymore. He still worked in the mill, but he no longer swept the floor. He no longer worked as hard or as long. He was the best player on the mill team, even though he was only thirteen and everyone else was an adult. He discovered that stardom had its perks. When he stopped in the company store, he was presented with his favorite drink—a Coke with lime juice—for free. When he hit home runs on Saturday afternoons, his brothers passed a hat in the stands and he'd take in twenty dollars—almost as much as he made working in the mill for a month.

Jackson began to see the mill for what it was, a dead-end. He saw his brother mauled by a machine in the mill. He saw the doctor set the bones badly. He saw his brother come out as a hunchback. He saw young men grow old in front of his eyes. He saw them drag themselves home to a little mill-owned house full of kids. He saw men without fingers, men without hope.

He saw the future and it scared him.

But he had baseball. He took to holding a bat out in front of him, holding it by the end of the handle, holding it out for as long as he could to strengthen his arm. Then he'd switch it to the other arm. He also took to staring at that candle with one eye at a time. Joe Jackson wanted to do everything he could to become a great hitter, and then, just maybe, he would be able to escape the jaws of the mill.

Not long after they came to Washington Heights, Ramirez's parents separated. Ramirez sometimes lived with his mother, other times with his father. He showed little interest in learning English, and his neighborhood offered him little incentive, since 90 percent of the kids at George Washington High are from the Dominican.

"I've been coaching youth baseball for twenty-five years," says Mel Zitter. "I've had over twenty kids sign pro contracts. I've had twenty other kids with the same talent as Manny, only they didn't make it."

Why?

"Too scared to leave the neighborhood," he says. "Not as dedicated and disciplined as Manny. You have to give this kid a lot of credit for accomplishing what he has in Cleveland. A lot of these are street kids, and the street often gets them before they can get out."

Zitter coached Ramirez for three years in summer leagues.

"He would talk to me afterwards about every at bat, about the pitches he hit and what he missed," Zitter says. "I always wish he could carry over the sophistication he has when hitting to the rest of his life."

During his senior year, the *New York Times* called him "The Hit Man," his nickname from school. He batted .615 with 14 homers in 22 games, enough to inspire the Indians to make him their number one pick in the 1991 amateur draft. Despite the wealth and notoriety he has received, Ramirez is perceived as friendly and humble by those who have known him the longest.

"He is more sensitive and more aware of the criticism coming his way than you think," Zitter insists. "Most players think they are much better than they really are—with Manny, it's the other way. Behind that smile is a good kid who is not a very confident person."

•

Baseball carried Jackson out of the mill and to the South Carolina town of Greenville, where he signed with a local minor league team. In the early 1900s, most minor league teams were independently owned, not affiliated with major league teams as they are today.

Jackson was barely aware of the big leagues. To him, Greenville *was* the big leagues. He was being paid to play baseball. He was out of the mill. He had a girlfriend. He was making $75 a month, about three times what the mill paid. He felt rich.

And he hit.

Joe Jackson always hit.

It was with Greenville in 1908 that he became "Shoeless Joe." He had played a game in a new pair of spikes, spikes so tight they hurt his feet and led to severe blisters. But he played in them all afternoon, all nine innings. The next day he could barely walk, but there was another game. Jackson tried to play in his old spiked shoes, but the blisters were still too tender. Finally, he went to right field in his stocking feet. Jackson's team was playing in Anderson, South Carolina. In the seventh inning he delivered a key triple, sliding into third base with those stocking feet.

As he stood up and dusted himself off, a fan yelled, "You shoeless SOB, you."

Jackson once said, "I never played in my stocking feet before or after that, but the 'Shoeless' nickname just stuck with me."

In July of 1908, Jackson married fifteen-year-old Katherine Wynn. A month later, his contract was sold for $325 to Connie Mack of the Philadelphia A's.

Jackson was in the major leagues.

But he didn't like it. The players made fun of his drawl, his slow Southern walk. They discovered he couldn't read. They played tricks on him. They once convinced him to drink water from a bowl they had used to wash their hands. They mercilessly teased him when he lost a fly ball in the sun and the ball banged against his chest, knocking him to the ground. Jackson brooded. He felt stupid. He had no idea how to respond to his new teammates or how to deal with a fast Northern city such as Philadelphia. He felt like a linthead back at the mill, and he hated it. Remember that Joe Jackson grew up in a rural South that was only thirty years removed from the Civil War. That war shaped the opinions of people for the next fifty years. There were at least two Americas, and Joe Jackson could not understand a country with cities such as New York, Philadelphia, and Boston, where people talked fast, walked faster, and considered him a social reject. So it was not surprising that after a few weeks with the Philadelphia A's, he bolted the team and returned to South Carolina.

"He was the town hero down there," said Mack. "He was satisfied with his lot, being the center of attention. He really didn't want to come to the big leagues."

Mack tried to get Jackson to stick in Philadelphia. He returned to the team, but not for long. Mack tried to convince Jackson to accept a tutor so he could learn to read, but Jackson refused, saying, "It don't take no school stuff to help a fella play ball." Jackson spent the 1909 season playing in Savannah, Georgia, and part of 1910 in New Orleans. He was comfortable in both minor league cities because he was in the South and his teammates accepted him. And he continued to hit as only Shoeless Joe Jackson could.

During Ramirez's senior year in high school, the *New York Times* made him into a local legend. The newspaper did an eight-part story on Ramirez and his high school team. Tribe scout Joe DeLucca was at nearly every game. He loved the swing. He saw Ramirez trying to play third base, and didn't think that would work—but Manny at the bat? No way he'd miss. DeLucca sent one glowing report after another to Tribe scouting director Mickey White. White traveled to Washington

Heights and fell in love with Manny at the bat. Next to stop by was general manager John Hart.

As Hart walked toward the field, he heard a crack of the bat. It was the special kind of crack, the kind that comes when the ball hits what is known as the "sweet spot," the part of the barrel of the bat where the best wood is found. It was the kind of crack you hear from a big leaguer, a Frank Thomas or Albert Belle. Hart's neck jerked. He was at least 300 feet from the field, but the crack rang in his ears.

"Manny?" Hart asked White.

"Manny," said the scouting director.

What they saw in the game was more line drives from Manny. This was in the spring of 1991. The Indians were in the process of losing a franchise-record 105 games. The Tribe had the thirteenth pick in the amateur draft. The safe selection would have been a college player who could help immediately. But scouting director Mickey White pushed Hart to select Ramirez. Yes, he's raw. Yes, his English is terrible and he'd need several years in the minors. Yes, he dropped out of high school without graduating—actually, this was a positive because the Indians didn't have to worry about him refusing to sign a pro contract to accept a college scholarship. There would be no college for Ramirez.

But the kid was the greatest young hitter White had ever seen. He was so excited about Ramirez, he was comparing him to Hank Aaron.

The Indians drafted him in the first round. They signed him for $300,000. They sent him to their Class A rookie league team in Burlington, North Carolina, where Ramirez felt in the American South like Jackson did in Philadelphia.

Ramirez was lost and scared. He finished with a .650 batting average as a senior in high school, but hit only .250 in his first month at Burlington. He ran up $800 in phone calls back to New York. He sulked and didn't run out fly balls. One night after he was hitless in four at bats, he came into the clubhouse and announced, "I'm going home. I don't like it here."

His coaches and some teammates tried to comfort him. They convinced him to stay. For all his turmoil that first season, Ramirez ended up with a .326 batting average and 19 homers in 59 games at Burlington.

Even frightened and lonely, Manny Ramirez still hit.

In August of 1910, the A's sold the contract of Jackson (who was playing in New Orleans) for $325 and an outfielder name Bris "The Human Eyeball" Lord. Mack believed Jackson would be a star in the majors, but knew it would never happen in Philadelphia because Jackson was afraid to return, afraid the other players would make fun of him.

Jackson reported to Cleveland in 1910 and immediately was accepted. In his first at bat, he hammered one of his blue darters that tore the glove right off the second baseman's left hand. He hit. He was cheered. He was one of the few bright spots on a lousy team.

He also was two years older than on his first trip to Philadelphia. At the age of twenty-two, he began to understand there was real money to be made in the majors. This was where the best players were found, and he was among the best. His wife, Katherine, liked Cleveland because they found a house within walking distance of League Park and the neighbors were kind to them, more like people in the South than those who lived in Philadelphia. She attended almost every game. She left in the seventh inning to go home and prepare dinner, so it could be served when her husband walked through the door about an hour later. This was the age of afternoon baseball. In the evenings, they strolled through what was then an upper-middle-class neighborhood by League Park. The houses were rambling, with large porches. The people were friendly, inviting them over for coffee, iced tea, and pieces of pie. Jackson was happy. He batted .387 in his first year with the Tribe.

His teammates didn't think it was strange when he carried a five-gallon jug of corn liquor on the road; he loved to sit on his bed, munching animal crackers and washing them down with the Old Panther Juice. They found it amusing when he stuffed twenty-dollar bills in the lining of his coats so he wouldn't ever be without money, even if he lost his wallet. They tolerated it when Jackson tried to act as if he could read; he'd look at a newspaper or magazine, then hand it to someone and say, "You should read this—great stuff." In restaurants with teammates, he'd let them order first and then pick from some of their choices for his meal selection—although he'd claim to have spotted it on the menu.

The Indians tried to convince Jackson to take reading lessons, but he refused: "None of my people had schooling, and besides, I won't like it around no books." He also knew he had his wife, Katherine, to read things for him—but he was not about to tell them that. Sometimes, the Indians bat boy read the sports page to Jackson, dropping by the player's house so none of the other athletes would know—and the bat boy never talked about it until Jackson left the team.

The Indians had a problem with a young Ramirez.

His defense and baserunning were atrocious. The one difference between Jackson and Ramirez was their attention span on the field. Jackson rarely missed a sign. He rarely was picked off base or made an error. He was a smart player.

While Ramirez worked very hard on his defense, it remained erratic. He was capable of great plays, but would botch easy ones simply because he didn't concentrate. The Indians wanted to keep him in the minors longer to improve in these areas, but he hit so well they were forced to promote him to Cleveland.

When Ramirez came to the Indians, he and young Dominican pitcher Julian Tavarez tried to borrow $60,000 from *Akron Beacon Journal* baseball writer Sheldon Ocker. Why?

Because they wanted a motorcycle. This led to a long explanation from Ocker:

1. Motorcycles don't cost $60,000.
2. Baseball writers don't make millions of dollars.
3. Even if he had $60,000, he wouldn't carry it around.

With the Indians, Ramirez stuffed $100 bills in his glove compartment so he'd always have money. He racked up a string of traffic violations, having his license suspended. At one point, he had two different Social Security numbers and two different driver's licenses from different states. He rented movies from video stores and forgot to return them, incurring huge bills.

Then, there was the night of the O.J. Simpson car chase through the streets of Los Angeles. Ramirez saw that and asked, with great concern, "Is Chad in trouble?"

He meant Tribe pitcher Chad Ogea, whose last name is pronounced O.J.

In 1996, teammate Kevin Seitzer missed a couple of weeks with appendix surgery. When he returned to the team, Ramirez was excited to see him back. He came up behind Seitzer and lifted him off the ground, putting his hands around Seitzer's waist.

Seitzer screamed in pain.

Ramirez quickly put him down.

"Manny," said Seitzer. "I just had an operation there."

"Oh," he said. "I thought you had heart surgery."

But Jackson and Ramirez had hitting in common.

As former Indians outfielder Jack Graney said of Jackson, "He never knew what the pitch was that he hit or if the pitcher was a righty or lefty."

Ramirez took the same approach. See the ball; hit the ball.

After five years with the Indians, Jackson was traded to the Chicago White Sox on August 21, 1915. The Indians were a lousy team with major debts. The White Sox paid $31,500 for Jackson—the most any team had ever paid for a player up to that point.

In 673 games with the Tribe, Jackson batted .374.

The trade changed his life. While he continued to hit in Chicago and was loved by the fans, he was never fully accepted by his teammates, who considered him a hick. Did this lead to his alleged involvement in the fixing of the 1919 World Series? Certainly, his desire to be one of the boys led him to hang around with the guys who were discussing the fix, and he did take $1,000 and put it under his pillow—and then he played wonderfully in the World Series, batting .375.

If the Indians had been smart and hung on to Jackson, they'd have been a powerhouse in the 1920s. Imagine Joe Jackson and Tris Speaker in the same outfield.

Instead, Jackson was booted out of baseball after the 1920 season. He was thirty-two years old, still in his prime. He returned to South Carolina, where he ran a liquor store. He died in 1951 at the age of sixty-three.

At the age of twenty-six, Ramirez broke through with 45 homers and 145 RBI in 1998. While his defense will never match Jackson's—Shoeless Joe's glove was known as "The place triples go to die"—Ramirez has developed into an above-average outfielder, despite his occasional lapses of attention.

The year Jackson was banned from baseball, he batted .382. He hit 12 homers and drove in 121 runs, both career highs. We'll never know what kind of numbers Jackson would have posted if his career had continued. Baseball was just coming out of the dead ball era; Jackson might have become one of the top power hitters in the early 1920s. After all, Babe Ruth once said he patterned his swing after Jackson's.

There are many similarities between Jackson and Ramirez. Like Jackson, Ramirez seeks the approval of his teammates, even if he isn't always sure how to get it. The difference is that Ramirez should have a chance to play a full career, playing well past his thirty-second birthday, which was the end of the line for Jackson. Assuming the Indians are able to keep Ramirez, he could do for them what Jackson might have been able to accomplish if Shoeless Joe had never been traded—namely, become the best Tribe hitter, ever.

# CHAPTER 6

# 1920 Season

IN THE YEAR my father was born, the Indians won the pennant and their first World Series.

It was 1920, and Cleveland became a baseball town.

"I always like to see a pennant where it is appreciated," wrote James Isaminger in *The Sporting News*. "Cleveland virtually declared each playing day a holiday. The players must know the whole city is behind them. There is more baseball talk in Cleveland than New York. Cleveland is the home of the old-fashioned fan who is rampant and roistering. . . . It is refreshing to step from the fog of scandal into this buoyant exuberance of a people who still believe in the game."

Then again, the 1920 Indians would make anyone love the game.

But first, we must talk about 1916.

The country was on the verge of the First World War, or what was supposed to be the War To End All Wars. The Indians were still owned by Charley Somers, whose family literally pulled millions of dollars out of the ground. The Somers money came from coal mines—not that Charley Somers was about to wear a helmet and hold a pick in his hand. He was more likely to be seen in a hundred-dollar suit and a derby. He ate at the best restaurants and liked action—a true sportsman, as they said back then.

Today, he'd be the kind of guy who has his own private suite in Vegas, a free limo waiting for him at the airport, the guy who is always comped by the house so they can get him to the tables. But at the turn of the century, there was no Las Vegas as we know it today. But there was baseball, especially the upstart American League, which was almost as big a gamble. Somers threw his cash into this new venture. Somers was so taken with the idea of baseball, he lent cash to Charles Comiskey so he could finish the construction of Comiskey Park in Chicago.

Let's stop right here to observe that when an owner wanted a new ballpark, he built it himself—and paid for it!

Doing something as responsible as that would get you thrown out of the brotherhood of owners today, when owners expect taxpayers to pay for new stadiums and then allow the teams to use these baseball palaces virtually rent-free. But in Somers's era, if an owner didn't have the money for the park, he didn't demand the taxpayers eat the bills; he did it the old-fashioned way—he hit up his friends and relatives for cash. At one point, Somers loaned money to four different American League teams just to help the new owners get started and strengthen the new league. And to think that baseball owners today still can't come to any sort of decent agreement on revenue sharing. So Charley Somers was one heckuva guy, at least as far as baseball's owners were concerned. Still, he was not much of a baseball man. He never had a pennant winner, and from 1900 to 1916, he had more losers than winners. But by all accounts, Somers had a grand time just being the owner—

buying his players drinks, playing cards, and otherwise being a very likable gent.

There was, however, a problem: the mines.

The mines were running out of coal.

Charley Somers didn't worry about it. He'd dig more mines, find more coal, make more money. If only the bankers would float him a loan. The bankers were like everyone else: They liked Charley Somers. But they also were bankers. They were men with sharp pencils and bottom-line eyes staring hard at his books. They were men who squinted at the world from under green visors, men who had about as much sense of fun as a pile of charcoal.

"Charley," they said. "You owe us $1.7 million."

That was a staggering sum in 1916. Maybe like $100 million today.

"Charley," they said. "Something has to go, either the coal mines or the baseball team."

In 1915, the Indians were 57-95 and drew only 159,285 fans. The 1997 Tribe drew more than that for a four-game series, any four-game series. So you can understand how Charley Somers was losing his butt on the baseball team.

In 1916, America knew the world war was coming, despite politicians insisting they would never send this country's fine young men across the ocean to crawl in damp trenches and be cut to bloody ribbons by these newfangled machine guns or have their lungs turned to fire by gas.

Army drill teams were assigned to each baseball franchise to teach the players the fundamentals of marching and other military skills. The sergeants took players into the outfield before games, their bats serving as rifles. They twirled their bats, they lifted their spiked shoes—and boy, did they ever march.

As this was happening, a group of Charley Somers's friends met in a Chicago watering hole to try to figure out how to bail out the man who had lent most of them money. Pounding on the bar was Ban Johnson, president of the American League.

"Gentlemen," he said. "The bankers are forcing Charley to sell the Cleveland club."

There was tongue-clucking, shaking of heads, and stories of how bankers weren't fit to eat dirt and drink sludge.

Johnson agreed with that sentiment, but it didn't change the facts. Something had to be done to help Charley. Also at the bar was Charles Comiskey, the owner of the White Sox and the man who was still in the baseball business partly because of Somers's loan.

Now, he was the Old Roman, yet another Grand Man of the Game.

Also around the bar were Sunny Jim Dunn (don't you love these names?) and Paddy McCarthy, a couple of Johnson's cronies.

"You," said Johnson, pointing at Sunny Jim. "You, Jim Dunn, are the next owner of the Cleveland club."

About all Sunny Jim knew about baseball was that Johnson gave him free tickets to the games.

"How much money can you put your hands on?" asked Johnson.

"I don't know," Sunny Jim said. "Maybe $15,000."

"I can come up with with $15,000 or maybe $20,000," said McCarthy.

McCarthy and Sunny Jim were partners in a construction business in Iowa. Suddenly, they were about to be the next owners of the Cleveland Indians.

"Hey, I can come up with $10,000," said a voice behind them. It belonged to John Burns—the bartender!

Ten grand was ten grand, so Burns the bartender was in.

Sunny Jim Dunn and Paddy McCarthy begged all their friends for loans. Comiskey kicked in some cash. Johnson found some investors. Sunny Jim then handed over a check for $500,000 to Charley Somers, enough to keep the bankers happy while he rebuilt his coal business.

This story has several happy endings.

Somers became a millionaire all over again, thanks to rising coal prices and the new demand for it during World War I. Sunny Jim Dunn was stunned at how easy it was to raise money for his baseball team, and he wasn't afraid to spend it on players.

Even the Army drill team worked.

In 1916, the Indians finished in sixth place in the American League. At the end of the season, a competition was held among all the teams to determine who marched the best and could do all those fancy rifle maneuvers with their bats. And when it came to marching, the 1916 Indians finished in third place, right behind the St. Louis Browns and Washington Senators. For winning it all, the Browns split $500 amongst themselves, and the Indians received $100 for their fine footwork.

The 1917 Indians had an outfielder named Jack Graney, who later became the first radio voice of the team. But in 1917, he had a dog named Larry, who did neat dog tricks.

Larry was so good at his tricks that the Indians took him on the road, so he could do them between innings to entertain fans across the American League.

Late in the 1917 season, Larry died of unexplained causes. All we know is what *Cleveland Press* sportswriter Whitey Lewis wrote: "His death resulted in deep grieving by all the Redskins."

Sunny Jim Dunn & Friends became the official owners of the Indians on February 21, 1916. They knew they had to have a star to attract some fans.

By 1915, Tris Speaker was a true superstar. He was a centerfielder who hit close to .400 and caught everything in the park.

"Tris played the shallowest center field I've seen," recalled veteran Cleveland sportswriter Hal Lebovitz. "I seldom saw anyone hit the ball over his head."

Speaker played such a short center field, that nearly every season in his career there was a game where he'd sneak behind the runner leading off second base . . . catch a throw from the pitcher . . . and complete a pickoff play!

Imagine being a runner caught napping off second base because the center fielder slipped in behind you. In 1918, Speaker recorded two unassisted double plays when he caught line drives in center field, then ran to second base, touching the bag before the stunned runner could return. His Hall of Fame statue simply reads, "The greatest center fielder of his day."

He could hit, too.

In 1915, Speaker batted .322 and helped the Boston Red Sox win the World Series. But Sox owner Joe Lannin was a man of the 1990s; even though his team won the World Series, he didn't make enough money, so he decided to hold a fire sale of his stars. He tried to cut Speaker's salary from $18,000 to $9,000. Speaker refused to sign, refused to report, and vowed to stay on his ranch in Hubbard, Texas, where he was considered an excellent bronco buster and roper. He also was a man who consulted with his mother on contract talks. He told his mother he was willing to settle for $15,000—a $3,000 cut. His mother thought that was more than reasonable.

The Red Sox did not.

The Red Sox shopped Speaker around baseball to the highest bidder, and the Indians stepped in with $55,000 and two players—Sad Sam Jones and Fred Thomas.

Now comes the part where you really have to love Speaker.

First, he wanted a $10,000 bonus to report.

Very 1990s, right?

But get this: He demanded that it come from the $55,000 that the Indians sent to Boston.

"I believe I'm worth $10,000 of the purchase price," he said.

The Red Sox were outraged. They threatened not to pay. Speaker then threatened not to play. Everyone made threats in loud voices, which made for excellent newspaper stories.

But in the end, greed ruled—as it usually does. Boston finally coughed up the $10,000, figuring $45,000 and two players was still a good deal.

The Red Sox were wrong.

In fact, Speaker began to play for the Indians before he even signed a contract with the team. He liked Sunny Jim Dunn and promised to work the details out later. All he wanted was the ten grand from the Red Sox, then he went on to win the 1916 American League batting title as he hit .386. Sunny Jim was so thrilled with his new star, he gave Speaker a contract for $15,000.

By the 1920 season, Speaker was the player-manager and earning $30,000. He also was about to change baseball in Cleveland forever.

Until I began looking back through this family album of a baseball team, I never realized how the 1920 Indians got caught up in the backwash from the stench of gamblers and the 1919 Black Sox scandal. Baseball's deep thinkers spent much of 1920 trying to convince their fans that the games weren't fixed, even as the fixers continued to play for Chicago. The Indians finished two games ahead of the White Sox, three in front of the Yankees to win the American League pennant.

Yet one unidentified White Sox player told *The Sporting News*, "We would have won the 1920 pennant in a walk if those fellows had played fair."

He meant the eight White Sox players accused of doing business with gamblers to throw the 1919 World Series. The player also told *The Sporting News* that, even in 1920, pitcher Eddie Cicotte was told to lose some games or gamblers "would do violence to him."

*The Sporting News* even ran some stories asking if the World Series should be abolished, because it was "evil" due to the fact so many fans bet on it. Betting would always leave the gamblers' fingerprints on the games, making you wonder if there would ever be an "honest" World Series. No one ever ac-

cused the 1920 Indians or National League champion Brooklyn
Dodgers of throwing games, but as the 1920 World Series
began in the first week of October, at that same moment, the
Black Sox trial was convening in Chicago. Pitcher Eddie Cicotte
wept in front of a grand jury, saying he took $4,000 from gam-
blers to help pay off the mortgage on his farm. First baseman
Chick Gandil, one of the key links between the players and
the gamblers, refused to speak. White Sox owner Charles
Comiskey mailed $1,500 checks to his players who were sup-
posed to have been "on the level" in the 1919 World Series, the
$1,500 being the difference between the winners' and losers'
share.

Into this baseball world, my father was born.

And into this baseball world, Tris Speaker and the Indians
came to the rescue.

Speaker proved to be a true leader.

Slim Caldwell could have told you as much.

Slim was a knuckleball pitcher with a terrible drinking problem—even for his time, when booze and baseball
flowed together. Speaker decided the mistake made by other
managers was trying to keep Caldwell *sober* all the time. In
Caldwell's contract with the Tribe, Speaker wrote, "After each
game he pitches, Ray Caldwell MUST get drunk. He is not to
report to the clubhouse the next day. The second day, he is to
report to Manager Speaker, and run as many times around the
park as Manager Speaker stipulates. The third day, Caldwell is
to pitch batting practice. The fourth day, Caldwell pitches a
game."

With this method, Caldwell won 20 games.

And boy, was he glad about the clause ordering him to get
wasted.

In his first game at League Park, Caldwell was struck by
lightning, and knocked flat. Everyone ran to the mound. But
somehow, Caldwell got up and finished the game. Maybe it's

true God keeps an extra eye on drunks. As soon as that game ended, Caldwell dashed to his favorite watering hole—all in keeping with the manager's orders.

In many ways, the 1920 Indians were a typical Tribe team: Tragedy lurked just beneath the surface.

Early in the season, the wife of star pitcher Stanley Coveleski suddenly died of unexplained causes. Even knowing that his wife had just passed away in Shamokin, Pennsylvania, Coveleski refused Speaker's offer to skip his start. He went out, beat the White Sox, 13–6, then took a train home to bury his wife.

The flag at League Park was flown at half-mast. Coveleski had a 24-14 record in 1920, but his teammates insist he could have won 30 games were he not depressed for a month after his wife's death. Coveleski was a coal miner and spitball pitcher. "I went into the mines at the age of twelve," he once said. "There was nothing unusual about a twelve-year-old Polish kid in the mines for seventy-two hours a week at a nickel an hour. What was strange was I made it out."

Control was the key. Coveleski would rather take his eye out with a stick than walk a batter. He learned how to make a baseball do as it was told by practice, only his practice was throwing rocks at tin cans. In 1920, he pitched one game where not one of his pitches missed the strike zone in the first seven innings.

Think about that.

Seven innings, not one ball.

On August 16, 1920, shortstop Ray Chapman was drilled in the temple by a pitch from sidearmer Carl Mays. This was before hitters wore helmets. A day later, the scrappy shortstop was officially pronounced dead—and remains the only major league player ever to be killed on the field.

The League Park flag was again at half-mast.

Chapman played the guitar and sang songs on those twelve-hour train trips. But after his death, the Indians never sang on trains again.

Not until right before the 1920 World Series.

Not until it was decided that the best way to remember Chappie in the World Series was to sing a song on the train as the Indians made their way from Cleveland to Brooklyn for the opening game.

After Chapman's death, the Indians had no shortstop. The pennant hung in the balance, and Speaker found a kid named Joe Sewell. He was a graduate of the University of Alabama who had played only 92 games as a minor leaguer in New Orleans. Chapman was the most popular man on the team. Replacing him wouldn't have been easy for an established big leaguer. But to bring in a kid, a college kid into a dressing room of farmers, miners, and dockworkers—what was Speaker thinking?

When Sewell arrived in Cleveland, he either forgot his bat or it was lost on the train. A first baseman named Tioga George Burns looked at the nervous college kid with no bat.

He said, "Kid, try this one. Just don't break it."

It was a 44-ounce beauty, dubbed Black Betsy.

It became the only bat Sewell used in his 14-year major league career. And get this: in 7,132 major league at bats, he struck out only 114 times—and he stayed with that one bat.

Joe Sewell batted .329, stepping in for Chapman. Yes, it was that kind of year, Tribe fans.

Here is why the players loved Speaker: When an opposing pitcher threw at the head of one of his teammates, the player-manager would come out of the dugout, screaming, "You do that again, and you'll never get out of this park alive!"

The pitcher would see Speaker's wild eyes and clenched fists. They would remember his hard, spikes-high slides into second base and how he muscled that $10,000 out of the Boston Red Sox.

As they said back then, Tris Speaker was not a man to be trifled with.

The Brooklyn Dodgers won the 1920 National League pennant by seven games. Their manager was Wilbert "Uncle Robbie" Robinson, a fat man who was quick with a smile, a joke, or a song.

You can say he ran a loose ship.

You can even say he and his players read newspapers in the dugout during boring games.

You can say he tried to have discipline, as Uncle Robbie started the "Bonehead Club," to punish players for mental mistakes. Only he became the charter member when he posted the wrong lineup for a game.

No one accused the players in the 1920 World Series of conspiring with gamblers, but not all of them were exactly the sharpest knives in the drawer. Before the seventh game, Brooklyn pitcher Rube Marquard was arrested for scalping tickets in a hotel lobby. He had a pair of box seats, and wanted $300 for them. A Cleveland detective was more than willing to talk business, then slap the cuffs on the Brooklyn pitcher. Marquard was fined $3.80, then reported to the park.

Now get this: Marquard was to start the seventh game for Brooklyn.

And get this: Uncle Robbie actually got mad, so mad that he scratched Marquard and started Burleigh "Ol' Stubblebeard" Grimes instead.

The Indians shaved old Stubblebeard, 3–0.

The Indians beat Brooklyn, 8–1, in Game 5.

Tribe second baseman Bill Wambsganss (shortened to Wamby to fit in newspaper box scores), recorded the only unassisted triple play in World Series history.

Famed author and sportswriter Ring Lardner wrote all

there was to say about the play: "Kilduff and Miller got base hits off Bagby, then Mitchell cleaned the bases with a line drive to Wambsganss."

The 1920 World Series was a best-of-nine affair.

The Indians were up, 4–2, heading into the seventh game at League Park. The assumption was that the Tribe would lose, taking the series back to Brooklyn for an eighth game.

Why?

So both the players and owners would make more money from an extra game.

Tris Speaker had other ideas. He not only cared about the Indians, but the state of baseball. He believed in an honest game, and he wanted to win the series in front of his home fans, who had been selling out League Park for every Series game. He asked Stanley Coveleski if he could start the game—even though he had only two days rest instead of his usual three.

Coveleski took the ball, beating Brooklyn, 3–0.

In the World Series, the man called "The Silent Pole" had a 3-0 record with an astonishing 0.67 ERA. The man who lost his wife early in the season pitched three complete games. It was a World Series where Cleveland's Elmer Smith hit the first postseason grand slam in history and Jim Bagby was the first pitcher ever to homer in the World Series.

While Tribe fans rushed the field after the World Series was won, Speaker headed into the stands with the ball used for the final out. Behind the dugout, he found his mother, and presented her the baseball.

The two embraced as photographers snapped their pictures, making Speaker Cleveland's favorite son.

# CHAPTER 7

# League Park

LEAGUE PARK was my father's favorite ballpark.

It was at the crossroads of two streetcar lines on East 66th Street and Lexington Avenue. The park was built there because the Robison family owned the Indians—and the streetcar lines.

It was the park where Babe Ruth hit his 500th home run and where Cy Young won his first game. It was where the Indians won their first World Series and where Tris Speaker got his 3,000th hit.

It was where my father took the streetcar, arriving early so he could find a spot where he could peer through a hole in the fence at the game for free.

"I was one of the original members of the Knothole Gang," he said. "My mother would pack me peanut butter sandwiches. That was lunch. This was the Depression. We didn't have any money."

His mother worked cleaning "rich people's houses in Shaker Heights." His father lost his job at an ironworks company for a few years, but took a streetcar to a designated location, where he was picked up by a truck and taken out to the country to pick crops such as mushrooms. My father had paper routes and did odd jobs.

But there was always baseball.

His parents took my father and his sister Pat to amateur games at Woodland Hills Park. It was a Pluto tradition on Sunday afternoons. No TV in the home. No money for movies. No car to drive. You walked. You took the streetcar. You looked for free entertainment, and baseball at Woodland Hills Park was a big part of that.

But most of all, my father loved League Park and the Indians. He followed them in the *Cleveland News*. He schemed to find free tickets to games. League Park was really where my father learned to love baseball. In our family, you can turn the pages of the album and see three baseball houses—League Park, Municipal Stadium, and Jacobs Field.

Because of his stroke, my father never made it to Jacobs Field.

Because of my age, I never made it to League Park.

"The two places are a lot alike," said Hal Lebovitz.

Lebovitz would know. As a kid, he was a vendor at League Park. As a young man, he covered the Indians at the Stadium. Still a working journalist in his eighties, Lebovitz now watches the team at Jacobs Field. I know my father wished he could have said the same thing. He longed to see the Indians in a new ballpark, especially a ballpark that is so much like the one where he first embraced the game. After my father's stroke, I found myself talking to Lebovitz as I would my dad; I could ask him the questions I wished I had taken the time to ask my own father. Like my father, Lebovitz took the streetcars to the games at League Park. He sometimes stood out beyond the right field wall during batting practice, waiting for baseballs to be hit into the street. Catch a ball and return it to the team, and you were given a free ticket to the game.

And that right field wall—my father loved that right field wall. It was 297 feet from home plate, but it was forty feet high. The last twenty feet was chicken wire held up with steel beams.

"The balls would just rattle off that wall," my father used to say.

Lebovitz also remembers the crazy bounces off that wall. Hit below the wire, and the ball shot off the concrete. Hit on the wire in some spots, and the ball dropped straight down to the base of the wall. Hit one of the beams, it could go any-where—straight back at you, or even at a 90 degree angle, all depending upon where it banged off the beam.

"On a ball hit to right field, the right fielder, center fielder and second baseman all ran out there trying to figure out how the ball would come off the wall," said Lebovitz.

It was a wall that rewarded short, high fly balls to right field by turning them into 300-foot homers. But it knocked down twenty-foot-high line drives that would have carried out of most other ballparks. A few hitters smote line drives that were so hard, they just stuck into the wire fence above the wall.

As if that wasn't eccentric enough, the left field foul pole was 378 feet from home plate. During much of its existence, dead center was 460 feet from the batter.

My father would arrive at League Park several hours be-fore the game. He'd wait outside the right field wall to catch a ball during batting practice, his ticket to the game. If not, then he'd peek through the fence.

He never said how he did that.

"I know," said Lebovitz. "You could watch the game *under* the right field wall."

Under? The Knothole Gang actually watched the game *under* the fence?

"You'd lie down on your belly and peek under the fence," he said. "Mostly, you'd see the players' shoes."

League Park opened for business in 1891, with the street-cars stopping a mere twenty feet from the main gate. It sat about 9,000. In 1910, the park was expanded to 27,000 seats. It was reinforced with steel and an upper deck was added. The Indians played most of their home games at League Park until the end of the 1946 season.

It was like Jacobs Field in that the fans could walk around the park and usually stop and have an excellent view of the game. Many of the seats were astonishingly close to the field. The moment a fan came through the tunnel, he saw the green grass and the huge wall looming so close in right. He saw the scoreboard where kids hung numbers on nails. The place just reeked of hot dogs on the grill, beer in sweaty bottles, and most of all, baseball. This wasn't a stadium, it was a ballpark.

My father and Lebovitz came to the Indians in the 1930s. Depression baseball. It was a time when ballplayers lived in your neighborhood, a time when 20 percent of the workforce was unemployed, yet newspapers routinely printed the home addresses of Tribe players. A *Plain Dealer* story about outfielder Joe Vosmik read, "He is Bohemian with blond hair, hazel eyes and lives at 3655 East Boulevard." No one thought to go to their homes and rob the athletes when a game was on or when they were on the road, even in the darkest hours of the Depression. Ballplayers were your neighbors, and most didn't consider themselves that much better than you.

"I was about sixteen years old and I saw Earl Averill coming out of a jewelry store one day," said Lebovitz. "He was one of my favorite players. I was so nervous, I had to force myself to talk to him."

But Lebovitz did. And Averill learned that Lebovitz was a vendor at League Park. The next thing he knew, Lebovitz was riding to the park with the Tribe's star outfielder.

"It wasn't a big deal," said Lebovitz. "At least not to Averill. I never forgot it. I even remember going to a game by streetcar, looking up and seeing Charlie Gehringer and some of the Detroit Tigers sitting right across from me."

Even future Hall of Famers took streetcars to League Park during the Depression.

"Every schoolkid in Cleveland used to get free tickets for

one game a year," Lebovitz said. "The boys would try to talk the girls into giving them their tickets, or making some kind of trade."

In the middle 1930s, the Indians were only averaging about 5,500 fans per game.

"On days when they had an overflow crowd, they'd put a rope inside the wall in center and left field," recalled Lebovitz. "The fans would stand behind the rope. You'd stand in the outfield and watch the game. You felt like you were looking over Earl Averill's shoulder."

There was something else.

"After games, they allowed kids to run around the bases and in the outfield," Lebovitz said.

The field wasn't a sacred shrine. It was a ballyard, and ballyards are for kids.


Baseball in the 1930s to men such as Lebovitz and my father was much like baseball in the 1960s and 1970s to the Curse of Rocky Colavito generation—we were too young to realize how truly lousy those teams and players were in Tribe uniforms. In the 1930s, the Indians never finished closer than 12 games out of first place. For those Tribe fans who remember "Don't Knock The Rock," that mediocre refrain sounds depressingly familiar.

The difference is the faces.

When you look at the players from the 1960s and 1970s, they look like many of the athletes of today. They are not quite as big and bulked up, but they are modern men. Some black. Some white. Some Latino. They are the post-Depression, post–World War II generation.

Compare them to the men in the 1930s. All of these men are white, and few are the sons of affluence. They have the faces of farmers and miners, of men who were new to America. They are hard, lined faces with prominent jowls and noses. They are faces of thirty-year-olds, yet they look closer to fifty.

Bad food, long train rides, and too much beer. Bags under the eyes.

There also are the faces of the twenty-somethings, the young stars who looked like they were still in high school. Huge ears stick out from baseball caps tilted cockily to one side. They have wide eyes, and many of them have buck teeth. They don't look much like pro ballplayers. They're just kids. But within ten years, most of them would be in their early thirties—already owning the lined, weathered faces of middle age.

This was the Depression. How bad was it? In 1935, Hall of Famer Cy Young was discovered clerking at a dime store in Newcomerstown, Ohio. He was sixty-eight years old and living in a small room at a modest hotel. Despite 511 victories and being one of the highest paid players of his day, Young had seen his savings wiped out in the stock market crash.

In 1935, the Tribe also fired the manager.

In the 1930s, the Indians were always firing the manager. At the All-Star break in 1935, the Indians were in fourth place, but they'd lost eight of their last nine games. Manager Walter Johnson was being blasted in the newspapers and by some of his own players as a former superstar who didn't understand the struggles of the average player. Johnson once said he "never had a sore arm," and apparently expected the same from his Tribe pitchers. Johnson also was unhappy with several sportswriters, and had stopped granting them interviews.

One of the Tribe's best players was center fielder Earl Averill, but he was out for three weeks because he was burned on the right hand when a New York fan hit him with a firecracker. Cleanup man Hal Trosky was in the midst of a horrible slump at bat, and suddenly he had trouble catching the ball at first base. He also was beginning to suffer from the migraine headaches that would eventually cut short his career.

Things were so depressing with the Indians that the players took out an advertisement in all three Cleveland newspapers stating, "We, the members of Cleveland Indians, want the fans to know we are not a team split wide open by dissension, arrayed against our manager."

It didn't help.

A month after the All-Star Game, Walter Johnson was fired. Perhaps the greatest pitcher of his era, he couldn't get his message across to the players.

In the 1930s, the perception was that Cleveland was always firing its manager—and the fans seemed to take out all their frustrations over the Depression on the man in the Tribe dugout.

"To be booed by the Cleveland fans is to booed by the best in the business," wrote Shirley Povich in the *Washington Post*. "There may be no truth to the report that Cleveland game-goers eat their young, but they don't stop very short of being carnivorous where Cleveland managers are concerned. But a Cleveland manager has not only the wolfish fans to contend with, he must battle an unpredictable front office and a hyper-critical Cleveland press. . . . Here, the baseball writers treat the game something akin to life and death."

The Indians had four different managers in the 1930s. They actually had only one losing season, but the team usually was out of contention by the end of August. Meanwhile, the fans and sportswriters grumbled.

"We only hire the manager, the public fires him," said Tribe owner Alva Bradley.

The same could have been said by the Indians from 1960 to 1993.

My father was very patient with those Tribe teams in the 1960s and early 1970s. Sure, he'd become frustrated when Richie Scheinblum was brought up from the minors, with the expectation that he'd be a .300 hitter with 30-homer potential—and he batted .186 in 1969. But mostly, my father would give a deep sigh, the reaction of a man who had seen all this before.

His favorite player was Hal Trosky, who came to the Tribe in 1934 and hit .330 with 35 homers and 142 RBI—in his first full season. In 1936, Trosky hit .343 with 42 homers and what remains a franchise-record 162 RBI.

"He was going to be a great, great player," my father said. "Another Lou Gehrig. I played first base, and I wanted to be just like him. But those headaches . . ."

In the late 1930s, Trosky began to suffer from severe migraines. Bob Feller thought it was the result of stress.

"I know the fellows are counting on me," Trosky told the *Cleveland News*. "I know that I can't always make good for them. I'm all right until I get on that field. Then my head starts hammering."

He also played first base with all the grace of a blacksmith strumming a harp.

"An awkward fielder on grounders, he was a fine receiver of thrown balls," wrote the *Cleveland Press*. "But he was sensitive to criticism from the stands, and admitted as much."

Or as veteran Cleveland sportswriter Franklin Lewis wrote, "Trosky is a worry wart who can't give his best efforts if he's upset. . . . World affairs worried him. He fretted [over] imperialism in Germany. He became a neurotic who was caught between a mental fog and a physical bog. Eventually, he quit baseball. . . . Headaches, stomach ailments, leg injuries, shin splints, etc., figured in his final decision."

You hear the stories of Trosky and you realize that not everyone in the Depression was the strong, silent type. Trosky sounds like a man of this age, torn and sensitive, wanting to please but fearing he'll always fall short. In 1939, he batted .335 with 25 homers and 104 RBI—excellent numbers, but not Lou Gehrig, not up to the standards he'd set early in his career.

By 1941, the headaches and anxiety had turned his bat to mush. He played in only 89 games and had 11 homers.

He was done, retired. And he was only twenty-eight years old.

He had grown up on an Iowa farm, and he went back to that farm in the hamlet of Norway, Iowa—the same farm where he first learned to hit by taking the handle of a hoe and whacking corncobs like a coach hitting fungoes. When Tribe scout Cy Slapnicka first spotted Trosky, the hulking farmboy was hitting with his hands crossed. In other words, he was batting right-handed—but he had his left hand on top, rather than the right, which is how left-handed hitters hold the bat. The Indians turned him into a lefty hitter to match his hands. He was right there, standing on the cusp of greatness, and it all fell apart. He returned to that farm angry about not making an All-Star team, as he could never beat out Jimmie Foxx and Hank Greenberg for a spot. He seethed over being labeled as one of the "Crybabies," who led a revolt against manager Oscar Vitt in 1940. He asked the Lord why all the headaches, which sometimes made him feel nearly blinded at home plate. His guts churned with every boo from the stands.

In 1970, my father's favorite player was Tony Horton, another talented but tormented first baseman whose career was cut short because he was unable to cope with the pressure of baseball in Cleveland. I don't think that was a coincidence.

In the 1930s, my father's Tribe had stars. But like Trosky, they were flawed people. The ace of the staff in 1936 and 1937 was Johnny Allen.

"The shirt," my father said. "He wore this shirt with the sleeve ripped. Then they complained and made him take it off. He never was the same pitcher after that."

Trosky with his headaches, Allen and his shirt. No wonder my father had the perfect training for a Tribe fan in the Curse of Rocky Colavito generation. Allen was believed to be one of the first pitchers to throw a slider. And like many of his fellow pitchers today, he believed he was always underpaid and was not afraid to gripe about it. He battled with general managers, managers, and umpires. His temper was such that the Yankees gave up on his obvious talent, and traded him to the Indians before the 1936 season. Eager to show the Yankees how stupid and shortsighted they were in casting him aside, Allen became a 20-game winner for the Tribe. "I have no use for New York and I want New York to know it—and you can quote me," was his refrain to sportswriters.

In 1937, he won his first 15 decisions and then lost, 1–0, on the last day of the season. If he had won that game, it would have tied an American League record for consecutive victories. But the Indians could manage only one hit for him.

For 1936 and 1937 his record was 35-11 and he was rated as one of the top pitchers in baseball. He also drove his manager to distraction. For a while, he'd only pitch to Frankie Pytlak, whom he considered his personal catcher. He had a bar fight in 1936 when he was fined $250 for "getting drunk, creating a disturbance, breaking up furniture, attacking hotel [employees] and for raising hell in general," explained Tribe manager Steve O'Neill.

The *Cleveland Press* reported that Allen "went on a binge at the Brunswick Hotel bar where after several minutes of elbow-bending, he discovered the stools were not large enough to sit upon. Allen bowled over several stools, berated the bartenders and finally became altogether too playful for the welfare of the bar furnishings, not to mention the customers. . . . He later became involved with a hotel porter. When the hotel porter refused to be cowed, Allen reached for a fire extinguisher and fired it point blank at the porter."

For good measure, he saw a man on a stepladder repairing a ceiling fixture—and pulled the ladder out from under the poor fellow, hammering the walls with the ladder as the repairman fell down.

But what about the shirt?

Allen wore an old sweatshirt that was slit at the sleeve of his throwing arm, so it would flap as he pitched. Early in June of 1938, Boston manager Joe Cronin complained that the shirt distracted the hitters, and he wanted Allen to change it. Umpire Bill McGowan—who'd had several run-ins with Allen before—was glad to agree with Cronin. Allen scoffed. The umpire insisted. Allen walked off the mound, into the clubhouse—and didn't come back out. Manager Oscar Vitt tried to coax Allen back to the mound (with a regulation shirt), but Allen refused. A frustrated Vitt fined the pitcher $250.

The shirt was later sold to the Higbee department store for—you guessed it—$250. The store put it on a dummy, and baseball fans flocked to see it. Allen returned to pitching, but according to my father, he was never the same.

Actually, Allen was 14-8 in 1938, the year he lost his shirt. That was down from 20-10 and 15-1 in his first two years with the Tribe, but he was still a fine pitcher. Losing his shirt did not lead to Allen's decline; a sore arm was the culprit. While Allen would not reveal the cause, Frank Gibbons of the *Cleveland Press* reported, "He slipped in the bathtub during an All-Star Game in Cincinnati."

So it was for the Tribe in the 1930s. The teams usually looked better on paper than they played on the field. The front office found it easier to fire the manager than make a major personnel overhaul. Meanwhile, frustrated fans such as my father continued to wait until next year, knowing that the team had not won a pennant since 1920.

But there was something romantic about the 1930s Indians to men such as my father. The ballpark was cozy. Following the team (despite its disappointments) was much better than watching the stock market. Baseball dominated the sports scene in Cleveland, as the Indians were the only pro team worthy of discussion. Just as the mediocre teams of the 1960s turned me into a Tribe fan, those 1930s Indians made my father a lifetime member of the Chief Wahoo nation.

Today, League Park still stands—sort of.

It's just the grandstand along the first base line. There is just one set of crumbling stone bleachers. The walls are scarred with graffiti as gangs fight to be noticed in the place where everyone from Ruth to Gehrig to Speaker to Feller once played. You see names spray-painted on those walls, names that mean nothing except to the gangs in the area: CEDA, BLOB, BIG MAN.

On the corner of East 65th and Lexington where the Indians office once stood is a small recreation center fighting to bring dignity to this neighborhood. There is a little gym and a community center.

There is even a baseball diamond, where Little League teams play, and the Indians are one of the sponsors trying to bring the game back into the inner city. The infield is all dirt, the outfield mostly crabgrass and dandelions. Recently, the city of Cleveland has spent some money shaping up the field so you can try to field a ground ball without worrying about your teeth being knocked out.

But the right field wall is gone. So is the center field scoreboard, the left field bleachers, and the streetcar lines.

When the Indians left for good after the 1946 season, League Park was turned over to the city. The city had little use for it, and soon it fell into despair and disrepair. It wasn't worth the money to maintain it, so it was mostly torn down by the early 1950s. The Browns still practiced there until 1964, changing under the one set of grandstands that remains.

This breaks Lebovitz's heart.

"I wish they had made it into a special field for the best amateur teams to play," he said. "It was such a great place. To me, it wasn't just a ballpark, it was heaven."

My father couldn't have said it better.

# CHAPTER 8

# Feller & Wright

IT WAS a night when I wished my father could be right there, sitting with me in the press box at Jacobs Field. It was Game 4 of the 1997 World Series. Jaret Wright was pitching for the Tribe, and I found myself next to Bob Feller and Hal Lebovitz. My father always respected Lebovitz as a writer, and he loved Feller.

"I saw him pitch at Woodland Hills Park," my father often told me.

Woodland Hills Park is an area on the East Side of Cleveland with a few baseball diamonds, basketball courts, and tennis courts. My father met my mother on those tennis courts. He played baseball on those diamonds, which were nearly across the street from his house.

"And I saw Bob Feller pitch there before he was with the Indians," my father said.

I always nodded. I didn't doubt my father, but I also was confused by it. Why would Bob Feller have been pitching at

some amateur field? My father said he was pitching for Rosenblum's, one of the top amateur teams in the Cleveland area.

"Fastest pitcher I ever saw," said my father.

As Bob Feller sat next to me, watching Jaret Wright, I
asked him about the game my father claimed to have seen.

"It happened," Feller said.

What happened was that Feller was signed by Tribe super-
scout Cy Slapnicka in 1936. Rather than send Feller to the minors, Slapnicka brought the kid to Cleveland to work out. Then
he arranged for the seventeen-year-old Feller to pitch for Rosenblum's against a team from Akron called Atlantic Foundries.

Feller pitched 12 innings. He struck out 16. He drove in
the winning run with a base hit to pick up the 3–2 victory.

I thought about this as Feller watched Wright in the 1997
World Series. I thought of how there aren't the renowned amateur teams such as Rosenblum's anymore, teams that drew
crowds of 500 or more to their games. I thought of how the Indians would never arrange for their prize prospect to pitch for
an amateur team, and they sure wouldn't let him throw 12 innings.

And then I saw Wright, and I thought of how Feller had
done so much in his career, but had never won a World Series
game. By the fifth inning, it was clear what would happen: The
Indians had a 6–1 lead over the Florida Marlins, and Wright
was destined to be the winning pitcher. Feller stared hard at the
kid, looking for just the right words.

Finally, he said, "Twenty-one years old and he's gonna win
a World Series game."

When the Indians walked off the field with a 10–3 victory,
Feller shook his head.

"That was the one thing," he said.

He meant winning a World Series game. The twenty-one-
year-old Wright already had one—and Feller has none.

"He'll look back on this later," Feller said. "Then he'll really appreciate it."

Feller had watched Wright pump new life into the Tribe's World Series dreams. He'd watched the kid hold Florida to three runs in six solid innings. He also had watched Wright beat the Yankees, not once but twice in the 1997 playoffs. Feller was like most Tribe fans, searching his memory banks trying to recall when the team last had a young pitcher like Wright.

"He's got a good body for a pitcher," said Feller. "Reminds me of Virgil Trucks."

Feller paused, realizing not many fans would remember Virgil Trucks, who pitched in the 1940s and 1950s.

"Tom Seaver," said Feller. "The kid is built like Tom Seaver."

Wright is 6-foot-2 and 230 pounds. Feller likes pitchers who look like linebackers, and he thinks there's nothing wrong with a pitcher having "a big butt," assuming it's not the size of a Jeep Cherokee. Some fans have compared Wright to Feller— but mostly fans who never saw Feller.

"Bob, he doesn't throw as hard as you," said Hal Lebovitz.

"The kid does have a good arm," said Feller.

That's a real compliment, because Feller thinks little of today's pitchers, especially their arm strength. He tells you how they just don't throw hard—and they don't throw hard because they don't throw enough. He thinks they baby their arms. He's tired of seeing twenty-five-year-old pitchers with their arms wrapped in ice as if they were old men.

"Between starts, I pitched batting practice," he said. "Once in a while, I even pitched in relief. I threw almost every day. The arm is a muscle. The way to make it stronger is to use it, not baby it."

And after pitching his 240 innings in a season (he did that nine times), Feller would put together a winter barnstorming team and play in small towns nearly every day. He'd pitch a couple of innings in each of those games because he was the man the fans paid to see. It was common for him to pitch twenty-eight out of thirty days in the winter.

●

Feller spends night after night in ballparks across the country as he makes appearances in minor league parks, signing autographs for a few bucks. He sees a lot of games, but he sees few good fastballs and even fewer pitchers he likes. But Jaret Wright is different. Of all the pitchers to come through the Tribe farm system in the last fifty years, Wright is one of the few to draw kind words from Feller.

In the late 1950s, Herb Score was supposed to be the next Bob Feller, but he was struck in the eye by a Gil McDougald line drive.

In the 1960s, Sam McDowell may have thrown as hard as Feller, but McDowell was plagued with drinking problems.

In the 1970s, 1980s, and most of the 1990s, no one came close. And Wright probably won't, either. But it's interesting to compare the two right-handers. Wright grew up in Southern California, son of former major league pitcher Clyde Wright. His father won 100 games from 1966 to 1975 with three different teams. He once threw a no-hitter. Clyde Wright also ran a school for pitchers in Anaheim, and Jaret obviously was his star pupil. At the age of eighteen, Wright had more than a blistering fastball; he had poise. He had a compact motion and surprising control for a young pitcher. On the advice of scout Jay Robertson, the Indians made Wright their first pick in the 1994 draft. Robertson then predicted, "Jaret Wright will throw harder than Roger Clemens, harder than Tom Seaver—maybe harder than anyone, ever." Robertson obviously was caught up in the moment, and his comments helped Wright squeeze a $1.3 million bonus out of the Tribe, the biggest in team history.

By contrast, the Indians found Feller in Van Meter, Iowa. His father owned a 320-acre farm, and had been a semipro pitcher around 1900. Nearly eighty years before *Field of Dreams*, Bill Feller cleared a cornfield and built his own baseball diamond on a hill overlooking the Racoon River. Bill Feller taught his son to pitch behind a barn. In the winter, they moved the games of pitch-and-catch into the barn, where the father had rigged up lights and a heater. Then Bill Feller unleashed young Bob on area players on his own baseball field at the farm.

Feller's hometown of Van Meter is twenty miles from Des Moines. According to a 1937 story in *Collier's,* in Feller's youth, "An active walker could touch every house in town within 15 minutes. . . . There is no bus service, no movie house, no drug store, no pool hall. Population is 410. It's on the Rock Island railroad. A train west stops every morning at 8:36, one east every evening at 7:37, but only when flagged. . . . His high school class numbers 14."

The Indians discovered Feller pitching in an amateur tournament in Dayton, and they signed him at the age of seventeen. He had just finished his junior year in high school. That led to his debut at Woodland Hills Park, which was so impressive that Slapnicka arranged for a new showcase.

This time, it was an exhibition game at League Park against the St. Louis Cardinals. Growing up in Iowa, Feller was a Cardinals fan. This was 1936, and the Cards were only two years removed from the 1934 World Series. They still had Dizzy Dean, Pepper Martin, Joe Medwick, Rip Collins, and most of the famed Gashouse Gang. Feller pitched three innings, struck out eight, and threw nothing but fastballs. As Whitey Lewis wrote in the *Cleveland Press,* "He wound up as if he were following the contour of a large pretzel. Then he kicked his left leg high in the air, up in front of his face. Then he threw fastballs. No curves, just blazers. Eight Cardinals went down swinging—or ducking—in those three historic innings."

After the game, All-Star Dizzy Dean was asked to pose with Feller for photographs. Dean said, "Ask this kid if he'll pose with me!"

The Indians formally put Feller on the roster. He struck out 17 in one game, tying Dean's record. He also walked nine and hit a batter. He fanned 15 in another start. His final record was 5-3 with a 3.34 ERA and 76 strikeouts in 62 innings. Remember, Feller was only seventeen, not even a high school senior.

After the season, there was a controversy about Feller's status when he signed, as the Indians had signed Feller to contracts for minor league teams for which he never played. He was still in high school when the Indians signed him for one dollar and an autographed baseball of the entire team. Commissioner Kenesaw Mountain Landis could have declared Feller a free agent, and Feller could have become the biggest bonus baby in baseball history to that point. After all, he had proven he was nearly unhittable on the major league level at seventeen. But Feller told Landis he wanted to stay with the Indians. "I don't want to play anywhere else," he insisted. Had Feller and his father made a case for free agency—as any agent, friend, lawyer, or even serious fan would have advised them if this happened today—Landis probably would have disallowed the Indians' contract. Feller would have probably received at least a $100,000 bonus. But based on Feller's plea, Landis fined the Indians $7,500 and allowed them to keep Feller.

"Loyalty to your team meant something back then," Feller said, then signed a $10,000 contract with the Tribe.

Jared Wright's advisers bled the Indians for the last dollar, threatening that he'd go to college if the team didn't pay him at least $1.3 million. Wisely, the Indians came up with the cash. No one blamed Wright and his advisers. That's how business is done today.

But Feller shows that wasn't always the case.

As Feller watched Wright, he spotted the flaw that would haunt the young Tribe pitcher in 1998.

"I'd say the kid throws maybe ninety-five miles an hour," he said. "You just don't see kids with arms like that. But he does need a curveball. He needs to pull down the shade."

That is Feller's favorite expression for throwing a curve—you snap it straight down, just as you do a window shade.

"The kid develops a curve to go with the fastball, then

he'll really have something," said Feller. "But I don't know if anybody teaches the old-fashioned, straight overhand curve."

Feller was known for his fastball, but he'll tell you the curve was his best pitch.

"I started throwing it when I was eight years old," he said. "It was by accident. I was playing catch with my father in the barn, and I snapped my wrist when I threw the ball. It spun and curved. My father made me do it again—and again."

And Feller had a marvelous curve.

"Eight years old, I started with that curve, and I never hurt my arm with it," he said. "I threw all the time, every day. I could get the curve over for strikes better than I could my fastball."

Feller paused.

"I got more strikeouts with my curve than anything else," Feller said. "This kid can do the same."

By his nineteenth birthday, Feller was using that curve in the big leagues. He also was winning 17 games. He made 36 starts, completing 20 of them. He threw 277 innings and led the league with 240 strikeouts.

When Feller was watching Wright beat Florida, Wright was only twenty-one years old. It was his third victory of the postseason. Naturally, Tribe fans were hyperventilating and throwing around comparisons with Feller and other great Tribe pitchers.

On that night of October 22, 1997, the Indians took Wright out of the game after six innings and 103 pitches. In his rookie season, the Indians wanted to keep Wright under 100 pitches per start. He was so young, so valuable.

"They never counted pitches when I played," Feller said. "Some games, I'll bet I threw 125 pitches, maybe more."

"A lot more," said Lebovitz, the sportswriter sitting with Feller.

"Maybe 150?" asked Feller.

"More like 175," said Lebovitz. "Who knows? No one worried about it."

They also didn't go to the bullpen. When Feller was twenty-one years old, he had a 27-11 record and completed 31 of 37 starts. He even saved four games. By Wright's age of twenty-one, Feller had already won 82 games and completed 89 games. Which is why it's hard for Feller to gush over Wright, or anyone else.

"But I do like the kid," Feller said. "I talked to him for ten minutes in Miami during the World Series. I saw him sitting by the pool last week, soaking up the sun. He was real nice, listened to what I said."

And what did Feller say?

"I told him that he better learn how to hold runners on base," Feller said.

The Tribe coaches have been saying the same thing.

"If you watch the kid in the stretch position, he holds his arms out away from his body," Feller said. "Looks kind of awkward to me. That could be part of his problem, how he holds his hands."

Any other advice?

"I told him to get a good curve," Feller said. "Pull down the window shade. The kid's curve is kind of flat right now. A good curve can make him a helluva pitcher."

What did Wright say?

"He thanked me," Feller said.

But in 1998, Wright didn't listen. Not to Feller. Not to the Tribe coaches who tried to teach him that curve. He had won a World Series game at the age of twenty-one. He believed a fastball was enough, and discovered otherwise as he had a 12-10 record and a 4.72 ERA. He started twice in the postseason, was hit hard and lost both games. Like so many others, he discovered it's not easy being the next Bob Feller.

Feller started two World Series games, and never won.

That's the only hole in the résumé for this man with three no-hitters, six 20-game–winning seasons, and 12 one-hitters.

"I felt like a guy who turned twenty-one years old and

couldn't wait to vote, but there was no election," Feller said. "You can't vote when there is no election. I couldn't win a World Series game [after 1948] because I never had another chance to pitch in one."

Feller's best shot at a World Series win was his first. He opened the 1948 World Series against the Boston Braves and lost, 1–0, to Johnny Sain. Feller insists that game should still be going, that Tommy Holmes never should have had a chance to drive in the winning run with a single because Feller had picked pinch runner Phil Masi off second base.

"The umpire [Bill Stewart] just missed it," he said. "We had him dead to rights."

Films of the play back Feller's version.

"Part of the reason the umpire missed the play was my fault," said Lou Boudreau, the shortstop and player-manager. "The umpire was from the National League. He wasn't used to our pickoff play, which we used a lot. Before the game, I should have told him to watch out for it."

Stewart seemed to be as surprised as the runner when the throw came to second base. The umpire just didn't react, and finally called "safe," because he realized he had to rule *something*. Of course, the Indians didn't score off Sain, either.

"Actually, all I would have had was a 0–0 tie," Feller said.

Feller started Game 5 of that 1948 series and was smacked around in an 11–5 loss to Boston. The only other time during Feller's career that his team appeared in the World Series was 1954, but Feller was thirty-six years old and a spot starter behind the Big Three of Bob Lemon, Mike Garcia, and Early Wynn. Tribe manager Al Lopez decided to pass on Feller and stick with his Big Three. The Indians were swept in four games by the Giants. And 1954 was Feller's last good year, as he had a 13-3 record and 3.09 ERA. He was 4-8 over the next two seasons and retired at the end of 1956.

While Wright's numbers will never compare to a young Feller's (whose will?), he had an 18-7 record in that year of 1997 counting his minor league and postseason games. It was a year that began at Akron's Class AA Canal Park in April and ended in late October against the Florida Marlins.

"The kid has a good arm," repeated Feller. "You're born with a fastball. I've never seen anyone develop one. It's the same thing with hitters: Either you can hit a good fastball, or you can't."

Wright has a very good fastball, especially because he can throw it over the plate.

"He has confidence," said Feller. "He doesn't pitch scared. Doesn't nibble at the corners."

Feller smiled.

"But he needs that curve," he said.

He'll need more than that to be another Feller.

Six times Feller won at least 20 games. Six times, he led the league in victories. He struck out 18 in a game. He struck out 348 batters in 371 innings in 1946. Neither Wright or anyone else will ever do that. Modern managers just won't allow their pitchers to throw that many innings and that many pitches.

Feller won 266 games, yet lost nearly four full seasons to the Navy during World War II. He lost four years between the ages of twenty-three and twenty-six, four very prime years. In 1940, he was twenty years old and he threw a no-hitter against the Chicago White Sox on opening day, the only opening day no-hitter in baseball history. The temperature was 30 degrees. And remember, Feller was only twenty years old, but he went the distance—with no one counting pitches, no one worrying about protecting his arm. And no one will probably ever do that again, because most managers today wouldn't allow their pitchers to throw nine innings in the first game of the season, even if the pitcher had a no-hitter going. They'd fear the guy's arm wouldn't be strong enough to handle it, especially in 30 degree weather.

"Back then, we just threw," said Feller. "We didn't think so much."

Part of Feller sees someone such as Wright and wonders

why this kid can't consistently win 20 games, why he can't throw 250 innings, and why everyone "just babies these pitchers' arms."

He knows the answer. That's how the game is played today.

"But that doesn't make it right," he said.

# CHAPTER 9

# Boudreau

Lou Boudreau.

Over and over, I heard that name from my father.

Lou Boudreau, the boy manager. Lou Boudreau, the greatest shortstop in Tribe history. Lou Boudreau, the last man to lead the Indians to a World Series title.

"There probably will never be another Lou Boudreau," my father once said.

He's right, and he's not alone in thinking that.

I received a letter from a woman named Kris Evans, who wrote that her father became a Tribe fan in the 1940s, during Boudreau's prime.

"When I was a kid, some twenty years later, I remember him sitting on the porch on dark summer nights, listening to the game on the radio. His cigarette flickered in the night. A beer was at his side. About the seventh inning when the Indians would blow a lead (if they had one), he'd turn off his radio in disgust and go to bed," Kris wrote. "My dad and I had an uneasy relationship. I never forgave him for not being wealthy. I never forgave him for wanting me to work in a restaurant when I wanted to go to college. . . . I resented his attitude for years. . . . He worked fifty years for the same company. . . . He was a dreamer, a contradiction—a chain-smoking beer drinker who knew all the lines to Poe's 'Annabel Lee'. . . . I remember him taking me to ballgames at the old Stadium, and I remember seeing Tony Horton hitting a home run. Blue Moon Odom was pitching. He bought me books by the bagful. He taught me to read the funnies when I was six. Then I became a parent and learned having kids is making mistakes. We grew closer. He taught my son how to figure out earned run averages. That was in July. By October, he couldn't even remember who my son was—cancer is like that. He died at seventy, a frail feather of man. He didn't leave me or my sisters much money or any real estate, but we all can read a box score."

It's funny what we remember, what our fathers leave us.

For Kris, it was the box scores, the memory of Tony Horton hitting a homer, and the Indians losing a lead as her father listened on the porch. But baseball doesn't start with us, with our memories; it goes back to our parents, or maybe even our grandparents. Just like many children today have come to the Indians because of Omar Vizquel, Jim Thome, and Manny Ramirez, our fathers and grandfathers had heroes, too.

Probably no player was more a hero to Tribe fans than Lou Boudreau. That's because there will never again be a twenty-four-year-old shortstop appointed manager of the Indians—or at least let's hope not. Imagine Omar Vizquel starting at shortstop and managing the team, too. Actually, if you had to pick a player-manager from the Tribe's roster, it probably would be Vizquel; as general manager John Hart has often said, "Omar is the heart and soul of our team." Manager Mike Hargrove has called Vizquel "the leader of the infield."

But Vizquel as player-manager?

"Not me," he said. "No way. I knew he was a great player. I saw his name in the media guide, having all these records."

But Boudreau also was the manager.

"That, I can't believe," Vizquel said.

Boudreau became the Tribe manager at twenty-four years old.

"Never," Vizquel said. "I knew a lot about baseball at twenty-four, but manage, too? Why did they do that?"

It's a good question.

In the 1990s you can understand why Vizquel would never be a player-manager. The game is too complex, the egos too much for one man to handle—especially while trying to play shortstop. But even in 1942, it made no sense for the Indians to make their twenty-four-year-old All-Star shortstop their manager. Why make your best player the manager? And your best player isn't even twenty-five? What happens if you have to fire the manager? You can't just fire your best player. You can't give him away. So do you trade him? Do you ask if he'd be willing to stop managing and just play? If you do that, would the player be willing to take a pay cut? Even if his pay stayed the same, would he listen to the new manager? Would he resent someone else telling him to bunt or to take a day off? Would the players he once managed come to him with their gripes about the new manager?

It's one thing to take a star such as Tris Speaker and make him a player-manager toward the end of his career. But to do it with Boudreau, who had been in the majors only three seasons?

Dumb. Dumb. Dumb.

Sometimes, a team can have dumb luck, which the Tribe did with Boudreau. But understand this right now—making Boudreau the player-manager at the age of twenty-four was just plain dumb. It was something only the Indians could do. So how did they get themselves into such a position that they expected a kid shortstop to bail them out?

You have to look at what happened to the Tribe after Speaker resigned as Tribe manager after the 1926 season.

Actually, Good Guy Tris found himself in a mess in 1926. He was part of an investigation of players who may have fixed a game in 1919, the same year the Chicago White Sox threw the World Series. Ty Cobb was another, and he resigned as player-manager of the Detroit Tigers. Cobb and Speaker were told to "retire" by American League president Ban Johnson. Both players were later cleared and came back with other teams as players, but this ended Speaker's fine managerial career with the Tribe.

In 1927, a new era of baseball began in Cleveland.

Speaker was gone. The team was sold by the estate of Jim Dunn to a millionaire named Alva Bradley, who also was president of the Cleveland Chamber of Commerce. It's a long story, but in the words of Bradley, "I bet this is the first time a million dollars and a baseball team ever changed hands in a bathroom!"

Yes, the Indians were sold in the bathroom of a hotel suite, Bradley sitting on the toilet—thankfully with his pants up, the seat down. Word is the boys shook hands over the sink. Bradley walked out of the bathroom and proclaimed, "I'm the perfect man to own the Indians—I know nothing about baseball!"

To prove it, Bradley banned radio coverage of Tribe games in 1933 because it was the Depression, and he thought the games being on the radio would hurt attendance—way to take care of your fans who couldn't afford to come to the park, right?

With that kind of thinking, it's no wonder Bradley's group couldn't find a manager it liked. When Speaker "retired," the Bradley group had to find a manager for the 1927 season. From that point on, they always seemed to be looking for a manager. Managers came and went, three years being the usual lifespan. In the 1930s, it was so bad that Cleveland was called "the Graveyard of Managers" by baseball writers across the country.

Then came Oscar Vitt.

Just listen to the name: Oscar Vitt. Does that *sound* like a nice man? Oscar Vitt. A man with that name probably is destined to grow up with a chip on his shoulder, especially if he grows into one of those "feisty" utility infielders in the big leagues. Usually, when you hear the word "feisty" attached to a guy's name, it means he's a pain in the butt. He's a bowl of green oatmeal. Oscar Vitt was all that and more. If you listen to the men who played for Oscar Vitt, they will tell you that Oscar Vitt wasn't a manager, he was nails dragged across a blackboard. He was a dentist's drill.

Not because he was an idiot.

It was worse. According to players, Vitt was two-faced. Vitt looked you in the eye and lied—then talked about you behind your back. A smile to your face, then a dagger between the shoulder blades. Another of his charming traits was to talk about himself in the third person. Vitt called himself "Old Oz." He'd tell writers and players, "Old Oz sure could hit that ball."

A check of the records revealed Old Oz was lucky to have a big league job. He batted .238 with only four home runs in 10 big league seasons. As a player, Oscar Vitt was just another guy, except he got himself noticed by talking louder than most everyone else.

Vitt was hired to replace Steve O'Neill, the catcher turned manager who was considered too soft, too much a friend of the players. The Tribe front office found Vitt managing in the minors for the Yankees, where his 1937 Newark Bears team ran away with International League title. Of course, that team was stacked with young Yankee talent, and New York had the best scouts and spent the most money on its farm system. Oscar Vitt was hardly the reason the Newark Bears were an International League superpower, although you'd never know that from talking to Old Oz.

So you bring a guy with Yankee arrogance to Cleveland, a guy who thinks he's going to set all these hayseeds straight.

He had about as much tact as the gout.

When Bob Feller was being bombed on opening day, Vitt paced the dugout mumbling, "How am I supposed to win with *that* guy?" and he said it loud enough for the other players to hear.

He once took the venerable Mel Harder out of a game by asking the veteran pitcher, "Just when do you plan on earning your salary?"

He had a theory that the best hitter in the lineup should bat sixth, which didn't sit very well with slugger Hal Trosky. He also once told a slumping Trosky, "You may as well go home, for all the good you're doing us."

Feller said Vitt would tell the hitters, "You know, the pitchers are killing us."

Then he'd tell the pitchers, "You know, we can't win if our guys don't start to hit."

Feller claimed Vitt's wife was an astrology fan, and Old Oz consulted her (and the stars) when it came to making out his lineup and pitching rotation. Even if that wasn't true, the fact that the players believed it was enough to sink Old Oz. When the Indians were losing, Vitt harked back to his days with the Newark Bears, and claimed they were a better team than the Tribe—something else the players were no doubt thrilled to hear. You're Bob Feller, Mel Harder, or Hal Trosky, a legitimate star—and your manager is saying you'd be lucky to play for his old minor league team in Newark? Why would anyone like Old Oz?

In the late 1930s, the Indians had one of the most talented teams in baseball. Many thought they could compete with the Yankees, but that never came to pass. Vitt had records of 86-66 and 87-67 in his first two seasons—not bad, but the players insisted they were winning despite their manager.

Vitt's third season was 1940, and the players couldn't take it. The Indians were the most miserable winning team in baseball history. They had been picked by most experts to win the pennant, and Feller even opened the season by throwing that no-hitter against the Chicago White Sox. But Vitt hated his players, and the players certainly wished he'd awaken one morning and gargle with battery acid so they'd never have to hear his voice again.

For a supposedly bright guy, Vitt could be a total stonehead. He was stunned that all his vile words uttered in what he thought was "a strict confidence" continued to make it back to the players whom he attacked. The fans didn't like Vitt, either—not because he had all the tact of an IRS agent with a migraine, but because the Indians were underachieving. Vitt was booed regularly.

On June 13, 1940, the Nazis invaded Paris—and the Indians had what is believed to be the first player rebellion.

A dozen members of the team went to owner Alva Bradley, asking that Vitt be fired as manager. They suggested coach Luke Sewell take his place. The spokesman was Mel Harder, considered one of the most pleasant, easygoing men ever to wear a Tribe uniform.

"Mr. Bradley, we think we have a good chance to win the pennant," Harder said. "But we'll never win with Vitt."

Other players spoke and said much the same thing, as an hour of Vitt stories filled the room.

"If this ever gets into the newspapers, you guys are in trouble," said Bradley. "You'll be ridiculed for the rest of your life."

Turned out, Bradley was right.

It did get into the newspapers, as the *Plain Dealer*'s Gordon Cobbledick broke the story. Bradley was in a bind. He was leaning toward firing Vitt, but it would appear he'd bowed to the pressure of his players. The inmates would be running the asylum. He would be considered a scarecrow of an owner, bowing to the whims of his pampered players. Remember, this was 1940, fifty-seven years before Penny Hardaway assembled the Orlando Magic in a hotel room and asked the players to vote on the future of coach Brian Hill. The players voted for Hill to be fired, then Hardaway called the general manager with the result. The only difference between the Indians of 1940 and the 1997 Magic was that Hill was canned.

What the Indians did in their meeting with the owner was to save Vitt's job. Suddenly, fans cheered the manager, who put on a Shakespearean performance of the hero who has just been wronged and had no idea why. Reporters around the country attacked the Indians as "Crybabies" and demanded Bradley back his manager. The typical response was like this one in the *Detroit News:* "It could happen only in Cleveland. One manager [Steve O'Neill] lost his job because he didn't get mad at his players and another manager may lose his job because he did. If Alva Bradley were a baseball man, he'd tell his temperamental incompetents to get rid of their shortcomings and silence Vitt."

In Cleveland, the press tended to play it cautious. Franklin Lewis demanded in the pages of the *Cleveland Press* that Vitt resign, but Lewis said the Tribe couldn't fire Vitt because it would "establish a precedent that would handcuff every future manager of the club." Most Cleveland scribes refrained from ripping the players or the manager—a sure sign they agreed with most of what the players had to say.

The day after the rebellion became public, Vitt was given a standing ovation from the 18,000 fans—the first warm greeting he'd ever received in Cleveland. Then the Indians swept a doubleheader. They won four of their next five games after the mutiny attempt. Bradley stuck with Vitt. The team even signed a statement reading, "We the undersigned publicly declare to withdraw all statements referring to the resignation of Oscar Vitt. We feel this action is for the betterment of the Cleveland Baseball Club."

A copy of the statement was printed in Cleveland newspapers.

The fans and writers continued to attack the players. Some fans dressed in diapers and walked around with lollipops and suckers as the Indians took batting practice. In Detroit, someone rigged up a washline and hung baby clothes near the Tribe dugout. It was common for the players to be pelted with rotten fruit and vegetables when they played on the road.

The players and Vitt hardly spoke for the rest of the 1940 season. The team finished 89-65, one game out of first place. Vitt "resigned" at the end of the season. Roger Peckinpaugh returned to manage the team in 1941. Peckinpaugh had also done a tour of duty as manager from 1928 to 1933.

The team fell to 75-79 under Peckinpaugh.

At this point, the Indians needed yet another manager—and the front office had no idea where to turn.

This part of the story is hard to believe.

Lou Boudreau was at his Champaign, Illinois home when he read about Peckinpaugh not coming back as the Tribe manager for 1942. Boudreau had seen Vitt. He had seen Peckinpaugh. He thought, "Could I be any worse than those guys?"

This is a twenty-four-year-old talking, and by all accounts a very polite twenty-four-year-old. He was spending his time after the 1941 season as freshman basketball coach for the University of Illinois, where Boudreau had been a star in basketball and baseball. The 5-foot-11 Boudreau had even played a little pro basketball. He thought about his young career. He had been captain of all his teams in both high school and college.

Why couldn't he manage the Indians?

He wrote a letter to Bradley and stated his case. Yes, he was young, but he had always been in a leadership role.

It came down to ego. Boudreau thought he could do it. Only as he was about to drop the letter into a mailbox near George Huff Gym on the Illinois campus did he begin to have some doubts. He was the youngest player on the team and had been in the majors for fewer than three full seasons. Who was he to tell guys ten years older what to do?

"I almost didn't mail it," Boudreau recalled.

But he did, figuring the Indians wouldn't hire him anyway. But three days after he mailed the letter, Bradley called; he wanted Boudreau to come to Cleveland to meet with the team's board of directors.

At this point, Bradley was out of ideas.

He had owned the team since 1927 and, fifteen years later, he was still looking for his first pennant. He had been through three managers in the last five years. He'd had a player revolt. He even had begun repeating himself when it came to managers, hiring Peckinpaugh twice.

Now this kid Boudreau wanted the job.

"I don't think he's ready," Bradley told the board of directors. "But I'll let you talk to him and decide."

Boudreau already was the most popular player on the team with both the fans and the money men on the board. They were intrigued with the idea of Boudreau as a player-manager. Maybe it would help sell some tickets.

Before Boudreau departed for his interview in Cleveland, his wife, Della, gave some unsolicited advice: If they offer you the job, turn it down. She thought he was too young, that managing and playing would put too much pressure on him. Something would have to give, probably his performance on the field.

Boudreau thought of all this as he faced the money men in their suits. Some of them sucked on cigars. Smoke filled the air. Over and over, they asked Boudreau why he wanted to manage. Over and over, Boudreau told them he had a degree in physical education and planned to be a high school or college coach when he was through playing. He talked of always being a leader, the captain of his teams.

The twelve directors sent Boudreau out of the room. A quick vote was held, 11–1 against making Boudreau the manager. The only man backing him was George Martin, who was chairman of the board of Sherwin-Williams paints. Martin wanted Boudreau. He was enamored with Boudreau's confidence. He knew it would be a move that would generate debate among the fans, and that Boudreau was popular with the local reporters.

"We need some attention on this team, good attention," Martin said.

The directors talked about it. Oscar Vitt. The Crybabies. The national joke the team had become, and how Peckinpaugh could do little to change that in 1941. They sucked on their cigars. They swilled some gin. They were men who knew a lot more about the bottom line of a bank book than what happens in the dugout and clubhouse. They talked about Boudreau being a handsome guy and how women liked him. Maybe he could bring more women to the park. Maybe being young, he could attract younger fans.

If Boudreau being the manager could help sell more tickets . . .

Why not?

That became the question.

Why not Boudreau? Why hire an older retread such as Burt Shotton, the only other candidate? These men were desperate. They hoped to make a public relations splash now and prayed they wouldn't be drowned in the backlash later. They took another vote and Boudreau won, with the stipulation that he hire Shotton and some other veteran baseball men as coaches. His salary was raised from $5,000 to $30,000—yes, this was an era when the manager earned more than most of his players.

"Now that he has a two-year contract, Boudreau will plunge into the titanic job of reconditioning the Indians," wrote Gordon Cobbledick in the *Plain Dealer.*

Bradley began to sell hard, insisting no Cleveland player is "so respected by the players, press and public. Lou is smart, a great ballplayer, a fine young man and a leader."

But could he walk on water? That's what many thought it would take to manage the Indians in 1942.

"The new field manager doesn't drink or smoke and his language at all times is polite and restrained," wrote Cobbledick. "But on the field, he is a firebrand."

There were stories of fights Boudreau had with runners who tried to spike him or his second base partner, Ray Mack.

The Cleveland reporters generally welcomed the hiring. After the chaos of the Vitt era, along with the utter tedium of the other managers, they were anxious to see if Boudreau could pull it off. If nothing else, they knew the Boy Manager was a national story and they were in the middle of it. Surprisingly, most sportswriters from other cities welcomed the move, and were anxious to follow it. Several stated that if any twenty-four-year-old could be a player-manager, Boudreau was the one.

Boudreau caught a break.

It was called World War II, and it broke out two weeks after he was named manager. Pearl Harbor was bombed. Bob Feller enlisted in the Navy. Other key players were headed to the service.

Because of his arthritic ankles, Boudreau was exempt from the draft and he remained player-manager of the Tribe. Because of the war, Boudreau's job was safe under almost any circumstances. He was one of the few major stars still playing stateside. With talent coming and going to the service, it was hard for any team or manager to construct a strong roster. The war bought Boudreau time to learn how to manage. He found out the hard way that signs such as THERE'S NO "I" IN TEAM were not welcome in a major league clubhouse. He found his signs ripped up and splattered with tobacco juice.

He also discovered that reporters didn't consider themselves to be part of the team. Because the writers appeared to like Boudreau, the manager said, "I'd like to read your stories before you send them in just to make sure there's nothing that will hurt the club." Veteran scribes such as Cobbledick gave the new manager his first facts-of-life speech, informing the manager that writers were paid by their papers, not the Cleveland

Indians. Boudreau was a quick study. He didn't put up any more rah-rah signs. He didn't push the writers, and instead made sure they had plenty of access to him and the players. He also told the players he had no objection "to moderate drinking or card playing." He realized he was managing men, not a bunch of college freshmen.

From 1942 to 1946, the Indians had only two winning records under Boudreau. But he was an All-Star shortstop, popular with the fans and writers. The world was at war, so there were more important things to do than fire the manager of the Indians, especially since he was their best player.

All of that changed on June 21, 1946, when the Indians were sold to Bill Veeck, who loved his shortstop but didn't like his manager. The problem was that Boudreau was both. The Indians had an 80-74 record in 1947, Veeck's first season. To Veeck, this wasn't good enough. He had spent every dime he had (and a lot of his friends' dollars) to buy the Indians. He needed them to win, now. He needed big crowds to pack the 80,000-seat stadium. With Veeck being the master promoter, the Indians drew a franchise record 1.5 million fans in 1947 for a team that finished a distant fourth.

Veeck wanted more.

More wins. More fans. More from his manager. He approached Boudreau about remaining as shortstop, but not managing in 1948. Boudreau wanted to keep both jobs or he wanted out. Veeck considered Boudreau "a hunch manager." He felt Boudreau managed like a player, basing many of his decisions on "a gut feeling," rather than sound baseball strategy. Those implusive decisions that buck conventional wisdom are great when they work, but they make the manager look foolish when they don't.

"My problem is, the best shortstop in baseball was not the best manager," Veeck once said. "At twenty-eight, he was still a faintly bewildered Boy Manager."

After the 1947 season, Veeck thought he had a deal set to

send Boudreau to the St. Louis Browns. The key man the Indians would receive in return was Vern Stephens, a power-hitting shortstop. Veeck was so sure the trade would become reality that he had Al Lopez stashed in a Cleveland hotel. At the press conference announcing the trade of Boudreau, Veeck planned to introduce Lopez as the new manager.

The Browns turned down the trade, partly because they had an offer of $300,000 as part of a trade with Boston for Stephens. Veeck had offered only $100,000, and the nearly broke Browns needed cash.

At that point, news of the trade hit the papers—not that the deal was dead, but that it was on the verge of happening. Tribe fans went into a frenzy. How dare Veeck trade Boudreau? The *Cleveland News* printed a ballot, asking fans to vote on the deal—and 90 percent said to keep Boudreau.

Veeck was loving it.

His trade had fizzled, but the rumor remained hot and had the entire city talking baseball. Fan after fan told Veeck to keep Boudreau. Writer after writer spent day after day discussing the merits of the trade. When it became apparent the publicity wave had begun to recede, Veeck called a press conference and announced, "Since the people are against trading Lou Boudreau, then I shout fervently that he will not be traded."

The owner sounded like a man of the fans, a guy who really cared what the customers said and was willing to bend to their will, even if it collided with his own judgment. Veeck turned what could have been a terrible public relations blunder into a way of making both himself and Boudreau even more popular with the fans.

It was all a con job.

He no longer had a deal for Boudreau pending. He was bringing Boudreau back for the 1948 season regardless of what the fans said. It wasn't Veeck or the fans who killed the trade, it was St. Louis. Veeck then had another press conference, announcing Boudreau's new two-year contract.

Winter ticket sales soared. And Bill Veeck looked like a genius.

Boudreau led the Indians to the 1948 World Championship. He was the American League MVP as he hit .355 with 18 homers and 106 RBI—all career highs. Boudreau spent the summer trying to prove Veeck wrong. Veeck told everyone that the Indians won the 1948 pennant late in 1947, when he decided to listen to the fans and not trade Boudreau. He even was credited with being the first baseball executive to say, "Sometimes, the best trades are the ones you never make."

But privately, Veeck still considered Boudreau a dubious manager. As Veeck once wrote, "Lou is the best manager who ever hit .355."

Veeck's vice president was Hank Greenberg, and the former Tiger star:

1. Didn't like the idea of a player-manager.

2. Didn't think Boudreau was a manager.

3. May have wanted to manage the team himself, at least according to Boudreau.

Greenberg and Boudreau would have stormy meetings in Veeck's office after games, with Veeck serving as moderator and sometimes referee. Boudreau believed Greenberg was second-guessing him in order to belittle him in the eyes of the owner. Greenberg thought he knew more baseball than Boudreau. He also claimed he didn't want to manage the team, but just to teach Boudreau a few things about managing. At the time, Boudreau was thirty years old. Greenberg was thirty-six, and still considered Boudreau a kid, at least when it came to managing. As for Veeck, he seemed to enjoy being in the same room while these two baseball greats argued. He found it invigorating and entertaining, while Boudreau just thought it was grating and belittling. Greenberg believed it was frustrating, because Boudreau would not listen to his advice. These meetings began in 1947, and continued through the end of the 1949 season, when Veeck sold the team. Boudreau believed he was through after Veeck departed because Greenberg remained as general manager. In 1950, the Indians finished fourth, but had a fine 92-62 record. Greenberg still fired Boudreau the manager and released Boudreau the shortstop.

Boudreau played a couple of more years with Boston, and also managed the Red Sox, Kansas City, and the Cubs with little to show for it—but none of that would linger in the memories of Tribe fans from his era. To them, Boudreau will always be the Boy Manager, the man who turned many of them into baseball fans.

# CHAPTER 10

# At War

My FATHER often told me that my generation has no idea
what it's like when the world is at war. We don't know what it's
like to wonder if our shores are safe, if our neighbor is a spy, or
if we'll ever see our husbands and fathers again. Most of us
have lived through Vietnam, the Gulf War, and other military
actions, and some of us have lost loved ones in those places. But
nothing ever quite gripped the nation like World War II. My
father went into the Army. Just about every healthy male between the ages of eighteen and forty ended up in the military.

Pearl Harbor did that.

Hitler did that.

"Even Bob Feller was in the Navy," my father said. "Just
about all the best baseball players were in the service. Bet you'd
never see that today."

He's right.

Those who served are our fathers, our uncles, or our
grandfathers. Some are no longer with us. Others are shoved
away in nursing homes, where they sit, waiting.

Waiting for what? The next meal? The last meal?

To many of us, they are just old men—invisible men. My
father told me how he was one of the fortunate ones. He spent
nearly four years in the Army, yet never fired a shot in anger.
Heck, he never even left America.

"I played a lot of baseball in the Army," he said. "I went
from one base to another, playing on the teams. Once, I was assigned to a unit that was supposed to be shipped overseas. The
base commander got me a temporary Section Eight [suppos-
edly because of mental problems], so I could stay at his base
and play in a big tournament. They did that for a couple of the
better players, said we were crazy so we could play baseball."

My father paused.

"My unit went to the Battle of the Bulge," he said. "Not
many of them came home."

Those who did were often helped by my father. He was in
medical reconditioning. He worked with men with missing
limbs, men who once could march fifteen miles on coffee and K
rations, then charge up a hill into a hail of enemy machine gun
fire. Now they were trying to figure out how to get out of their
wheelchairs and take a few steps. This was something he spoke
little about, trying to put these men back together. Was it because it was too depressing? Was there some guilt because so
many of his friends went to Europe or Japan, and not all of
them came back?

I don't know.

I didn't think about it much until right now—now that he
can't talk about it.

So I went to Bob Feller.

He was my father's favorite pitcher, and he can talk about
what it was like to serve.

"I heard about Pearl Harbor when I was driving over the
Mississippi River," he said. "Never forget it. Heard it on the
radio. I was going from my farm in Van Meter [Iowa] to meet

with Cy Slapnicka [the Tribe scout who was promoted to general manager]. That night, I told him I was joining the Navy."

Why?

"Because they had bombed Hawaii!" he said.

Feller was only twenty-three years old, yet he had already won 103 games for the Tribe.

"I didn't have to go," he said. "My father was dying of brain cancer. I had a sister and my mother to support. We had a farm. I was classified 3-C, and would have had a deferment from the draft."

So why sign up?

"Because it was my duty," he said. "Because I loved my country. And when you joined, you had no idea for how long. You just went in for the duration of the war."

Can you imagine many players saying those words today? How many of us would be willing to enter the military service not knowing when we'd get out? How many of us would leave our homes and families, never mind a tremendous, high-paying career as a baseball pitcher, to swab the deck on a battleship? Feller spent three years in the Pacific Ocean on the battleship *Alabama*. He ended up as a chief petty officer and a gunnery officer.

"I grew up with guns on the farm," he said. "I was very comfortable with them."

Feller mentioned something I often heard from my father—that the military was very boring.

"Hurry up and wait, that's the Army," my father would say.

"The Navy wasn't much different," said Feller. "It's not like the movies. You spend so much of your time doing nothing. We'd sit there on the ships, waiting."

They'd wait for orders.

They'd wait for mail call.

They'd wait for a chance to maybe play a little catch on the deck of the ship.

"Day after day, nothing would happen," Feller said. "Then the shooting would start, and it would be complete panic. In the back of your mind, you'd wonder if there was a bullet with your name on it. Or a bomb. Or maybe you'd be killed in a freak accident."

Feller said the *Alabama* didn't lose one man in combat.

"The worst were the kamikazes," he said. "They'd come at you right out of that noonday sun. You never really saw them, but you heard their engines and saw the sun reflecting off their wings. Not one of those planes crashed into us. We splashed them all."

And Feller was one of those pulling the trigger.

"I don't say that to brag," he said. "But I'm very proud that none of our men were killed in battle."

Then Feller talked about the accidents.

"Men would be knocked overboard by the guns, or they'd slip off the deck . . . all kinds of freak things," Feller said. "Veterans don't talk much about that, how so many were killed in things that had nothing to do with combat. On the *Alabama*, we lost thirty-five men like that."

Today, that would be a scandal. In World War II, it was just part of the price that had to be paid.

"Because our very existence was threatened," Feller said. "Just think if we had lost that war. As it was, over 405,000 of us were killed in the war. But we won because of sacrifice and teamwork. There was a great sense of purpose from the officers to the enlisted men to the civilians back home."

Feller then talked about the unique 1942 All-Star Game, and it was held in Cleveland.

"And they brought a bunch of us back to play in it," he said.

When it came time for the 1942 All-Star Game, there was a problem. Many of the best players were in the military service. Some had joined after the bombing of Pearl Harbor, others were drafted. Some of those who weren't in the service and were still playing ball were viewed with suspicion. Women asked, "How come these young, healthy ballplayers aren't in the Army, but my husband the accountant had to go?"

Joe DiMaggio found out about that. This is a man who received standing ovations simply for walking into a restaurant. He was a hero, an icon, the epitome of grace and class on the diamond. But in 1942, DiMaggio was being booed.

Why?

Because DiMaggio was swinging a bat in Yankee pinstripes while other stars such as Feller, Mickey Cochrane, and Hank Greenberg were wearing government-issued uniforms and learning how to march with a rifle.

During World War II, President Franklin Roosevelt wanted major league baseball to continue. The game certainly wanted to go on. There were fans. There were ballparks. There was money to be made for the owners. And there would be an All-Star Game, even if some of the All-Stars weren't in the game back in 1942. The owners decided to have one game on July 6, 1942: the American vs. National League. It would be played at the Polo Grounds in New York.

But what about the boys in the service, the players who would have been All-Stars if the war hadn't come along? Well, there would be a second All-Star Game for them. The winner of the American vs. National League game in New York would come to Cleveland, and the next day that team would meet a team of the best players who were in the military.

Proceeds from both games would go to the Ball and Bat Fund for servicemen.

•

Headline: DRAFT KEEPS GRIP ON MARRIED MEN.
It was a July 6, 1942, story about married men being drafted and the effect on their families.

•

On that same Monday, July 6, 1942, stars such as Feller and Frank Pytlak gathered at Cleveland Municipal Stadium for a morning practice. They were waiting to see what team they'd face—the AL or NL. Until 1942, All-Star Games had always been played in the afternoon. But baseball officials thought a night game would mean more fans, and more money for the Service Fund. So they started the game at 6:30 P.M.

Only they forgot something: the war. There was a war going on, right?

In 1942, there was a real fear that the Japanese or Germans might bomb American cities. The Japanese had hit Pearl Harbor. The Germans had their submarines off the coast of Long Island, Louisiana, and elsewhere. So cities had blackouts, periods where the electricity was shut off and everything went black. If there had been a real bombing raid, a blackout would make it more difficult for pilots to spot their targets.

"Mayor Fiorello La Guardia proclaimed a total blackout for New York City [three hours after the start of the game]," wrote Gordon Cobbledick in the *Plain Dealer*. "It's estimated this reduced the crowd by 5,000 as the average citizen had no desire to be caught in a crowded baseball stadium during a blackout, or try to make his way homeward over pitch-black streets."

The city of New York and major league baseball didn't communicate well on this matter.

"The selection of the blackout was purely arbitrary on La Guardia's part," added Cobbledick. "Tomorrow night would have done just as well . . . as a result of Little Flower's thoughtlessness, Commissioner Judge Landis decreed the game must end by 9:10 P.M., regardless of the score."

•

Headline: JAPS IN ALEUTIANS BOMBED 5 TIMES: "Pressing their attack whenever weather permitted, Army bombers have made five new attacks on the

Japanese in the Aleutian Islands, the Navy said today."

•

The first All-Star Game was played in two hours and seven minutes at the Polo Grounds.

Weren't those the Good Old Days?

But it started about fifty minutes late because of rain. The crowd was 33,694, considered disappointing.

"There were mitigating circumstances holding down the crowd," wrote *The Sporting News.* "There were heavy afternoon showers. New York's baseball-loving mayor chose this night for his second 30-minute blackout test. The game was completed just two minutes before the blackout. The gas shortage in the East and the doubling of admission prices were other reasons given for the 16,000 empty seats."

The Tribe's Lou Boudreau homered and played brilliantly at short for the American League, which pulled out a 3–1 victory. After the game, players showered and reporters tried to interview them in the pitch-black dressing rooms. The fans were forced to remain in the stands for all thirty minutes of the blackout immediately following the game. The amazing part of this story is that the fans did as they were told. There was some griping, but the people just sat and waited for a half hour in the dark.

No one even lit a match.

•

Headline: SCRAP RUBBER IS USED FOR NEW BASE-BALLS: "The Spalding Company admitted it had been necessary to use scrap rubber in the cores of baseballs since last January instead of the pure crude rubber it formerly employed. Players from both leagues had been protesting the balls are not as lively."

•

Headline: FDR SEES TIRE SEIZURE AS NEEDED:
"President Roosevelt told the country his job was to
save the nation, not just the tires or rubber or cars. If
the war lasts long enough, he might have to take every
tire in the country."

•

It would be more than an All-Star Game in Cleveland.

The celebration began on July 4, with a rally at Cleveland
Stadium. Over 81,000 people showed up, not for baseball, but
to support the men in uniform. They saw parades of Army and
Marine soldiers, of tanks and jeeps and trucks. There were cannons and over 180 military vehicles.

And flags.

Everywhere you looked, there were the Stars and
Stripes.

Over 500 men stood near home plate. They were
inductees, men joining the various military services.
Men from Cleveland, men with bags at their sides. They
raised their right hands. They took the oath of loyalty, pledg-
ing to protect their country. The 81,000 fans stood and
cheered.

Together, the inductees marched off, a band playing "Yankee Doodle" and then "God Bless America."

When the inductees left the Stadium, the lights were
turned off. Fans were asked to light matches and stand in a moment of silence and prayer for the war movement.

•

Headline: STRIKE NAZIS NOW BELIEVED TIR-
ING: "The Allies threw fresh troops into a battering
assault on weary Axis forces which were being
pounded on their small strip of desert position by

the heaviest aerial attack ever seen in the Middle East."

•

The war had been tough on the Indians.

Not only did they lose Feller, their best pitcher, they lost fans.

"League figures show Cleveland has suffered the biggest drop in attendance compared to all other teams," reported *The Sporting News*. "The turnstiles are approximately 125,000 clicks behind their pace of 1941."

Tribe owner Alva Bradley wanted a big crowd for the All-Star Game, and he convinced 140 companies to buy tickets. Selling tickets wasn't easy; prices were raised $1 to pay for War Stamps, a contribution to the war effort. And baseball just didn't seem that important anymore, not compared to the war. *The Sporting News* even noticed the change at the ballparks: "In the old days, the great majority of athletes and fans slouched during the National Anthem. Next time you attend a game, watch how rigidly erect everyone now stands."

Cleveland papers appealed to fans to support the ballplayers in the military. The star soldiers were managed by "Lieutenant Mickey Cochrane," as the papers now called the former Tiger catcher and manager, and they openly rooted for the armed forces team to win.

Two hours before the game, troops from the Marines and Coast Guard marched across the diamond. More tanks, trucks, jeeps, and cannons followed.

Two heavyweight champs were there: Lieutenant Jack Dempsey of the Coast Guard and Lieutenant Commander Gene Tunney of the Navy.

Before the game, there was a two-minute blackout.

"One's neighbor disappeared into the inky darkness," wrote Fredrick Lieb in *The Sporting News*. "Only the gray outlines of the stands were visible on this moonless night. It made one feel alone with one's god."

•

Headline: MILL CREW SETS RECORD: "Carnegie-Illinois Steel said that a 75-man crew manning a plate mill in its Gary, Indiana, plant really celebrated Independence Day. The crew worked from midnight to 8 A.M., turning out an all-time record for [steel] production, giving the other shifts something to shoot at."

•

Feller started for the servicemen. He wore an N on his uniform, because he was stationed at Norfolk Naval Base.

It would be nice to report that Feller was sharp and the military men beat the American League All-Stars. But as a *Plain Dealer* headline stated: "Fans Learn Pitching for Country Comes First in War."

Feller was roughed up for four hits and three runs while recording only three outs. Right before the game, he received a telegram from Iowa, informing him that his father's brain cancer had grown worse.

When Feller was removed from the game in the second inning, he received a huge ovation from the crowd of 62,094. They remembered the newspaper headline of a few months earlier: "U.S. Navy Wins Services of Greatest Living Pitcher."

It was as if Feller were on the free agent market and the Navy outbid everyone for him. As for the game, the American League prevailed, 5–0, a game played in two hours and eight minutes.

About $70,000 was donated to the Army and Navy Bat and Ball Funds. *The Sporting News* called the game a "triumph for Cleveland and for Owner Alva Bradley. Tickets were $2, double the normal price. Finding 62,094 fans to buy them says a lot about Cleveland, patriotism and Indians fans."

1

My father, Sergeant Tom Pluto.

2

My father showing off his swing.

3

Lou Sockalexis was the original Cleveland Indian, but he actually played for the Cleveland Spiders in the late 1890s.

Old League Park, where my father learned his baseball.

Tris Speaker, "The Grey Eagle," played centerfield and managed the Tribe to the 1920 World Series.

Stanley Coveleski overcame the death of his wife in 1920 to pitch the Indians to their first World Series title.

Three great hitters of their era: Joe Jackson, Ty Cobb, and Nap Lajoie.

Bill Veeck, my
father's favorite
Tribe owner.

8

9

Frank Lane, the man who broke
millions of hearts by trading
Rocky Colavito.

The old Cleveland Stadium when it first opened in 1932.

Oscar Vitt, one of the most hated managers of the Tribe.

A young Bob Feller.

Bob Feller at twenty-six as a recruitment ploy for the United States Navy.

Tribe manager Lou Boudreau and his ace, Bob Feller, who was pitching for the Navy at the time.

My father's favorite Bill Veeck promotion: Good Old Joe Earley Day.

The Indians make history: A young Larry Doby gets the telegram informing him that the Indians have just bought his contract from the Negro Leagues. Doby became the first black player in American League history.

The famous photo of Vic Wertz's bald head.

Gene Bearden is carried off the field after beating Boston and sending the Tribe into the 1948 World Series.

18

19

The last Tribe World Series pennant.

Al Lopez was the Indians manager in 1954 when the team won a franchise-record 111 games. But in true Tribe fashion, the Indians were swept in the World Series.

20

21

Rocky Colavito's magic smile.

Yes, that's Roger Maris in a Tribe uniform.

Joe Charboneau and Herb Score, two promising players whose careers
were cut short by injuries.

One of my father's
favorite players, Tony
Horton. Unfortunately,
his career was shortened
by a mental breakdown.

The infamous Rose-Fosse All-Star-Game collision.

One of those rare moments
when the old Cleveland Stadium
was packed for baseball.

Kenny Lofton has been called
the best Tribe centerfielder
since Tris Speaker.

Few Tribe hitters have
ever swung as lethal a
bat as Albert Belle.

Carlos Baerga was the heart of the 1995 pennant-winning Tribe.

Jose Mesa saved a lot a games for the Indians, but he couldn't do it in the 1997 World Series.

The best Tribe defensive shortstop ever: Omar Vizquel.

A true clutch pitcher, Dennis Martinez beat Randy Johnson to send the Tribe to the 1995 World Series.

Jaret Wright's fastball impressed even Bob Feller.

Many Ramirez,
the Tribe's star
of the present
and the future.

Feller would lose all of three seasons (1942–44) and most of 1945 because of his service in the Navy.

He finished his career with 266 victories, and those years probably cost him a chance to win 350 games.

Don't think so?

He won 25 games in 1941 . . . and 26 games in 1946.

In the four war years, he had five wins.

"I don't worry much about that," he said. "I just know we did the right thing. We won the biggest game for our country."

Today, that sounds hokey.

But we never lived in a country of meat and gas rationing and one-armed major league outfielders. Most of us don't remember neighbors who had stars in their living room windows, signs they had lost a father, son, or husband in the war. Most of us really don't know what it's like to go to bed each night, praying that there would be no mysterious knock on the door the next day, no nice young man in a dress uniform delivering a message about a death on a beachhead halfway across the world.

To those like my father and Bob Feller, this was the biggest game of all—and they won.

For that, they deserve our respect.

# CHAPTER 11

# Veeck and the 1948 Indians

My FATHER LOVED Bill Veeck because he never wore a tie.

He loved Bill Veeck because he saw Veeck limping around the Stadium, greeting fans—many by name.

He loved Bill Veeck because he gave away things for free, and he loved Bill Veeck because he never would let anyone call him "Mr. Veeck."

Most of all, my father loved Bill Veeck because Veeck ran the Indians exactly as he would have.

"Bill cared about the fans," my father would say.

But this is more than the story of a man who buys a baseball team and then comes up with some nifty promotions. It's even more than the story of the man who owned the Indians when they broke a streak of twenty-eight years without a World Series appearance. This is the story of Cleveland after World War II, the story of men such as my father who grew up during the Depression, remembered breadlines and hobos riding the rails, remembered fireside chats and Pearl Harbor. They never forgot a president who reassured them, "The only thing we have have to fear is fear itself." They knew how many of their mothers had pictures of FDR in the living room—often right next to a picture of Jesus or the pope.

Bill Veeck bought the Indians in June of 1946, a year after the end of World War II. Veeck was thirty-two years old; he had been in the Marines, and was wounded when an artillery gun fell on his leg and pretty much smashed it. He spent twenty-eight months with his leg in a cast. Older men had created the policies that sent the country into the worst depression in its history. Older men allowed Hitler to fester and become a cancer. Older men didn't stop the Japanese from a surprise attack on Pearl Harbor. And older men sent young men such as Veeck and my father into military service right in what should have been the prime of their lives. Now, these young men were back from the war. They had survived the Depression. They had defeated Germany. They had defeated Japan. While blood was shed all over Europe and Asia during the war, not one drop was spilled in combat on our shores. These men came home from the war with a new sense of power, a sense of themselves. The Depression was over. The war was over. They had been on the front lines, making it happen. They had helped the country prevail. Now it was their turn to run things, and they had earned the right.

That's why Bill Veeck was almost immediately accepted in Cleveland.

In 1946, almost anything seemed possible if people just worked together. Hey, that's how we won the war, right?

That was Veeck's underlying message.

If we can win a world war on two different fronts at the same time, why can't the Indians win a pennant? And why can't the fans have fun while watching it happen?

You have to understand the state of Cleveland baseball in 1946. The team was owned by Alva Bradley, at least in the eyes of the fans. Actually, Bradley was the front man for a group that had owned the team for the previous nineteen years. They allowed Bradley to run the franchise. In those nineteen years, the Indians never won a pennant. They finished in second place just once, and that was in 1940 when the team revolted against manager Oscar Vitt. No one wanted to remember 1940 and the Crybaby Indians. But the problem was more than mediocre baseball. Bradley was a nice man, but a man with money. He was a "suit and tie guy," as my father would say. Bradley belonged to the Union Club, whose members seemingly didn't lose a dime during the Depression or spend a moment in uniform during World War II.

"The symbolism [of the owners] was of wealth and social affluence," wrote Franklin Lewis in the *Cleveland Press.* "The average fan has resented for years the society touch of the Tribe operation. Maybe this has been because of the large laboring class in Cleveland. Maybe the elements that form nationality groups and civic clubs bristled because the team operators were from the other side of the tracks. . . . The citizen, arguing his baseball in a streetcar or a bar, got to blaming the owners for the ills of the Indians."

Whatever it was, it annoyed most fans like a perpetual stone in their shoe.

Enter Veeck, who was perceived as the kind of guy who'd argue baseball in a streetcar or a bar—and he went around Cleveland doing just that! That was how he spent a week before he bought the team, riding in cabs and streetcars and stopping in bars, asking people what they thought of the Indians. He found they loved their baseball team but loathed the owners. He was shocked to learn how ownership had failed to understand its customers.

For example, in 1946, none of the Tribe games were on the radio. Not a single one. Why? Because the owners still took the elitist attitude that fans would rather listen to a game for free on the radio than buy a ticket and watch it themselves. They actually believed radio coverage hurt attendance. This wasn't just a philosophy common to Cleveland; many baseball people had believed it. These guys worshipped at the altar of "Less Is More," and not just when it came to players' salaries.

Veeck saw so many little things he could do just to make life better for the fans—things that didn't cost much money, but they were things the old owners would never notice. When Veeck and Harry Grabiner put together a group to buy the Tribe for $1.6 million in 1946, Veeck was one of the most experienced thirty-two-year-old baseball men in the history of the game. His father had run the Chicago Cubs, and Veeck grew up at Wrigley Field learning every facet of the operation. He spent the early 1940s as general manager and part-owner of the Milwaukee Brewers, then a minor league team. He won an American Association pennant. He broke attendance records. He had outlandish promotions. He made the baseball establishment wince while he embraced the fans. He was the kind of guy who started some games at 8:30 in the morning for the benefit of those who were just coming home from working the night shift in the war plant. Veeck met them at the gate, handing out free Corn Flakes and coffee for breakfast.

These stories were immediately reported in Cleveland when Veeck bought the team. He had reporters following him around at his first game, and they saw him shake hands with the fans as they came through the gates. He spent five innings with the fans in the bleachers and discovered that no one could understand what was said by the public address announcer.

He promised a new sound system would be installed—and it was!

He promised the games would be on the radio even if he had to give the rights away—and they were!

He saw fans wiping off dirty seats with hankies and he ordered ushers to clean every seat before every game—and they did!

He promised women that their rest rooms would always be clean—and he had them cleaned every two innings!

In a change from the old administration, he promised that fans could keep any baseball hit into the stands!

The fans loved it!

It seemed that everything Veeck did had an exclamation point after it!

Veeck became an adult under FDR, and realized that the man was elected president four times partly because FDR understood the average citizen, even if he came from wealth himself. He knew their fears. He knew that much of what they wanted was a sense that someone in power was listening to them. Even though many of FDR's New Deal social programs didn't work out, there was a sense that the man was trying. He cared.

Veeck promised Cleveland a new deal for Indians fans. He brought in circus acts and fireworks for postgame entertainment.

Why?

"Because I like circus acts and fireworks," he said.

He had a night when he gave veteran trainer Lefty Weisman a wheelbarrow filled with $5,000 in silver dollars. All Weisman had to do was push it away. Of course, $5,000 in silver dollars felt like 5,000 tons to the elderly trainer. Fans roared as Weisman strained to move the wheelbarrow, but it wouldn't budge an inch. Then the fans stood and cheered when a tow truck came out from under the stands to help Lefty.

Fans liked the fact that Veeck gave 5,000 silver dollars to the trainer, a guy perceived to be a working stiff just like them. They liked it when Veeck dressed the ushers in new uniforms and gave them lessons in politeness.

"Such little deals as telephone service to the Stadium and ushers who don't look like fugitives from Dogpatch" was how Lewis characterized some of Veeck's immediate changes.

Veeck set up a telephone line that went directly to his

desk, no secretary to screen the calls. He advertised the number. He actually answered his own phone. Not every fan got through, but a surprising number did. Over and over, Veeck told his front office people, "There is nothing owed you!" Again, the exclamation point. He did not expect fans to show up simply because a team put up a sign reading: "GAME TONIGHT," then opened the ticket windows—which was the Tribe's old style of business. Over and over, he told his employees, "The fans are important." And over and over, he told the fans, "You are important."

Then he acted like he believed it.

"Bill Veeck was sitting in the Stadium bleachers on Sunday," wrote Lewis in the *Press*. "He wore his customary disguise, no tie, no coat, no hat and an open white sport shirt at the throat. . . . Veeck's immediate and close contacts with the common man, alias the short-sleeved client in the hard seat, is a studied pose, albeit a refreshing one hereabout where aloofness by ball club personnel and players has been the custom."

My father was like millions of Tribe baseball fans. He claims he met Veeck, shook his hand one day at the Stadium. Maybe he did. Maybe he didn't. But Veeck shook so many hands . . . and so many fans saw Veeck shaking so many hands . . . well, everyone assumed they'd shaken the hand of Bill Veeck, too.

Or else, they'd heard him speak.

Veeck averaged a public appearance a day during the season, at least two a day in the off-season. Breakfasts, lunches, dinners, late-night gatherings—if you wanted a speaker, you probably could get Veeck. Just don't expect him to wear a tie.

Veeck also cultivated the press. He gave them incredible access. He floated rumors. He understood their job and wasn't afraid to give them a story. Unlike many of his peers even to this day, Veeck knew how to generate several days of stories. If he was working on a trade, he'd whisper it to a couple of writers. A speculation story would run about the deal. Then he might tell them that the deal had hit a snag. Bang, a second story. Then, he'd tell them the deal was back on, and it was about to be made. Bang, a third story. Then, he'd have the press conference announcing the trade that had already been announced as happening in the newspapers that day. So what? The papers had to cover the press conference. So bang, that was a fourth story. So he turned one trade story into four stories by the time the deal was officially announced. Then there would be follow-up stories the next few days. He could turn a decent-sized trade into a week's worth of stories in the dead of winter, when baseball needed to be in the papers to help sell tickets.

He put the games on the radio by telling stations, "You can broadcast all or any of our games. If you get them sponsored, just pay me what you think is fair."

How could stations resist an offer like that?

It went on and on.

"They said I couldn't pull bush-league stunts like giving away livestock as I did in Milwaukee," Veeck wrote in *Veeck As in Wreck.* "So I gave away livestock in Cleveland and the fans were delighted."

There were flagpole sitters. There were orchestras playing before games. There were Ladies Days where women received nylon stockings for some games, or orchids for others. There were vaudeville acts. There were special nights for straight-A students and their teachers.

"I remember looking out the window after a game had been rained out," Veeck wrote in his book. "I saw a couple of hundred out-of-towners waiting disconsolately for their train at the Pennsylvania Railroad depot. I called down to the locker room and asked Boudreau and Feller to dash over and talk with them until their train came."

Can you image any manager or star player today agreeing to visit with fans after a rainout? Can you even imagine any owner having the guts to ask them to do so? Veeck did, and then Feller and Boudreau actually met those fans.

●

Veeck had been around baseball his entire life. He knew that what he called "bread and circuses" couldn't sustain the team forever. Yes, he drew a franchise record 1,057,289 for a sixth-place team in 1946, a team that was 36 games out of first place. In 1947, the Indians improved to 80-74, but still were a distant fourth place, 17 games behind the Yankees.

They drew a stunning 1.5 million.

To accommodate the fans, he moved all the games to the 80,000-seat Stadium, even though League Park had been part of the sale of the team. Veeck gave League Park to the city of Cleveland. With only 27,000 seats and in need of major repairs, it wasn't worth his time and cash to keep it.

By 1948, Veeck realized he had to give the fans more. He had to put a winner on the field.

He recovered from the fiasco of nearly trading Lou Boudreau to the St. Louis Browns by giving Boudreau a two-year contract extension as player-manager. Why not? He had no other hot deals going, so make a show of keeping the man. Give him a vote of confidence, play to the fans. While Boudreau knew much of this was a charade, he decided to make the best of the shotgun baseball marriage—mostly, because he had no choice. If he wanted to be a player-manager, Cleveland was the only place that would happen.

Veeck also figured that if he acquired enough good players, he'd win even with Boudreau as the manager. Veeck made deals. He obtained veteran second baseman Joe Gordon from the Yankees for promising pitcher Allie Reynolds. In the long run, New York got the best of the trade, but without Gordon teaming up with Boudreau in the infield and supporting the manager in the clubhouse, the Indians never would have won the 1948 pennant.

Nor would they have won a pennant without Gene Bearden.

After the 1946 season, Veeck was hospitalized as his right foot was amputated, his war wound never having healed properly. He recovered for a month, then celebrated his return to the land of the baseball living by showing up at the baseball winter meetings in Los Angeles. On crutches, he worked the lobby and the bars. He talked trade and impressed writers with his stamina. Here was a guy who'd had his foot cut off only four weeks earlier, a guy on crutches, and all he cares about is making the Indians a better team.

The fans loved these stories.

Even more remarkable, they were true.

He made a five-player deal with the Yankees that was deemed "minor" by most Cleveland writers. For the most part, it was of little consequence—except for what happened to one man in one miraculous year.

That man was Gene Bearden. He had a 15-4 record in Class AAA in 1946. He was a left-handed knuckleball pitcher, of all things. Casey Stengel had recommended Bearden to Veeck. Stengel had managed Bearden in 1946 at Oakland of the Pacific Coast League. Veeck had never seen Bearden pitch, nor were any of the Tribe's scouts especially high on him. Even the audacious Veeck never claimed he knew Bearden would be the Tribe's missing link to a pennant. In 1947, he pitched only one game for the Tribe, facing four batters—one walked and two got hits. His ERA was 81.00. He returned to the minors, where he had a 16-7 record.

And then, in 1948, Bearden won 20 games, threw six shutouts, and led the American League with a 2.43 ERA.

Veeck was also gutsy enough to sign Larry Doby, the first black player in the American League. So much has been written and said about Veeck, yet this part of the man often is overlooked: Bill Veeck was a fine judge of baseball talent. He made shrewd deals. He relied on the advice of people who knew what they were talking about. With Veeck, there was always lots of sizzle—but the man also knew how to make a good steak.

For men in Cleveland such as my father, 1948 was a dream year. It was like winning World War II all over again. The Indi-

ans had the core of a fine team: Boudreau (shortstop), Jim
Hegan (catcher), Ken Keltner (third base), Dale Mitchell (left
field), and pitchers such as Bob Feller and Bob Lemon.

Veeck's moves put the team over the top.

Gordon was a team leader and the best defensive second
baseman in the history of the franchise. He also hit for power.

Doby became a force in center field, both with his glove
and his powerful bat.

At midseason, Veeck realized the Indians needed another
pitcher. When he had signed Larry Doby in July of 1947, he received a telegram from Satchel Paige, simply stating, "I can
pitch and win for you."

That always stuck with Veeck, who considered signing
Paige in 1947 but feared he'd be ridiculed because Paige was at
least forty years old, or maybe fifty. Who knew? Veeck was sin-
cere about breaking the color line in the American League, and
he knew this was no time for a sideshow. By the middle of
1948, it was different. Several black players had followed Doby
into the American League. And the Indians needed a pitcher.
People kept telling Veeck, "Satch can still pitch." And Veeck
could sign him without having to give up a player.

On July 7, Veeck brought Paige to Cleveland for a tryout.
He didn't tell Boudreau beforehand, because he knew the man-
ager would be vehemently against it. Paige pitched against
Boudreau in an empty Stadium, and showed enough that
Boudreau reluctantly agreed with Veeck that signing Paige
wasn't a terrible idea.

No, it was a brainstorm.

Paige had a 6-1 record for the Tribe with a 2.48 ERA. Two
of his wins were shutouts. Several of his starts drew over
70,000 fans. Veeck and Paige were perfect for each other, as
they played with reporters about everything from Paige's
age—"Could be forty, could be fifty"—to his marital status—
"Just say I'm in great demand."

In 1948, everyone was an Indians fan.

Veeck would stare out his office window, watching the fans mob his ballpark, pouring down the West 3rd Street Bridge. He continued to set off fireworks and give away everything from cows to flowers. His team was in a three-way fight for the pennant with the Yankees and Red Sox, and Veeck was the toast of the town. He still met fans. He found a way to shake hands, despite being on crutches.

Boudreau had a career season. He seemed to spend much of the summer determined to show Veeck that the owner was wrong, that he could manage this team and still be a superstar at the same time. While Veeck still shook his head in utter disbelief at some of Boudreau's on-field managerial moves, he marveled at how this man not only ran the team, but delivered one clutch hit after another and was nearly flawless at shortstop.

For Veeck, everything was working—even the trade he couldn't make.

"The closest thing we've had to the 1948 season was October of 1997, when the Indians had all those close games in the playoffs," said Hal Lebovitz. "The only difference was, we had a summerful of games like that."

After the regular season, the Indians and Boston Red Sox both had 96-58 records, necessitating a one-game playoff. Against Veeck's advice, Boudreau started Bearden with only one day's rest in the most important game of the season. The manager picked Bearden over Lemon or Feller, who had far more rest and experience. But Bearden was hot, and the knuckleball was easy on his arm. Besides, Boudreau just *knew* Bearden was the one. It came straight from his heart, as did most of his decisions. The Indians went into Fenway Park and played one of their best games of the year when it meant the most. To make sure his decision about Bearden was the right one, Boudreau had four hits, including two home runs. He was 4-for-4 with three runs scored and two RBI. Bearden went the distance in the 8–3 victory. Boudreau's gamble had paid off.

Then came the World Series, which seemed almost anticlimactic. The town never was quite able to catch its breath with these Indians. Nor could anything stop them. First, they beat the Boston Red Sox in a one-game playoff to make the World Series, then they defeated the Boston Braves in six games to win the world title.

The Indians of 1948 were not a great team. They were a good team with several players who had great years. They were a team that caught the fans' attention, and then were swept up by the crowds at home. Veeck had installed an outfield fence to make the Stadium more inviting to home run hitters—but he also needed the fence to hold back the standing-room only crowds. Yes, close to 80,000 seats weren't enough on some nights.

They drew 86,288 fans for Game 5 of the World Series, their last home game in 1948. The team set a baseball record by drawing over 2.6 million fans, this in an era when 1 million was considered outstanding.

But like most things in Tribe history, 1948 didn't last.

Bearden lost control of his knuckleball and became just an ordinary pitcher in 1949 and was traded in 1950. Paige faded in 1949. Boudreau began to show his age as a player. In 1949, he was thirty-two. He batted only .284 with four homers.

But worst of all, Veeck's wife sued him for divorce, and he had to sell the team in November of 1949 to pay the settlement.

Just like that, Veeck was gone. And so was the magic.

When my father spoke of 1948, it wasn't just Boudreau and Bearden and Paige. It wasn't even just Bill Veeck.

"It was Joe Earley," my father said.

Who?

"Joe Earley," my father repeated. "He was just a guy, a fan. Veeck gave him a night."

A guy name Joe Earley had written a letter to the editor of the *Cleveland Press*. Earley was a night watchman at a local Chevy plant. He wanted to know why the Indians always had special nights for ballplayers and other people who really didn't need a night instead of for fans like him. He signed the letter, "Good Old Joe Earley."

Veeck saw the letter and declared the Indians would have "Good Old Joe Earley Night."

He gave away 20,000 orchids flown directly from Hawaii to the first 20,000 women through the gates. He gave away three stepladders to the same fan, and four rabbits to another fan. He gave away a broken-down old horse, which the *Plain Dealer*'s Chuck Heaton called "a fugitive from a glue factory."

Then it was Joe Earley's turn.

Veeck announced the Indians were presenting Good Old Joe with a house done in "Early American architecture." And from center field, here came a truck pulling an outhouse. Next, Good Old Joe was to receive a grand, fully equipped automobile. And out came a rusty old Model T, a circus car that backfired and the bumpers fell off. A few more gag gifts were rolled out.

Then came the real loot.

A new Ford convertible, a truckload of appliances including a refrigerator, washing machine, and dryer. My father was one of the 60,405 fans at the Stadium that day. He didn't receive a gift, but he understood what it was like to be Joe Earley. In 1948, Bill Veeck and the Indians had made him feel special.

# CHAPTER 12

# Larry Doby

BILL VEECK had good intentions. He had the guts and vision of a revolutionary and the heart of a missionary. But his planning stunk.

That is the real story behind the Indians and the signing of Larry Doby. It never should have worked. Keep that in mind as you read this. Doby survived against far greater odds and obstacles than those facing Jackie Robinson. Most of us don't know that. Most of us just know that Larry Doby was the second African-American to play major league baseball. Because he was second, it was supposed to be easier.

"Why would it have been?" Doby has often asked. "What would have changed? I signed eleven weeks after Jackie did with Brooklyn. We still have problems with race today; why would it have been different in 1947?"

Good questions.

In 1947, Bill Veeck had just bought the Cleveland Indians and was mortgaged to his eyeballs. The team was boring, snoozing through a .500 season. It played in an 80,000-seat stadium. Veeck pulled out all of his promotional stops, blowing up fireworks, giving away used cars, having a band strolling the aisles, handing out flowers on Ladies Day. He was also losing money. He needed a crowd, anything for a crowd. He also needed a good team. He had seen enough of the Negro Leagues to know Jackie Robinson wasn't their only star. In fact, he didn't even think Robinson was the best black player he'd seen, and Robinson was batting .300 and stealing bases for Brooklyn.

Bill Veeck needed to do something.

Imagine you are Larry Doby.

You are twenty-two years old, playing second base for the Newark Eagles. You are leading the Negro National League in hitting at .415. You grew up in Paterson, New Jersey. You played with white kids in a world that was as integrated as it gets in the 1930s. Your neighborhood was a true melting pot with Irish, Italians, Jews, and blacks. You were the only black on the high school football team. You were one of two blacks on the basketball and baseball teams.

But that was fine. You were treated like another kid on the team, period.

You then spent four years in the Navy, where the units were segregated but a black man was still allowed some dignity. You were stationed at an island in the South Pacific called Uluthi when you heard on the radio that Branch Rickey had signed Jackie Robinson to a Brooklyn Dodgers contract. You heard Robinson would start his career in the minors with Montreal. You never dreamed you'd be the second black player. You did want to play baseball; you played some service baseball with Mickey Vernon, a first baseman with the Washington Senators. Vernon wrote Senators owner Clark Griffith, asking him to sign you.

He heard nothing back.

In 1946, you were discharged. You went home to New Jer-

sey and began playing baseball for the Newark Eagles. You
played well. You didn't think much about Jackie Robinson or
playing in the majors; your plan was a couple of years in the
Negro Leagues, then maybe a high school coaching job some-
where. You are twenty-two. You have been married for ten
months. Your wife has a job with the phone company. In fact,
she became the first black operator in New Jersey. One day, a
guy named Lou Jones shows up. He is a black man, about forty.
He says he is a special assistant to Bill Veeck, and the Indians
have been scouting you for a couple of months.

"I wouldn't be surprised if you are in Cleveland in two or
three weeks," Jones said.

You hear those words, and you can't breathe.

You are afraid.

Afraid it might not be true.

Afraid that it might indeed be very true, and your life will
never be the same.


Now you are Lou Boudreau.

You are twenty-nine years old, both the manager and All-
Star shortstop for the Indians. This is your sixth year as manager of the Indians. You no longer are the Boy Manager. Only
twice has your team finished over .500.

Veeck is in his first year as owner. You know he doesn't
think much of you, at least as a manager. He has told friends,
"Lou is a hunch manager . . . he manages by the seat of his
pants."

Now it is July 3, 1947. Veeck has called you into his office.

"Lou, we are going to sign a new player," he says.

"Who?" you ask.

"Larry Doby," says Veeck. "He's a Negro."

You take a deep breath. You have nothing against black
players. But why now? Is Veeck that desperate to draw some
fans? The Dodgers did it right with Robinson. They let him
play at Class AAA Montreal in 1946, allowing him to acclimate

himself (and his teammates to him) in the minors. Robinson then went to spring training with the Dodgers in 1947. He opened the season with Brooklyn. He broke in gradually, slowly earning respect.

But why sign Doby now, on July 3? Is this some kind of Fourth of July stunt?

"What position does he play?" you ask.

"He's a second baseman," says Veeck.

You say nothing. But this makes no sense. Joe Gordon is your second baseman, and he's an All-Star. You have never seen Doby in your life. You don't know where to play him. You keep reading in the newspapers that your "job status is in question." You don't look at Doby as a pioneer. You don't see him as black. You see him as one of the trickiest problems you'll ever face as a manager.

Oh, he also can play some shortstop, you're told.

Great, you think. I'm the shortstop.

What am I supposed to do with this Larry Doby? It's not a question you ask because he's black; it's what any manager would ask if he was told he had a new player coming to his team at midseason, a player he'd never seen before and a player whose position is one you don't need filled.

Bill Veeck called the players together to tell them of his plans to sign Doby. He told them he would not tolerate any racial slurs, and he said anyone using the word "Nigger . . . well, you can leave this room right now because Larry Doby is going to be a bigger star than any of you."

Blank faces stared at Veeck.

He knew what they were thinking. They were wondering why the owner was shoving this kid down their throats; they were thinking it was a gimmick.

Whitey Lewis, sports editor of the *Cleveland Press*, was with several other writers, meeting with Veeck, when Veeck dropped his little announcement.

"We've signed a new player," Veeck said. "His name is Larry Doby."

Veeck paused.

"He's a Negro."

For a moment, it was so silent, Lewis could hear the pens scribble. Then Veeck said that Doby would join the team in two days.

Why now?

"Why wait?" asked Veeck. "Negro players are on the way to the majors, and I want to get the best available Negro boys for Cleveland while the grabbing is good. Our scouts rave about him. We want to sign him before someone else does."

Lewis immediately caught a train from Cleveland to Newark. He saw Doby play in a Fourth of July doubleheader, hitting a home run. He is fast, Lewis thought, but so skinny. And so young. If he were Veeck, he wouldn't sign Doby—or if he did, he'd send him to the minors. The player who Lewis was really impressed with was the shortstop.

"Our reports on that guy are mixed," Veeck told Lewis. "We don't want to bring more than one colored player into the league at this time—besides, he is too old."

Lewis wrote down the shortstop's name, anyway: It was Monte Irvin, who later became a star with the New York Giants. Then Lewis found out that Veeck had paid $10,000 to the Newark Eagles for Doby—and agreed to pay another $5,000 if Doby made it through the 1947 season. He arranged to ride back on the train with Doby. He waited at the Newark station. He was 6-foot, 180 pounds but looked about sixteen years old, all arms and legs.

Lewis thought, "He's just a kid. Jackie Robinson is a man. Jackie is twenty-seven. This poor kid has no idea what he's getting into."

Doby sat next to Lewis at the train station. He wore a new black sport coat, a gray shirt buttoned to the neck and no tie. He said little and mostly picked imaginary lint off his lapels. In his story, Lewis wrote, "He has red-brown skin, kinky and short hair. He is typically Negro in appearance."

Then he added, "He is plain scared."

Lewis remembered an announcement he heard during the Newark game. It gave the time of "the anti-lynching meeting."

He wished Veeck had signed Irvin and Doby. They both were good players, both could help the Indians—and it would be easier for Doby if he had a friend.

Instead he will be so alone.

You are Larry Doby.

You try not to pay much attention as Veeck tells people you'll "be a better player than Robinson." You admire Veeck when he says, "I see no reason why a Negro player shouldn't be given as much a right as a white man to make good in our league."

They put you on a train from Newark to Chicago, where the Indians are playing the White Sox at Comiskey Park. You carry the travel bag and about fifty dollars in cash, gifts from your old Newark teammates. You also have the weight of their dreams with you, right in that bag. For them to make it, you have to make it. Jackie Robinson isn't enough. There must be more than one, or baseball will find a reason to close the gates.

You arrive in Chicago and try to check in at Hotel Del Prado, where the Indians stay.

No coloreds allowed, you are told at the desk.

The Indians scramble, and they find you a room at the Hotel Dusable, described as "in the heart of Chicago's Negro Belt."

You are Lou Boudreau.

You meet Doby for the first time and you think, "He's just a frightened kid."

Reporters want to know when and where he will play. How do you know? You've never seen him.

"At short or second," you say. "That is where they tell me that he belongs."

The reporters tell you that makes no sense, the Indians already have stars at second and short. You shrug. You say nothing. You have no idea what to do with this kid, or why Veeck wants to make this move now. You wonder, is this a way to make it easier for him to fire you at the end of the year? Even though you don't say a word, the reporters wonder the same thing.

You are Larry Doby.

They take you into an office at Comiskey Park, where they have you sign a contract with the Indians. Bill Veeck smiles. You shake hands. All you remember is being blinded by the flashes from all the cameras. You see Lou Jones, Veeck's special assistant. You know Jones is supposed to be your friend, keep you out of trouble and show you the ropes.

You hear Jones tell reporters, "I don't think we have to worry about him getting in trouble by talking too much or saying the wrong thing. He doesn't speak a half-dozen words in an hour."

Jones enjoys the spotlight. He is a minor celebrity himself, having been married to actress Lena Horne. Veeck is smiling. Jones is smiling. You try to smile, but it doesn't work. You have never met Veeck before this day. You start to call him "Mr. Veeck," but he stops you.

"You call me Bill," he says. "I'll call you Lawrence."

No one else ever called you Lawrence, but you like that. Veeck is your boss, a white man, but he wants you to call him by his first name—and he will call you by your formal first name. That is the nicest thing anyone says to you on your first day with the Indians.

Then Bill Veeck tells you the rules:

Don't get in any fights.

Don't acknowledge any insults.

Don't even look back at an umpire if you think he made a bad call.

Don't sign any autographs for white women. You realize Veeck doesn't want any racial incidents. He tells you if someone sees you sign an autograph for a white woman, they might think you are trying to get a date with her—and that would be trouble.

You listen to all this and wonder if you are even allowed to breathe.

You are Lou Boudreau.

You're glad for small favors. At least you don't have to cut someone to make room for Doby, because you had a roster spot open for a few weeks, ever since pitcher Roger Wolff was sold to Pittsburgh.

During batting practice, you take Doby around the field, introducing him to each player, one on one. You have decided to try him at first base, and the players know it.

Some players refuse to shake Doby's hand.

You are Larry Doby.

You see the hard stares. You feel the cold-fish handshakes. You know that many of the players are from the South. You sweat, just standing there in your woolen Cleveland uniform with No. 14 on the back. That is the scene in the Cleveland dressing room on your first day on the job.

As Whitey Lewis wrote, "Most players' faces turned to the floor. Not even a single scuffle or solitary spike on the floor broke the horrible, tomblike muteness. . . . Then the Indians filed out of the room. Not one word was uttered. Larry Doby was welcomed to the big leagues."

You follow them onto the field. You wait for someone to play catch with you. No one does. A few minutes go by. They seem like hours. Later, you will recall this as one of the most humiliating moments of your life. Then Joe Gordon comes out of the dugout.

"Hey, you just want to stand there, or do you want to throw a little?" he asks.

In another time, another place, you'd have hugged Joe Gordon.

Bill Veeck was in Comiskey Park for Doby's first game. He saw a crowd of 18,062, and people told him, "It's the most colored we've ever seen here."

Black fans just stared at Doby as if he were a miracle in spikes. They applauded as he walked by. Veeck saw Doby sitting at the end of the dugout and hoped Boudreau would put him in the game. Why not? The team's record is 30-30. In the seventh inning, Doby went to bat as a pinch hitter. The black fans gave him a standing ovation. Veeck was gratified that many of the white fans politely applaud, too.

Veeck swore he could see Doby's knees shaking. He was amazed when the kid actually made contact, lashing a line drive just foul down the left field line.

Then he struck out on a pitch high and outside.

The black fans stood and cheered as he walked back to the dugout. Most white fans also clapped.

You are Larry Doby and your world has just ended.

You struck out.

You come back to the dugout, staring at your spikes. If someone says anything to you, you don't hear it. You walk to the end of the dugout, by yourself. You slump down. You put your head in your hands, praying you won't cry.

A moment later, you hear someone sit down next to you. You peek out between your fingers, and you see Joe Gordon, *his* head in *his* hands.

"I just struck out, too," Gordon says.

A Cleveland *Plain Dealer* editorial praised Veeck's signing of Doby: "Negroes have risen to stardom in other sports. If given the opportunity, they will do so in baseball. Veeck deserves to be congratulated. The fans will be pulling for Larry Doby to make good."

That's the response in nearly every paper you read. Furthermore, Cleveland fans were talking baseball again, which is exactly what Veeck wanted.

You are Larry Doby.

You have been in the big leagues for two days, and this is your first start. You see Boudreau going out of his way to play catch with you. You have a real friend in Gordon. A number of the players at least say hello, but a few others wish you'd turn into a lump of coal.

Boudreau tells you to start at first base, where you've played a few times in the Negro Leagues. But you don't have a glove, and none of the Tribe players will lend you theirs. A third party secures one from a player on the White Sox. You wonder about a teammate who won't give you his glove. You play that day before 31,566 fans, many of them black. They are so happy just to see you, and you know you represent something bigger than yourself—only you wonder if you are ready for and worthy of this mission. Baseball is hard enough.

You beat out an infield hit. You are 1-for-4, with an RBI and no errors. The Indians win, 5–1.

Your teammates go back to their hotel.

You go back to yours—alone.

You check the newspapers. They are kind.

Yes, some writers call you the "coppery colored boy," or the "mild-mannered colored boy." Others refer to you as the team's "new Negro player." The fans have been great. But you just wonder if you'll play much on the team, and if the players will accept you.

•

Bill Veeck received over 20,000 letters about Doby, most of them vile and racist. He didn't care; he knew he'd done the right thing.

You are Larry Doby.

You didn't know what major league baseball would be, but you never guessed it would be this.

*This* is not being allowed to eat in the same restaurants as your teammates.

*This* is not being in the same hotels.

*This* is feeling like the new kid in school, and none of the other kids want you there.

*This* is losing five pounds in your first week with the team because you are too nervous to eat.

*This* is a manager whose job is on the line, and he's not about to take a chance on you. Day after day goes by, and you seldom play. Six weeks after joining the Indians, you are 2-for-17. You are staying at the home of a black family in Cleveland. You don't hear the racial taunts, but your wife does, especially when she travels on the road with you. Helyn had come with you on the road for company, since you couldn't stay with the team in many cities. But what she heard in some parks made her cry, so she stopped going to the games.

At home, Bill Veeck makes you comfortable. He takes you and Helyn to the best restaurants. He says his door is always open, and it's true. He becomes a true friend. But Boudreau remains distant. Many players remain suspicious. You sit at the end of the bench for a team that wins as many games as it loses.

One day, you ask veteran coach Bill McKechnie, "Do I have a chance to make the grade?"

He assures you that you will.

At the end of the season, you have batted only 32 times, and you're wondering if you will even be invited back for 1948. Bill McKechnie tells you not to worry; he says you will be a fine big leaguer, an outfielder.

"Outfield?" you ask.

"Outfield," he says. "Center field. This winter, get a book on how to play the outfield and read it."

You do just that. It's a book by Tommy Henrich of the Yankees.

Bill Veeck came to realize he had made a mistake.

Doby was a good idea.

Signing Doby in the middle of the year with no place to play was wrong. For spring training in 1948, Veeck hired former Indians great Tris Speaker to teach Doby to play center field. He had six weeks under the Arizona sun to learn the position. He played it well, earning the respect of his teammates and confidence in himself. This was how it should have been done in the first place.

Doby hit .301 with 14 homers and helped the Indians win the 1948 World Series. He won Game 4 of the Series with a 400-foot homer, and was hugged by pitcher Steve Gromek in the clubhouse. The picture of the two men—one black, one white—ran all over the country and was a sign of acceptance for Doby.

Both men received a lot of hate mail about the picture. So did Bill Veeck.

You are Larry Doby, and you play with the Indians until 1956.

You remember a game in 1948 when you were thrown out trying to steal home, and some people questioned your intelligence. No one said it, but they were thinking that a white player would never do that.

You had another terrible moment when you lost a fly ball in the sun. You had sunglasses on, but forgot to flip them down. Sunglasses were new to you, because they weren't used in the Negro Leagues. The ball hit you on the head, and sportswriters had great fun with that. You can't help but think the criticism was a little harsher than it would have been if you had been a white player.

Some fans yelled "nigger" at you on the road.

One day, you slide into a base and an infielder spits tobacco juice in your face. This is 1948. You want to punch the guy, but you are still under orders to hold back.

You ignore it and you seethe.

You remember your parents telling you that sticks and stones may break your bones, but names will never hurt you. But these guys threw baseballs at you. They tried to spike you. They called you foul, obscene names.

It hurt.

All of it.

One of the best things Bill Veeck ever did was sign Larry Doby. He became a seven-time All-Star and the first black named to the American League All-Star team. He led the league in homers twice. He drove in 100 runs in five different seasons. But Veeck saw Larry Doby as a potential Joe DiMaggio, and he always wondered what Doby could have done had he not been under all the pressure, if he had just come along maybe ten years later.

"Larry had not been bruised as a human being," Veeck wrote in his autobiography. "He didn't have his nose rubbed in it [racism]. It hit him later in life, and it hit him at a time he thought he had it licked. It hit him hard. . . . He was not a man to shake off those slights and insults easily. He was very sensitive. If he didn't like an umpire's call, he'd back out and point to his skin, as if to say, 'You called that on me because I'm colored.' All the inner turmoil was such a drain on him."

One of the best aspects of baseball's celebration of the fiftieth anniversary of Jackie Robinson's breaking the color line was that it brought the spotlight back to Doby. It may have been 1997, but Doby was finally at center stage because Robinson had passed away. In Cleveland, he was able to tell his story, over and over, and have a receptive audience. In 1998, Doby deservedly was inducted into the Hall of Fame. Even for fans such as my father, fans who were there when it happened, only fifty years later did they come to appreciate all that Larry Doby endured.

# CHAPTER 13

# Nineteen Fifty-four

THE BALD HEAD.

That's my favorite image from the 1954 Indians.

It's Vic Wertz's bald head, and printed on it in black letters were these words: WE'RE IN. That picture ran everywhere when the Indians clinched the 1954 American League pennant.

WE'RE IN.

Every time I see that picture of Wertz's head, I think of my father—my very bald father. I think of how Wertz was a lumberjack of a first baseman, a hulking man who seemed destined to remain what he was with the Indians in 1954—a big, strong, bald man.

Like my father. Like so many of our fathers.

Tim Bartlett's dad was a lot like my father. A baseball fan. A man who could tell you that the key guy on the 1954 Indians is lost in Tribe history, a man who only lives in a picture of his bald head painted with the words: WE'RE IN.

"My dad died in 1994, right after he and my mother celebrated their fiftieth wedding anniversary," wrote Bartlett, a longtime fan. "It also was seventeen years after the massive stroke that forced his retirement at the age of fifty-seven. As the years passed, I learned all about the role reversals, the helplessnesses of not being able to give this man his physical abilities back. I shared the sadness with him of knowing the things he could no longer do. Dad developed diabetes after his stroke, and his limited mobility made it even harder for him to control the disease and his weight. Then circulatory problems ensued, and first he had a toe, then half a leg amputated—on his *non*-paralyzed side. I began to wonder how much this proud and strong man could endure. He and Mom worked and planned for him to return from the nursing home to their little retirement home by their fiftieth anniversary. They made it two years before his death, and I firmly believe he wasn't going to depart until he spent his golden anniversary with his wife. . . . I remember Dad dying before we could take him to a game in Jacobs Field, before the Indians won the [1995] pennant. I now have a son, whom Dad hasn't met directly. Evan was born after Dad's death, but I have taken him to games at Jacobs Field. It is comforting to be able to share the gift of baseball with my little Evan—passing it down to him as my father passed it to me."

For men such as my father and Tim Bartlett's dad, 1954 loomed as a benchmark, a key date in the history of the team. Tim's dad passed away a year before the Indians won their next pennant. My father's stroke meant he could only watch the games on TV.

To them, the 1954 Indians were much like the 1997 Tribe is to our generation. We never thought they'd beat the Yankees. They finally did, but then were devastated by what happened to them in the World Series.

Yes, there are differences.

The 1954 team won 111 games; the 1997 Tribe won 86.

The 1954 team was swept in the World Series; the 1997 team came within two outs of a victory.

But the end result was much the same. Utter shock. In both cases, the Indians finally beat the Yankees—and still didn't win the World Series!

That is something Tribe fans of nearly any age can understand.

In 1954, Tribe fans never thought it would come. This was a team in the process of winning what was then an American League record 111 games, yet it spent most of the season looking over its shoulder. Behind them were the Yankees. There always were the Yankees. Even when the Indians took a half-game lead with a 56-27 record at the 1954 All-Star break, the assumption was, "Just wait, the Yanks will catch 'em."

That's because the Yankees always seemed to catch the Indians. It didn't matter that Cleveland had the best pitching staff in the early 1950s with Bob Lemon, Early Wynn, Mike Garcia, Bob Feller, and the underrated Art Houtteman. It didn't matter that they had Al Rosen, who was the MVP in 1953. Or that they had Bobby Avila, an amazing second baseman and a .300 hitter. Or that they had Hall of Famer Larry Doby, a power-hitting center fielder, or Jim Hegan, considered the best defensive catcher in baseball. Or that they were managed by Al Lopez, who is in the Hall of Fame both for his work as a catcher and as a skipper.

No matter how much talent the Indians had, the Yankees had more. It didn't matter that the 1950 Indians were 92-62 . . . or the 1951 Indians were 93-61 . . . or the 1952 Indians were 93-61 (again) . . . or the 1953 Indians were 92-62 (again). The Yankees always won more games. The Yankees were always a little bit better, and seemed destined to stay that way, now and forever, amen.

This was the 1950s. In the 1950s, there were no gimmicks, no playoffs, no wild cards. It was a man's league; you played 154 games, then the teams with the best records in the American League and National League went to the World Series.

Second-best earned you the same spot as last place, home in
October.

Then came 1954. Glorious 1954. The year of the 111 victories. The year the Indians finally finished ahead of New York.
While the Indians didn't need all of those 111 wins, they
needed a monster year, as the Yankees still won 103 games.

"But we wouldn't have beaten the Yankees in 1954, either," said Al Rosen. "Not without Vic Wertz."

Big, bald Vic Wertz. He was 6-foot, 190 pounds of muscle.
He looked even larger and more strapping because of that bald
head.

"There just weren't many bald guys around back then,"
said Rosen. "It's not like today when guys shave their heads."

Wertz loved the attention he received from being bald. He
constantly had his picture in the newspaper. Guys made jokes
about it. He didn't care.

"That's because Vic thought he'd gone to heaven when he
was traded to us," said Rosen.

There's something else about Vic Wertz.

Remember the first game of the 1954 World Series, the famous catch by Willie Mays in dead center field of the Polo
Grounds? Remember how that one catch supposedly changed
an entire World Series, how it led to one of the biggest upsets
in baseball history?

Who hit the ball?

Vic Wertz.

Or how about this: Who was the only Tribe hitter to make
any noise in the World Series?

Vic Wertz, once again.

And who lived in the same apartment as Rosen and who
rode to the park every day with the Tribe's star third baseman?

The same Vic Wertz.

Today, Al Rosen is in his middle seventies, retired and living in Rancho Mirage, California. He is a smart, gracious, won-

derful man. He not only was a fine player for the Indians, he went on to a distinguished career as a general manager, helping teams in New York, Houston, and San Francisco into postseason play. For Rosen, 1954 should have been the best of times. The Indians won the pennant. He hit .300 and was the most popular man in town.

"But now, I see it was really the beginning of the end of my career," he said.

He was only thirty years old in 1954, at his peak.

"I should have been," Rosen said. "Except for the finger."

If you want to see Rosen at the bat, imagine Albert Belle. Picture the cold, steely eyes staring down a pitcher. Imagine the fire in his soul, the iron will demanding excellence. Al Rosen expected to get a hit *every* time. Outs ate away at him. They made him seethe. They forced him to practice harder, to concentrate even more.

"Al Rosen was like Albert Belle in that he was a perfectionist and very emotional," said veteran sportswriter Hal Lebovitz. "But Al was a much nicer man off the field and he always had time to talk to you."

It took Rosen three spring trainings to unseat Kenny Keltner as the team's starting third baseman. When he finally did make it into Cleveland's opening day lineup in 1950, he was booed. The fans loved and missed Keltner, who had played third for the 1948 championship team. But Rosen hit a home run that opening day in 1950, and he received a standing ovation by the end of the game. He called it his greatest thrill in baseball. By 1953, he was the American League's MVP. His 43 homers and 145 RBI led the league, and he missed the triple crown by one point as he batted .336.

"When the 1954 season began, I was at the height of my powers as a player," he said. "I was coming off an MVP year. I thought I could play that way again. In fact, I could have."

Except for the finger.

•

Here is why 1954 is so different than today. Can you imagine a guy who was the MVP of the league being asked to switch positions—to make room for a rookie?

So it was in the spring of 1954.

Rudy Regalado had one of those Tucson mirages, a spring training that made Tribe manager Al Lopez believe he'd found another Rosen. Regalado's best position was third. Lopez didn't like any of his first basemen, so Rosen agreed to make the change for the good of the team.

"It was not my best career move," he said.

For the first 35 games of the season, Rosen was solid at first, and he was putting together another MVP year. In those first 35 games, he had 11 homers, 45 RBI, and was hitting .375.

"We were playing the White Sox," Rosen said. "I was holding Ferris Fain on first base."

Jim Rivera was the batter. As the ball was delivered to home plate, Rosen and Fain both left the bag.

"I was playing behind Fain," Rosen said. "I heard the crack of the bat, but I lost the ball for a split second. The runner was shielding me."

Then he saw a white blur—a shot kicking up dust, coming his way.

Rosen put his glove down, just a second too late.

"The ball took a funny bounce," he said. "Instead of catching it with my glove, it banged against my right index finger."

He thought something broke, but wasn't sure. The finger swelled. He shook off the pain.

"I kept playing with it," he said. "We figured it was just a sprain or bruise or something like that."

Wrong.

"I'd broken it," he said. "It was a fracture, but they didn't find that out until a week later when I went to see a surgeon."

Rosen was not about to stop playing. The Indians were

winning. He was the MVP. A right index finger? Broken? The pain had to go away, right?

Wrong again.

In the next seven weeks, Rosen had only one home run and seven RBI. He batted a weak .259, as his once powerful swing was reduced to a wave of the bat. He never would have guessed that the right index finger would have so much to do with his swing.

"I couldn't get the finger around the bat," he said. "Some days, it just pointed straight up."

He also couldn't throw well, having to use more of his palm to hold the ball because the index finger wasn't able to supply any guidance. The more he played, the worse and weaker the finger became.

"Today, I'd have been taken out of that game right on the spot and taken to the hospital for X rays," he said. "They would have discovered the fracture, and probably put me on the disabled list for a few weeks, letting it heal."

But in 1954, teams didn't do that.

If the bone didn't stick out of the skin, you tried to play. Rosen was proud of his durability. He was not about to complain about the finger, even as he saw the swelling grow and the throbbing pain kept him up at night. Al Rosen was a tough guy. As a third baseman, the joke was that he caught more balls with his face than he did with his glove. He had broken his nose on a ground ball in 1954, one of thirteen times that happened in his career. Another ground ball took a wild hop and whacked him between the eyes with such force that his face swelled to the point where nearly both of his eyes were shut. He went to bed looking at the world through nothing more than slits. The next morning, the swelling remained. He held ice packs against his eyes all day, and somehow managed to play that night as some of the swelling subsided. Not much of this made it into the newspapers; it was so common for him, the nose was barely mentioned by reporters.

Rosen returned to third base in the middle of June because Regalado fizzled and was shipped back to the minors—and Wertz joined the Tribe.

"Thank God for Vic Wertz," Rosen said.

Even with the lousy finger, Rosen wanted to go back to third base. The Indians picked up Wertz on June 1, 1954, from the Baltimore Orioles. They traded a minor league pitcher named Bob Chakales for him. Tribe general manager Hank Greenberg acted as if he'd just acquired another Lou Gehrig. He said he'd been after Wertz for three years. He predicted Wertz would take over at first base and that he'd hit for power.

Some fans and writers said, "Wait a minute."

They said, "Wertz never played first base in his life, he's a right fielder—and isn't all that great in the outfield, either."

They said, "If Wertz is so good, why was he hitting only .202 with one homer?"

There were whispers that Wertz was "an old twenty-nine." Yes, he'd knocked in a combined 256 runs in 1949 and 1950, but that was four years ago.

So they were going to play this guy at a new position, and assume that simply by putting on a Cleveland uniform, he'd remember how to hit? And yet, that's exactly what happened.

"If they think I can help at first base, I'll play first base," said Wertz.

Sometimes he was more like a Secret Service man than a fielder as he seemed to wrestle ground balls to the earth before picking them up and finally tagging the bag. He sort of tiptoed on throws, feeling behind him with his foot for the bag. At one point, Al Lopez even suggested that Wertz take dancing lessons to improve his footwork. That never came to pass, but Wertz was willing to do it. He was willing to do anything for the Indians. He went out there every day with that big, floppy first baseman's glove. He took extra ground balls and throws until his bald head was coated with sweat. He didn't try to beat the heat in Cleveland with the same method he used in St. Louis:

With the Browns, he'd put frozen cabbage leaves under his cap while playing. But Wertz claimed the leaves actually boiled on top of his bald head, creating an odor that was even worse than a ballplayer's armpit. Leaving his cabbage leaves at home and playing for a contender, Wertz hit .275 with 14 homers and 48 RBI in 94 games in 1954.

"I wanted to be traded and I wanted to go to Cleveland," Wertz once recalled. "When I heard about the deal, I got so excited that I packed all my baseball equipment in my good suitcase and I stuffed my good suits in my duffel bag."

"Vic Wertz was like Al Rosen," recalled Bob Feller. "Tough as rusty nails."

In 1954, the Indians never faltered.

After the All-Star break, they won 15 of 18 games to put some breathing room between themselves and the Yankees. From August 6 to 19, they were 13-1. Wertz was the last piece for this great team, settling down the infield as Rosen returned to his natural position at third base. The pitching staff had an ERA of 2.78. Early Wynn and Bob Lemon each won 23 games, while Mike Garcia had 19 victories. Serving as the fifth starter on the team, a thirty-five-year-old Bob Feller was 13-3 with a 3.09 ERA, completing nine of his 19 starts. A couple of rookies named Ray Narleski and Don Mossi combined for 20 saves out of the bullpen.

It remains one of the greatest and deepest pitching staffs ever assembled.

The hitting wasn't bad, either.

Doby led the league with 32 homers and 126 RBI. Avila (.341) was the batting champ. What his teammates didn't learn until later was that Avila suffered from stomach ulcers during much of the season and was under a doctor's orders to drink a half-gallon of milk every day.

"Bobby looked like Cesar Romero and he was our only Latin player," recalled Rosen. "He could be a little moody. He was probably under more pressure than any of us realized."

Despite his finger injury, Rosen still hit .300 with 24 homers and 102 RBI.

These Indians were an interesting mix. Doby was the first black player in the American League. Early Wynn was part Native American. Mike Garcia was a Mexican-American, born in San Gabriel, California. Lopez was a Spaniard raised in Tampa, while Rosen was a Jew from Miami.

"We really didn't think much about the [racial] makeup of the team," said Rosen. "The nice thing was we truly were a team."

That team set a then major league record with 111 victories, eclipsing the 1927 Yankees, who had 110.

"No one cared about that," said Rosen. "We weren't out to make history. We just wanted to beat the Yankees."

Then came the World Series.


Over forty years later, Al Lopez is still not sure what happened. He sat in the dining room of his home, overlooking Tampa Bay. Al Lopez had seen just about everything in baseball. He once caught Walter Johnson. He managed a young Tommy John. He delivered bread from a horse-drawn carriage, and he is credited with creating the first bullpen bookends (the lefty-righty combination of Mossi and Narleski in 1954).

"We had Hall of Famers on that pitching staff," said Lopez. "And we were swept in four games?"

Lopez shook his head.

He had no answers in 1954. In 1995, when I spoke with him about it, he still had no answers. While obviously older, Lopez came across in 1995 much like he did in 1954—as a thoughtful man in horn-rim glasses whose inherent decency shone through an otherwise restrained personality. Lopez was a man you could trust. Lopez didn't tell stories out of school. He was a man who was driven out of the dugout by stomach ulcers. He just kept so much bottled up inside.

As *Sports Illustrated* wrote in 1954, "El Señor is a calming presence in the dugout. He gets in no bitter arguments, utters no fiery quotes and never chews out a player in front of others."

Mentioning the 1954 World Series caused a pained expression to cross the face of this fine man. It was utter agony, even though it was forty-one years later. Lopez thought about it for a long time, looking for an answer he knew he'd never find.

"The only thing I can say is, we had a slump at the absolute worst time," he said.

Which brings us to Vic Wertz and Willie Mays, Game 1 of the World Series. The Indians were enormous favorites, 9 to 5 by Nevada bookmakers. Bob Lemon started the opener, the same Bob Lemon who had an 11-game winning streak during the season and finished with a 23-7 record.

"The way I had my rotation set up, Lemon would pitch twice in the first four games," said Lopez, believing Lemon had to win at least one of those starts.

It looked like it would be that opening game at the Polo Grounds. In the first inning, the Indians took a 2–0 lead. Wertz drove in both runs with a triple. New York tied the game at 2–2 in the bottom of the third.

In the top of the eighth, Doby walked, Rosen singled, and Wertz came to the plate. To Cleveland sports fans, it will forever be known as The Catch, much like Earnest Byner's blunder against Denver in January of 1988 is The Fumble and Michael Jordan's heartbreaking jumper in the 1989 playoffs against the Cavs will always be The Shot.

The Catch came about because Wertz hit the ball to the wrong part of the Polo Grounds. Depending upon which account you choose, the ball either went 440 feet or 460 feet to dead center.

"It went off Vic's bat like a cannon shot," said Rosen. "I was on first base, and I was off at the crack of the bat. I wanted to score."

But as Rosen was running to second, he had a perfect view of Willie Mays in center for the Giants.

"I had this sinking feeling," Rosen said. "I could tell that if the ball stayed in the park, Willie would catch it."

It seemed Mays ran about 400 miles to track it down. He just turned his back to home plate and was gone, not even looking at the ball. To most fans, there was no reason to expect Mays to make that catch—but Rosen was not most fans. His Indians played the Giants about a dozen times each spring training in Arizona. He knew what Mays could do. He knew that in 1954, you did not hit the ball over the head of Willie Mays.

"I felt the same way," recalled Bob Feller. "So did most of the guys in the dugout. The wind was blowing in, and that helped Willie. Everyone said that was the greatest catch ever, but I saw Willie make better plays than that in spring training."

Wertz thought otherwise. A career American Leaguer whose teams trained in Florida, this was his first look at Willie Mays. He'd never seen an outfielder who could catch that ball.

"I never hit a ball that hard," Wertz said. "At least not one that was caught."

When Wertz came to bat in the eighth inning, he already had three hits in the game. He was facing reliever Don Liddle.

Wertz should have been the hero.

That should have been his fourth hit of the game, and the Indians should have taken at least a 4–2 lead into the ninth inning.

Instead, Mays caught the ball. Ran out from under his cap and caught the ball. He caught the ball at full stride, his back to the plate. He caught the ball because he seemed to know where it was going from the moment it left the bat. He caught the ball for one reason: The Indians just weren't supposed to win this game, or this World Series.

"I had rounded second base when Willie made the catch," said Rosen. "I had to cross back over second, step on the bag again, and hightail it just to get back to first base."

Doby, who was at second, was able to return and tag up and reached third on the play, but the Indians stranded Doby and Rosen.

Liddle was removed from the game after Mays's catch. Wertz was the only hitter he faced. "Well, I got my man," he said with a smile as he sat in the dugout.

"Thirty years after the catch, people still talk about it," said Wertz. "When it happened, it about broke my heart. But after a while, I kind of liked the idea that Willie caught the ball. If he hadn't, who would ever have remembered that I was the guy who hit it?"

With those words, Wertz sounded like a true Indian.

Two other words Tribe fans would never forget in 1954: Dusty Rhodes.

They didn't say the name, they spat it. They cursed it. They dreaded the day they ever heard the name. James Lamar Rhodes didn't even start; he was supposed to be an outfielder, but he was not on speaking terms with his glove. Mostly, Dusty Rhodes could swing the bat. He was a left-handed hitter in a park where the right field line was a child's dropkick away, only 260 feet. In the 10th inning of Game 1, Rhodes was summoned to the plate. His Giants had two runners on base. Hall of Famer Bob Lemon was still on the mound for the Tribe.

Rhodes hit the ball 261 feet to right field to win the game, 5–2.

Avila drifted back from his second base postion and swore it was nothing more than a pop-up, that he'd catch it. But the same wind that had seemed to knock down Wertz's drive shifted and lifted Rhodes's fly ball into that short porch in right field.

A three-run homer.

A "Chinese homer," as several politically incorrect reporters called it.

A wind-blown pop-up, said Lopez.

The crusher, said most of the Tribe players.

Wertz hits the ball 460 feet and gets nothing. Rhodes taps the ball and is the hero.

"It had all the harsh, crunching quality of a poached egg," wrote Franklin Lewis in the *Cleveland Press*.

In Game 2, Rhodes was sent to home plate to pinch-hit. Early Wynn decked him with the first pitch, put the ball under Dusty's chin and dropped his butt in the dirt. Rhodes stood up, didn't say a word—and lashed a run-scoring single. He stayed in the game and homered in the seventh.

Giants 3, Tribe 1.

Rhodes drove in two more runs in Game 3, the Giants winning, 6–2.

Things were so bad for the Tribe, the Giants didn't even need Rhodes in Game 4 as New York completed the sweep with a 7–4 victory.

During the 1954 regular season, Rhodes was a .341 hitter with 15 homers in only 164 at bats, mostly as a pinch hitter. In the World Series, Rhodes was 4-for-6 with two homers and seven RBI.

"The guy caught lightning in a bottle," said Rosen.

No doubt. For his career, Rhodes hit an undistinguished .253. In seven years, he had 54 homers. Later in life, he drove a bus.

"The 1954 World Series just was Dusty Rhodes's time on earth," said Rosen.

Over forty years later, Rosen was still stunned by what had happened in October of 1954.

"We had a chance to be one of the ten greatest teams of all time," he said. "For a team to win 111 games with all our great pitching and to lose the way we did, the clubhouse was like a wake for your best friend. A few guys cried, but most of us were just emotionally spent."

After that loss in Game 4, the 78,102 fans at Cleveland Stadium made this impression on Arthur Daley of the *New York Times:* "A breathless hush fell over this sprawling stadium. It was so quiet, you could almost hear a heart break. No one spoke a kind word about the deceased. The Indians died friendless and alone."

And there would be no more baseball life in October for another forty-one years.

Unlike his old manager and many of his 1954 teammates, Rosen has an idea what happened in that World Series.

"It was a letdown, pure and simple," he said. "All year, people kept waiting for us to fold and the Yankees to catch us. We always were the bridesmaids, and we were sick of it."

The 1954 Indians drove themselves to beat the Yankees, "and when we did, it was like winning the World Series," Rosen said.

When the Indians clinched the pennant, they did more than write WE'RE IN on the head of Vic Wertz. There was a parade through the streets of downtown Cleveland with over 250,000 fans watching the players rolling by in convertibles.

"Physically, we were in bad shape by the World Series," Rosen said. "I was limping on a bad hamstring. Doby also had a bad hamstring. He had been playing on it for a long time, and it was so raw from all the taping—well, they couldn't tape it anymore because it would tear the skin off. They took part of an inner tube, wrapped that around Doby's leg, and then taped over the tube."

Doby also had a badly bruised shoulder from a slide during the last week of the season. Wertz was the only Cleveland player who hit during the Series (8-for-16), yet he was playing with a severely bruised index finger. He wore a sponge in his glove to cushion the finger from the force of the baseball as he caught throws at first base. Wertz never told Lopez about the injury, fearing the manager would take him out of the lineup. But he always wondered if the finger had not been so sore, would that ball he hit to center field have cleared the wall instead of ending up in the glove of Willie Mays?

"You can talk about how we couldn't get a break, and we didn't," Rosen said. "But in the end, I just think our tank was empty. We had nothing left."

It didn't take long for the 1954 team to come apart.

Manager Al Lopez left after the 1956 season, feeling unappreciated by the fans and front office. Lopez managed the Tribe for six years, winning one pennant and finishing in second place the other five seasons.

Rosen batted .300 with 24 homers and 102 RBI in 1954, but he hit .273 with only 13 homers and 57 RBI after the May 25th fractured finger from the experiment of playing him at first base.

"I was never the same player," he said. "The finger never healed properly. I couldn't swing the bat normally. It became so frustrating that I probably quit before I should have."

Rosen played only two more seasons, retiring in 1956. He batted .267 with 15 homers and 61 RBI in the final year, and was the object of boos from the fans who blamed his decline for that of the team's.

Frank Lane was hired as general manager after the 1957 season, ushering in the Curse of Rocky Colavito after that and other terrible trades. Lane also drove Wertz out of Cleveland. In 1955, Wertz was still the Tribe's first baseman, but he was struck down with polio in late August.

"I've got two strikes against me, but I'm a long way from being out," Wertz told the *Cleveland Press* from his hospital bed in 1955. "I know I have polio, and I also know I'm going to lick it. They tell me this thing may end my baseball career, but I'll never believe it."

Wertz's problems began with what he called "a king-sized tummy ache." Then he began to feel weak. Eventually, he was sent to the hospital. Doctors originally thought it was an ordinary virus, then determined it was polio. He was placed in isolation. It took a week to determine there was no permanent paralysis. Nonetheless, doctors said he had "only a 50-50 chance" of returning to baseball. Wertz came back in 1956, hit 32 homers and drove in 106 runs. He was voted the Tribe's Man of the Year. In 1957, he made the All-Star team, hitting 28 homers and driving in 105 runs.

In 1958, Wertz missed most of the season with a broken ankle, and Frank Lane tried to cut his salary from $32,000 to $24,000.

Here was a guy who had bailed out the team in 1954 by playing first base, a brand-new position. He had come back from polio, played hurt, and was the captain of the team—and Frank Lane wanted to cut his salary by 25 percent because he broke an ankle. Lane then traded him to the Red Sox. Wertz hung on as a player until 1963. He also had a successful beer distributorship in Detroit, where he was known as "Mr. Miller Beer."

"Vic was involved in about every major charity in Detroit," said Rosen. "He raised millions of dollars for great causes, and he just wasn't the kind of guy to complain about anything."

Vic Wertz died in 1983 after heart surgery.

If I had to pick any player in the history of the Indians who reminds me of my father, it's Vic Wertz. Not just because of the bald head, although that's part of it. But there also was his willingness to sacrifice for the team, and the will to overcome polio. You hear so much about unsung heroes that the phrase ceases to mean much anymore. But these men have always existed. They are men like Vic Wertz, men like my father, Tim Bartlett's father, and so many other fathers who gave so much of themselves and asked for so little in return.

## CHAPTER 14

# Roger Maris, Rocky Colavito, and Frank Lane

HER NAME is Sue Mattocks, and she wrote me a letter about the Indians, her father, and Rocky Colavito.

"Every time I start to write this, I wind up crying," she wrote. "When I was born in 1947, my father was very disappointed. He wanted a son to teach about sports, and he got a daughter instead, his only child. Those were the days when girls didn't have organized sports, so he'd felt he'd lost his chance to pass on his love of baseball. In 1956, my parents divorced. My dad was suddenly faced with one-on-one time with his daughter. He decided to teach me about baseball, so we'd have something in common. At first, I went to the old Stadium just to be with him, but something happened on those trips: I developed a deep love for my father and for Indians baseball. When all my friends were playing with dolls, I was collecting baseball cards and playing catch with anyone I could find. Later on, when those same friends had pictures of Ricky Nelson and Elvis on their walls, I had Rocky Colavito and other Indians

players on my walls. . . . My father is very ill now. He has em-
physema and a weak heart and isn't strong enough to go with
me to see the Indians at Jacobs Field. Every time I go to a game,
I think of how much he'd enjoy that beautiful ballpark and our
wonderful team. But I guess he probably wouldn't enjoy it any
more than he did going to that big tomb of a stadium watching
a mediocre team, because he had his small daughter looking at
him with such love in her eyes because he showed her the
world of baseball."

For the fans who have just come to the Indians in the Jacobs Field era, it's impossible to understand what Rocky Colavito meant to Tribe fans in the late 1950s and 1960s. They look
at his statistics and see that he was a good player, but not a
great one. Albert Belle consistently had better numbers with
the Tribe. In 1998, Manny Ramirez had 45 homers and 145
RBI, more than any right fielder in the history of the franchise,
including Colavito.

Yet there is something special about Rocky Colavito to
those of us who were eating our first hot dogs with Stadium
mustard when Colavito represented hope and power to a franchise that was lacking in both areas.

Which is why so many Tribe fans still hate Frank Lane.

He was paranoid.
He was an egomaniac.
He lied.
He was foul-mouthed.
He traded Colavito.

But you probably know all that. You have to go back to
1959, back to a year when the Indians were in contention with
the White Sox until the final week of the season. That Tribe
team fell five games short of the American League pennant, but
it was a good team led by a young slugger named Rocky Colavito. There were reasons to make trades after the 1959 season,
but the one player you'd never trade was Colavito. Naturally,

Lane traded Colavito. He would not have been Frantic Frank Lane, or Trader Frank Lane, if he hadn't.

Frank Lane wanted to be known as the one guy with guts enough to trade one of the most popular players in the history of the franchise. Lane knew the trade would put him at center stage of the Cleveland baseball scene, and he craved the spotlight, the headlines. So he traded Rocky Colavito to the Detroit Tigers for Harvey Kuenn. It made no sense. Kuenn was older than Colavito. He hit for less power. He chewed more tobacco. He drank fewer chocolate sodas. He was uglier than Colavito, at least according to the women of Cleveland. But Harvey Kuenn had one big thing going for him—he was not Rocky Colavito. He would not steal Lane's luster.

Thinking about this trade nearly forty years later still makes the blood boil. Only Frank Lane would do this. Only Frank Lane would have traded a twenty-six-year-old Rocky Colavito to Detroit, a twenty-six-year-old Rocky Colavito who already had 129 home runs. Only Frank Lane would trash Colavito after the deal, starting with his assertion that "home runs are overrated." Or his insisting, "We've given up 40 homers for 40 doubles, but we've added 50 singles and subtracted 50 strikeouts."

"Only Frank Lane would have made that trade," said former Tribe pitcher Mudcat Grant. "Because only Frank Lane was that kind of idiot."

In 1959, the Indians were a contender because they led the league in home runs, runs scored, and batting average. They had an 89-65 record. Then they traded Colavito. Lane said the only people who'd really be upset were "the bobby-socks set." He meant teenaged girls such as Sue, who had Colavito's picture on their walls—much like many teenage female Tribe fans in the 1990s have posters of Omar Vizquel in their rooms.

That second-place team, that team with an 89-65 record with Colavito, dropped to 76-78 in 1960. The Indians would not contend for a pennant again until 1995. Actually, they were a contender in 1994, but the Curse of Rocky Colavito lingered for another year as baseball went on strike before the Indians had a chance to make the playoffs. So it took thirty-five years after the Colavito trade for the Indians to contend. It also led to an even worse deal after the 1964 season, when Gabe Paul was determined to bring Colavito back to Cleveland. In Colavito's last season of his first tenure with the Tribe, the team drew 1.5 million fans; five years later, the attendance was down to 653,293 and there were rumors of the franchise moving, with cities such as Seattle and New Orleans being mentioned. Colavito was brought back to sell tickets—and in the process, the Indians sold their future. They sent Tommy John, Tommie Agee, and John Romano to Chicago as part of a three-way deal to acquire Colavito from Kansas City.

Colavito was, by then, thirty-two years old. He had a great season in 1965 (26 homers, .287 batting average, and a league-leading 108 RBI while playing all 162 games and not making an error in right field). In 1966, he hit 30 homers but batted only .238. By 1967, his career was about over; at midseason, he was traded to the White Sox for a guy named Jimmy King, who was hitting .188.

In the meantime, Tommy John won 286 games after leaving the Indians.

Tommie Agee was a fine center fielder for 10 seasons.

Talk about the Curse of Rocky Colavito.

The second Rocky Colavito trade may have been even worse than the one in 1960, but you can blame all this on Frank Lane, too. He was the guy who traded Colavito in the first place. He started the Curse.

But there's even more.

Does the name Roger Maris ring a baseball bell?

Bet you didn't know that trading Roger Maris was the best deal Frank Lane made while he was in Cleveland. At least, that's according to Frank Lane. If there is a baseball hell, Frank Lane should be roasting like a marshmallow on a stick, being thrust into a bonfire. Just ask the guys who played for him. Just listen to Lane insisting, "The best deal I made for Cleveland was Roger Maris for Woodie Held and Vic Power." True, Lane said this right before the 1961 season, right before Maris would hit a then record 61 home runs. But it was right after the 1960 season, after a year when Maris hit 39 home runs, drove in 112 runs, and was the American League MVP. Lane traded away the guy who became the MVP and still thought it was a great deal?

In the 1950s, the Indians had the second-best scouting staff in the American League, right behind the Yankees. They had leathery-skinned men who looked at dusty diamonds through eyes in a perpetual squint as they watched baseball under the blistering summer sun. They knew where to find players. They found Herb Score in Florida, Rocky Colavito in the Bronx, and Roger Maris in North Dakota.

The trio of Score, Colavito, and Maris should have kept the Indians in contention at least through the middle 1960s. But Score was struck in the eye with a ball off the bat of Gil McDougald in 1957. He never reached what should have been his destiny—to be Sandy Koufax before baseball met Sandy Koufax. And Colavito was traded for Kuenn.

Then there was Maris.

This guy wasn't just a hitter, he was a natural, all-around athlete, as tough as the winter wind off the North Dakota plains. He also could have the same biting personality. A scout named Frank Fahey spotted Maris at an American Legion tournament in 1950. At that stage of his life, Maris was only 5-foot-8 and 150 pounds. But he had wrists quicker than the tongue of a snake. The ball was a lightning bolt off his bat. He played the outfield with grace and stole bases with ease.

Best of all, he was only sixteen.

A year later, Maris was up to 175 pounds. He was an all-state running back, good enough to be offered a football scholarship to Oklahoma—and that's as good as there was in the early 1950s. But Maris didn't like school and he wanted to play baseball. The Indians were the only team that pursued him hard, and they signed him for $5,000.

That's right, five grand for the man who'd break Babe Ruth's record.

If only Frank Lane . . .

But that came later.

In 1953, the Indians wanted to send Maris to Daytona Beach, their Class D minor league team. Made sense. Class D was the lowest rung on the Tribe's minor league ladder. Maris was only eighteen. Why rush him? But the Indians' Class C team was in Fargo, Maris's hometown. He demanded to be assigned to Fargo. The Indians hesitated. Maris threatened to quit.

"I'm going to Fargo," he told team officials. "Either I go there to play ball and live, or else I'll go there just to live and find another job. It's up to you."

The Tribe sent him to Fargo, and realized Maris could be as stubborn as the men and women who'd settled those inhospitable Northern Plains, people who refused to quit during the winter blizzards, the summer droughts, or the attacks of locusts.

In the off-season, Maris ran a gas station and was often seen at the pumps, pouring the high-test into a customer's tank and then cleaning the windows. Maris bulled his way through the Tribe farm system, sometimes insisting at the top of his lungs that he be promoted to a higher level—often before the Indians thought he was ready. He usually got his way.

By 1957, Maris was in Cleveland. He batted only .235 with 14 homers in 116 games, but he was only twenty-two years old. Furthermore, he had been hitting about .280 when he cracked two ribs while sliding into second base early in May. He later jammed a wrist and pulled a hamstring chasing a fly ball into a wall. He came back too soon, fearful of losing his job—and the bottom dropped out of his batting average. He never was fully healthy in the last two months of the season.

During the winter, Lane wanted Maris to play in the Dominican Republic for $1,000 a month. Maris refused, telling Lane it wasn't enough. Actually, he wanted to go home to Fargo, to lick his wounds and heal before spring training. But Maris was a man who didn't like to admit he was hurt, so he used money as an excuse to bypass winter ball. Lane was outraged, and many claim this dispute over winter ball was when Lane privately vowed to trade Maris.

"At that stage of his career, Roger reminded me of a young Brian Giles," said Hal Lebovitz. "He was a good all-around player. He knew he was going to be much better than he showed as a rookie. Did I know he'd be the one to break Babe Ruth's record? Never. But did I like him as a player and a person? You better believe it."

Despite his uninspiring statistics in 1957, nearly everyone who saw Maris liked his talent. They thought he could be pigheaded and gruff, and they thought he needed to grow up; they wished he wouldn't complain so bitterly. But they knew Roger Maris could play. They also knew there was nothing in his personality that would prevent him from becoming an excellent outfielder who'd drive in runs. Some scouts saw him as a guy who'd hit .280 with 20 to 25 homers and at least 85 RBI. He also could steal some bases and play all three outfield positions.

The Yankees were also watching. They'd do that back in the 1940s and 1950s. They'd target a young player on another team and scout him for years. The Yankees went as far as sending someone to Fargo to talk to those who knew Maris growing up, just so they'd have a complete report on him.

The Yankees were waiting.

They waited for the day the Indians became impatient. They waited for the day they could work a deal for Maris, whom they projected as a right fielder because of his strong, accurate arm. They also believed he'd learn to pull the ball as he approached his middle twenties, and his uppercut swing from the left side of the plate was perfect for the short right field porch in Yankee Stadium.

When Lane took over the Indians, they knew it was just a matter of time. Something about Maris would rub Lane raw, and then Lane would trade him.

So the Yankees waited.

"I played in Fargo in 1954, the year after Roger had played there," former Tribe pitcher Mudcat Grant recalled. "He was the Northern League Rookie of the Year in 1953, and I won the award in 1954. I heard from everyone that Roger would be a great player. Throughout the Indians farm system, you heard Roger Maris and Rocky Colavito, Roger Maris and Rocky Colavito. Those guys were the future. There was no way I ever thought either one of them would be traded."

The Yankees did, and they waited a little longer.

Before the 1958 season, Lane offered Maris a contract with a $1,500 raise. Maris returned it to Lane, ripped in half. Lane opened the envelope and let loose with a variety of cuss words in combinations never quite heard before in the Tribe's front offices. He vowed to "get Maris outta here." He had traded for veteran outfielders Minnie Minoso and Larry Doby, who returned for a second tour of duty. The Indians planned an outfield of Minoso, Doby, and Colavito. As for Maris, Lane thought the hotheaded kid could platoon with Colavito in right field. To understand the absolute absurdity of this plan, realize that the 1957 Indians were a sixth-place team with a 76-77 record. It was time to play the kids, to build. Instead, Lane was junking his youth movement in favor of Doby and Minoso, two players over thirty years old. He was going to hinder the development of Colavito and Maris by having them share one position. He wanted a quick fix.

Colavito started fast in 1958, and Maris slumped. He missed a week with a sore back, and manager Bobby Bragan accused Maris of being soft, not willing to play through pain. Maris didn't want a repeat of 1957, when he came back while still injured and didn't hit—and was criticized for it. Soon Colavito was playing nearly every day, while Maris brooded on the bench. Lane decided to trade Maris. The Yankees were interested. Lane vowed he'd never trade Maris to the Yankees.

"They offered Bobby Richardson," Lane said at the time. "I didn't want to make the trade because I'm not certain Richardson is better than Billy Moran."

Moran was the Tribe's starting second baseman. And guess what? Bobby Richardson developed into an All-Star second baseman. Billy Moran was another Eddie Leon.

Good move again, Frank Lane.

When Lane balked at New York's offer, the Yankees just waited some more. In June, the Indians were still a sixth-place team. Maris was batting only .225 with nine homers in 182 at bats. Lane found a taker in Kansas City. The A's offered Woodie Held and Vic Power for Maris.

"Two starting infielders for a kid sitting on my bench?" asked Lane. "I had to jump at that."

And he did, landing with both feet in his fat mouth.

Some of the Tribe's deep thinkers characterized Maris as "spoiled," and a "mama's boy." They talked about him pouting when he didn't get his way. Some of that was true—but it also was true that the Yankees were nearly drowning in their own drool trying to get this guy, and Lane should have realized that alone was reason not to trade him. When the trade was announced, it was a yawner in Cleveland; Maris was hitting only .225 and some fans thought he'd be nothing more than a perpetual prospect, another Rudy Regalado who was a bright star in the Arizona desert in the month of March, until the shine rubbed off in the realities of the major leagues.

With Kansas City, Maris was planted in right field. Every day, his name was in the lineup. And soon he was starting to show his potential—and doing it every day in nearly every way. While he batted only .247, he hit 19 homers in 99 games. For the 1958 season, he ended up with 28 homers.

He was only twenty-four at the end of the season. And the Yankees were still waiting.

In 1959, he batted .273 with 16 homers and 72 RBI. The Yankees made several offers to Kansas City for Maris, but they were rejected. In December of 1959, Maris was finally traded to New York in an eight-player deal where he—by far—became the most important piece. Lane was livid. He snorted. He shouted. He swore and stomped his feet, and everyone around him wished they were on another planet. Kansas City had deceived him! How dare they trade Maris to the Yankees? He never would have traded Maris to Kansas City if he had known the outfielder was going to end up in New York. On and on it went. Lane screamed, and Lane nearly cried. But most of all, he whined.

Everyone in baseball knew full well that Kansas City had once been the Yankees' top farm team, and it sometimes forgot that it was now an equal competitor, at least in theory. When it moved up into the majors, Kansas City *constantly* traded with the Yankees. If Frank Lane truly was shocked when Maris ended up in New York, he was the only executive in the game who was surprised by that turn of events. Whenever Kansas City had a player the Yankees wanted, the Yankees usually got him. The following members of the Yankees in the early 1960s first played for the old Kansas City A's: Ralph Terry, Ryne Duren, Clete Boyer, Bob Cerv, Joe DeMaestri, Hector Lopez, Art Ditmar, Bud Daley—and Maris.

Playing for the Yankees in 1960, Maris was the MVP with 39 homers and 112 RBI. Then, in 1961, Maris broke Babe Ruth's record with 61 homers. Through it all, Lane insisted he'd made a "great trade" unloading Maris.

In 1958 and 1959, Lane made 64 trades involving 140 players. In 1960, he traded managers—sending Joe Gordon to Detroit for Jimmy Dykes.

"He once tried to trade his entire roster for the roster of

another team," recalled Herb Score. "When Lane was general manager in St. Louis, he was ready to trade Stan Musial when the owners stepped in and stopped him."

Frank Lane preferred trading to winning. He acquired a young first baseman named Norm Cash from the White Sox, then traded Cash to Detroit for a minor leaguer named Steve Demeter before Cash ever played a game for the Tribe. Cash hit 373 homers in his Tiger career. Demeter's career with the Tribe was five at bats—as you'd expect, he was 0-for-5.

In 1961, while Maris was hitting those homers for New York, Cash hit 41 homers and batted a league-leading .361 for the Tigers. Colavito hit 45 homers and had 140 RBI—also for the Tigers. All of these guys could have been—no, make that *should* have been—with the Indians.

By 1961, all the Indians had to show for those deals were Vic Power and Woodie Held, who had more errors (37) than home runs (28).

Thank you, Mr. Lane.

"For a while, his trading Rocky turned me off to baseball," Sue Mattocks wrote. "Then I took my own children to a game in 1993, the last year at the old Cleveland Stadium. It took about ten minutes for me to fall in love with the Tribe all over again."

Sue is like so many of us. We go to the park now with our children, our nieces and nephews, and we think of when we were kids, when our fathers led us to the Stadium to see Rocky Colavito. Only now it's Manny Ramirez, or Jim Thome, or Omar Vizquel—players whose stories our children will pass down to their children.

# CHAPTER 15

# Our Place, the Stadium

I REMEMBER telling my father they were tearing down the Stadium.

He stared at me, wide-eyed, questioning.

I reminded him that the Indians had moved to Jacobs Field.

"Man . . . MAN . . . MAN!" he roared, waving his left hand, his good hand. He was telling me that he knew that. He'd watched the Indians on TV. He had seen Jacobs Field.

"They're going to build a new stadium," I said. "A new one for the Browns."

Those wide, questioning blue eyes stared hard at me again.

Then he remembered. Art Modell had taken the Browns away. The Stadium was just sitting there on the lakefront, empty.

"No one is playing there," I said.

He shook his head, sadly.

This was in 1996, three years after his stroke. In those

three years, I had gotten to know so much more about my father than in our first thirty-eight years together. I knew when he wanted the pillow moved behind his back. I knew when his foot ached and he wanted it rubbed. I knew just how he wanted to have his dentures cleaned, his body washed, and his face shaved. I knew things about my father that most sons would never know, because his stroke brought us closer together. And I knew what the Stadium meant to us, and that was why I couldn't tell him that parts of the old Stadium were being tossed into Lake Erie to create a reef for perch and walleye. At that stage, why tell a man that one of the best parts of his life was being reduced to rubble and dumped into the lake?

My father grew up in a Cleveland without a TV. He grew up in a Cleveland where most families didn't have cars, you either walked or took the streetcar. He grew up in a Cleveland where fruit and vegetables were sold out of the back of a wagon—a wagon pulled by a horse. He grew up in a Cleveland where the neighborhoods were defined by the ethnic group that lived there—Warsazwa Village, Little Italy, etc. He grew up in a Cleveland where people asked, "Where do you live?" and you'd answer with the name of a Catholic church. Tell someone you lived by St. Benedict's, and people knew you meant East Boulevard. Before his stroke, my father liked to talk of those days, but I didn't have the time to listen. No, I didn't have the patience to listen.

But I do remember him saying, "When the Stadium opened, it was a big deal."

That was in 1932.

My father was twelve years old.

The first baseball game played at the Stadium was on July 31, 1932. In that day's edition of the *Plain Dealer*, there was a story about Adolf Hitler gaining political strength in Germany, and of a presidential candidate named Franklin D. Roosevelt running on a platform to end the Depression and legalize beer sales.

Baseball in 1932 was different.

The Stadium was new, but Babe Ruth was old. He was thirty-seven years old, but still hit 41 homers. He still drove in 137 runs. He played in his last World Series. He took one look at the new ballpark in Cleveland and said, "To play in that out-field, you need a horse."

That's because there was no fence in the outfield. It was 320 feet down the foul lines; that never changed. But it was 463 feet in the power alleys. Yes, *463 feet* in the area of the park where most of the home runs were supposed to be hit. Virtually no one hit the ball 463 feet. As for center field, it was 470 feet away. You had a better chance of being struck by lightning than hitting a homer into the center field bleachers.

"A great park for triples," my father recalled. "And a great park for pitchers."

"In League Park, I felt like the fans were breathing over my left shoulder, but at the Stadium, I could *breathe,*" recalled Willis Hudlin, who pitched for the Tribe in 1932.

That was assuming Hudlin didn't get blown off the mound by a gust of Lake Erie wind. Yes, the Great Lake was just be-yond the center field bleachers. That was another attraction of the Stadium to fans, especially those in the 1930s who seldom traveled. You could sit in the upper deck behind home plate, watch the game below and also see the ships on Lake Erie. Even when my father took me to games as a teenager in the 1960s, there was something special about seeing the blue lake, the huge iron freighters and the delicate sailboats. Of course, that was when the weather was sunny, the wind calm—which wasn't very often.

But when the Stadium opened in 1932, it was stunning. It was astounding. It was *just so big.*

Listen to the early reviews:

"It's perfect."

"It's the only park where the spectators can see clearly

from any seat. Look at those people in center field. They can see every play."

"Not a barrier to block one's view. Comfortable chairs."

"The greatest baseball plant in the world."

It sounds like what some people said when Jacobs Field opened in 1994, but these platitudes came from the mouth of Judge Kenesaw Mountain Landis. Today, it sounds as if the good commissioner must have been puffing on contraband cigars.

No barriers? A clear view from every seat? Mr. Commissioner, the Stadium was held up by forty-four steel beams. That's forty-four beams in different spots around the ballpark, forty-four beams that made it virtually impossible to see the field from hundreds of seats.

By the 1980s, the Stadium was being voted the worst baseball facility in the country—partly because of those beams, and partly because of the wind and rain and fog and snow (yes, snow!) off the lake. Oh, and the bugs. In July, swarms of no-see-ums whirled in like locusts off the lake. Fans and players swatted those little bugs they couldn't see (but heard). Legend has it that Jim Kern had to leave a game when he swallowed a mouthful on the mound, but he always denied the story.

But no one talked about bugs in 1932 when the park opened.

That's because the Stadium overwhelmed the fans and players with its sheer size. It had 76,000 chairs. It had rest rooms that didn't back up (that would come later), and it had the smell of fresh varnish, new paint, and a world of promise.

It was the biggest baseball park in America, and it was in Cleveland.

Like most residents of the city, that made my father proud.

When the Stadium opened for its maiden baseball game on July 31, 1932, it was nearly overrun by a mass of humanity.

"The unbelievable happened, they filled the Stadium," wrote the *Plain Dealer.* "Game time was 3 P.M., but they started coming at noon. They came over the bluff at Lakeside Avenue and they came down the bridges to the lakefront. Some on foot. Some in autos. They came by bus and train. One man told a policeman he had come all the way from Louisiana to see the Stadium."

More than 25,000 cars and 1,000 buses and cabs created the biggest traffic jam the city had ever seen. But there were no newspaper accounts of arrests. Story after story stressed how the "mob" was "well-behaved."

Mel Harder started that day for the Indians.

"When I went to the mound and looked around at the crowd, it was the most awesome thing I'd ever seen," he recalled sixty years later. "I mean, 80,000 fans. It was hard to believe so many people could be in one place."

Harder's opponents that day were the Philadelphia A's and their star pitcher, Lefty Grove. To put it kindly, Grove was "crusty." To tell the truth, Grove was a miserable loser. He tore metal locker doors off the wall. He smashed water buckets with a baseball bat. He once ripped his own uniform off and shredded it—with his bare hands as if it were a newspaper.

As the Associated Press reported, "Robert Moses Grove was in rare form, and held the Indians to four scattered hits to win his 16th game. Mel Harder, the Indians' young righthander, was almost equally stingy."

"The final score was 1–0," recalled Harder. "In the eighth inning, I walked Max Bishop on a 3-and-2 pitch. I thought it was a strike. Mule Haas sacrificed Bishop to second. Then Bishop scored when Mickey Cochrane hit a fastball right off his fists for a single. It went right under my glove and up the middle for a hit."

One run was it.

"Our hitters were almost beat before the game [because of the size of the ballpark]," said Hudlin.

Not only was the Montana-sized outfield a problem, so were the fans in the bleachers. This was the era when male fans wore hats, suit coats, shirt, and ties to games. It was a warm afternoon, and the fans in the sun-soaked bleachers took off their coats.

"About 1,000 of them were in the bleachers and all but 17 wore white shirts," reported the *Plain Dealer*. Hitter after hitter complained that they lost the ball in those thousand white shirts.

The next day, the Indians and A's played again. And again the A's won, 1–0.

It didn't take long for it to become clear the Stadium was not "a baseball palace," as Landis and others insisted.

"After two games, the Indians don't care anything about their new home, for all it has brought them is 18 horse collars, as the boys now call goose-eggs, along with two defeats and cinders in their nifty motors, which are parked near the railroad tracks," wrote Stuart Bell in the *Cleveland Press*.

The second game at the Stadium drew only 21,218 fans (including 12,000 schoolkids admitted for free). By the seventh game at the Stadium, the attendance was 12,270 (only 5,945 paid).

In 1933, the Indians played all their home games at the Stadium and averaged slightly under 6,000 fans. That meant over 70,000 empty seats per game. The expense of keeping up such a huge facility for so few fans staggered the city's bean counters. By 1934, the Indians were back at cozy League Park for all but their Sunday games.

"Our hitters hated the Stadium more than our pitchers hated League Park," said Willis Hudlin. "They hit the ball 420 feet only to see it caught. They came back to the bench talking to themselves."

In 1939, some night games during the week also were played at the Stadium, but it wasn't until 1947 when Bill Veeck bought the team that the Indians took up permanent residence on the lakefront.

By 1948, when the Indians were setting attendance records, the Stadium was back to being considered one of the best baseball venues in the land. Players loved the excellent infield. Fans were happy with the extra seats and the wider concourses, at least compared to League Park. Bill Veeck had installed outfield fences so hitters had a fair chance to hit home runs.

The Stadium will always be a source of colliding emotions for me. It was Our Place, the place where my father and I felt the closest when I was young. I remember my father allowing me to skip school on opening day; he'd slip out from work and we'd head down to the Stadium. Some of those openers were more like February than early April with the frigid wind whipping off Lake Erie and that old steel and concrete building still seeming to shiver from the winter's chill. I remember my father continually buying us hot chocolates as we moved from one section to another, following the sun as it made its way around the park during those April afternoons—you could do that because there always were empty seats in that huge Stadium, even on opening day. I remember little things, like catching a foul ball off the bat of Alex Johnson. Okay, it bounced first, but I caught it on the hop. I don't remember much about the games or even the players; I just remember being with my father, his arm around me, a Tribe cap on my head.

It wasn't until my father had his stroke that I truly understood what the Stadium meant to us. The last year for the Indians at the Stadium was 1993. My father was spending the summer visiting his sister in the Cleveland suburb of Broadview Heights. We got together a few times a week, usually to go bowling and have lunch.

"I'd like to go to one more game," he said.

He meant one more Tribe game before the team left the Stadium. I was evasive. I said a lot of "Maybes" and "We'll sees." Truth was, I didn't like to go to a game unless I was working and hanging out with my buddies in the press box. I had become spoiled. I didn't think of all the times that my father may not have exactly felt like dragging himself off the sofa and taking me to an Indians game, but he did it. He did it because that was what a good father was supposed to do. He did it because he wanted to be with me. He did it because, as a fan named Phil Ferguson wrote, "It was a time when you could make up your mind to go to the game at the last second and just about always get a good seat. Nothing made me feel better than to hear my dad say, 'The Yankees are in town, want to go to a ballgame?' "

How I used to love hearing those exact same words from my dad.

But in 1993, I didn't think about how the Stadium was a special place to him, and that he would want to say goodbye to it. I didn't think that he was getting older, and who knew if his health would hold, or even if he'd live to see another season. I didn't think about him at all.

And in the end, I didn't take him to a game.

Sure, he could have gone on his own, but I was very slow to realize that he wanted to go, not just to a game, but to a game with me. That epiphany finally came to me when I was at the last Tribe game at the Stadium, October 3, 1993. By then, my father was back in Sarasota; he had suffered his stroke only three weeks earlier. I'd left his bedside a few days before to return to town to cover the final Tribe series at the Stadium.

Then I thought of him.

I thought of what the ballpark meant to us.

I thought of him pointing out Mudcat Grant to me when I was about five years old, and how Mudcat Grant signed my scorecard. I thought of how my father would buy general admission tickets for us, and how we'd sneak down to the box seats behind home plate in the middle innings when the ushers had become bored. He'd take us to the concession stand, load up with popcorn and Cokes, and then we'd walk right down to some empty box seats and settle in.

"Just follow me," he'd say. "We'll act like we've been sitting here all night."

My father would talk the game to me, but in a quiet fashion. He was more a gentle teacher than an overbearing expert. He continually told me that even the worst big league player was a great athlete compared to everyone in the stands. His one summer of minor league baseball in Welch, West Virginia, had given him a healthy respect for those men who played for pay.

During that final weekend at the Stadium, Tribe fans from all over the country flew in for the games. My best childhood friend, Frank Sarmir, came all the way from San Francisco. Fans talked of Herb Score, Bob Feller, Rocky Colavito, and even Albert Belle. They also talked of Super Joe Charboneau, Joe Azcue, Tom Veryzer, and Rudy Regalado. They talked of going to the games with their fathers, and how they wished their fathers could be with them for one last time.

I felt the same way.

# CHAPTER 16
# The Sad Saga of 1970

In 1970, my father thought the Indians had turned the corner. What he didn't know was that the new corner led to another dead-end street.

That's because 1970 was like so many seasons for the Curse of Rocky Colavito generation. It was the start of yet another rebuilding plan.

There was Ray Fosse.

Maybe he is nothing more than a faint memory, a blip on the Cleveland baseball scene, but in 1970 Ray Fosse was a reason to believe. He was the second-best young catcher in baseball, right behind Johnny Bench. He even was selected before Bench in the 1965 amateur draft, and no one screamed that the Indians had made a mistake.

Ray Fosse was that kind of player.

Tony Horton was supposed to be the Jim Thome of his generation. The Indians had a couple of kids as a keystone combination—Eddie Leon and Jack Heidemann—and they really had promise, or so we were told. The third baseman was Graig Nettles—not a bad player at all. Just ask any longtime Yankee fan. The Indians brought Steve Dunning right from the Stanford campus to the major leagues, and scouts said he had all the right stuff.

But in 1970, it turned out that the Indians were . . . well . . . the Indians.

Does the name Fred Lasher ring a bell?

He was a pitcher with the 1970 Tribe, a sidearmer who is just a footnote in Tribe history. But on the last day before the All-Star break, Lasher was facing Tony Conigliaro, and he plunked the Boston slugger in the back with a pitch. A week earlier, Lasher had vowed to "come inside" on Conigliaro, who was crushing Cleveland pitching. For good reason, Conigliaro was sensitive to this talk; three years earlier, pitcher Jack Hamilton had hit Conigliaro in the face, nearly in the eye socket. It almost ended his career.

When Lasher nailed Conigliaro, the batter rushed the mound. He karate-kicked Lasher in the leg, then clubbed him with a left hook.

Tribe catcher Ray Fosse flattened Conigliaro with a bullish tackle.

Ah, those rough-and-tumble Indians.

At the All-Star break, Bob Sudyk wrote in the *Cleveland Press*, "The Indians are in last place (38-48). They have won one fight (Vada Pinson over Stan Bahnsen), lost one (Conigliaro over Lasher on a drop kick) and had one draw (Washington's Frank Howard's call for peace when Graig Nettles threw his bat at the mound after he was decked by a Senator's pitch)."

Sounds like my Indians.

In 1970, about everything that could go wrong with the Indians did. It began in spring training, when Ken "The Hawk" Harrelson slid into second base and broke several bones in his right ankle. In 1969, Harrelson hit 30 homers. He'd miss virtually all of 1970, and hit only six more homers for the rest of his career before he retired in 1972.

Here was a guy the Indians acquired when he was twenty-eight, in what should have been the prime of his career. He was a teen idol in Boston with his floppy Beatles haircut, Nehru jackets, moon-rock jewelry, love beads, and everything else that was very late-1960s, and very silly when you look back at it today. When the Indians traded Sonny Siebert, Joe Azcue, and Vincente Romo to Boston for Harrelson (now we can say it was yet another truly terrible deal), Harrelson refused to report. He forced general manager Gabe Paul to raise his $50,000 salary to an unprecedented $100,000, the most in Tribe history. The Indians even muscled a local TV station into setting Harrelson up as the host of his own "mod" TV talk show.

This was supposed to generate interest in the Tribe.

But like most of the Best Laid Plans of Gabe Paul, this one ended up like the Rocky Colavito deals—take your pick, the first one or the second.

When the team reported to spring training in 1970, Harrelson and Tony Horton were expected to be a powerful 1-2 combination in the middle of the lineup. They had combined for 57 homers in 1969, and remember that 1969 was the tail end of the era of the pitcher. A guy with the capability of hitting 25 to 30 homers was considered like a 40–home-run man today.

Then Harrelson broke his ankle.

Broke his ankle in the middle of March.

Broke his ankle under the Arizona sun in a meaningless spring training game, sliding into second base.

Broke his ankle, and once again shattered the hearts of Tribe fans.

Meanwhile, Horton had held out for much of the spring of 1970. He made $40,000 in 1969. He asked for $60,000, hoping to receive $50,000. This was before agents and free agency. This was when teams could actually cut a player's salary—and did! This was an era when the Indians could offer their exciting young power hitter a $5,000 raise to $45,000—and not budge. Horton sat. He begged for another $5,000. He wanted $50,000, which was only half of what Harrelson was earning. Alvin Dark would not be moved. Yes, Alvin Dark, the team's manager, was also conducting contract negotiations with players. You don't want the players and manager haggling over money, because it creates hard feelings and suspicion. But Dark had won a power struggle with Gabe Paul, and ownership had allowed him to handle contract talks. And here was Dark deciding to show how tough he could be at the bargaining table by making his supposedly future star player miss three weeks of spring training over $5,000.

Don't you love these Indians?

Horton finally signed on March 18, 1969; a day later, Harrelson fractured his ankle. If Horton had stuck it out for only two more days, his value would have increased. Instead, he buckled at absolutely the worst time.

This ate away at him.

When the season opened, Horton was booed by the Tribe fans, who still hadn't forgiven his holdout.

All over $5,000.

That ate away at him, too.

Three weeks before the All-Star break, the big first baseman faced Yankee pitcher Steve Hamilton. The lefty had invented a pitch he called "the folly floater." It was like a slow-pitch softball delivery. He threw one to Horton, who popped out to the catcher. Horton crawled back to the dugout on his hands and knees, as if he were pleading for mercy. During the All-Star break, Horton spent all three days at Cleveland Stadium taking extra batting practice, the only Tribe player to do so.

Horton played his last pro game on August 28, 1970, when his mental demons became too much and he left the Indians (and baseball) forever.

At the age of twenty-five, Tony Horton's career was finished.

At the age of thirty, Ken Harrelson's career was history. And all of this happened in 1970, only there was more.

There was Steve Dunning. Outstanding pitcher at Stanford. Looked like a pitcher, 6-foot-2, 205 pounds. Threw hard. Mature guy. Should have been a good major league pitcher for a long time. The Indians made him their top pick in the 1970 amateur draft, signed him for $50,000 (a healthy sum in 1970), and brought him straight to Cleveland. No minor league seasoning needed for young Mr. Dunning. On June 14, 1970, Dunning started his first game for the Tribe. The front office hyped it as a special occasion. When Steven John Dunning is inducted into the Hall of Fame, you can tell your friends that you saw his first big league game. A lot of fans bought the sales pitch, as 25,380 showed up—about 15,000 more than normal. They watched him pitch five innings and be credited with a 9–2 victory over Milwaukee.

Cooperstown, here he comes.

But Dunning would have an 0-4 record in his next six starts. Not all of it was his fault; the Indians supported him with only four runs when he was on the mound in those six games. Still, it turned out Dunning really wasn't ready for the Indians. Not then. Probably not ever. His career record was 23-41 as he bounced around to five different teams in seven seasons.

Given all this, it's not hard to understand why Bob August wrote in the *Cleveland Press,* "No one was counting on the Indians anyway, but at their best, they can be as entertaining as a chimpanzee on a bicycle."

Believe it or not, Ted Williams (then the manager of the Washington Senators) insisted he liked the Indians as a contender in the future.

Turned out Williams was right, just twenty-five years premature.

•

The real reason Williams gushed about the Tribe was their catcher, Ray Fosse.

"Something seems to be stirring," wrote the *Cleveland Press*'s Bob August at the All-Star break. "There is a new hero named Ray Fosse, a solid young man who has hit 16 homers and shows no inclination to stop hitting them."

At the All-Star break, Fosse was batting .313 with 16 homers and 45 RBI. He also was a Gold Glove–caliber catcher. Best of all, he was only twenty-three years old. His teammates called him "Mule," because he was so durable.

"A baseball star has been born," wrote Hal Lebovitz in the *Plain Dealer*. "His name is Ray Fosse . . . Fearless Fosse."

Want more?

Consider this letter to the *Plain Dealer* from a fan named Bill Zimmerman: "Not only does Ray Fosse deserve to be an All-Star for his ability as a player, he also is a gentleman. Last year, despite a broken finger, he insisted on signing autographs for fans even though it obviously pained him to do so."

As Fosse headed to Cincinnati for the 1970 All-Star Game, it appeared the Indians had found their own Johnny Bench. Most Tribe fans know what happened in that fateful All-Star Game. They know that Pete Rose ran into Fosse at home plate. They know it was a frightening collision, as Rose lowered his shoulder and just flattened Fosse, who obviously never saw Charley Hustle coming.

But do you know where Fosse was the night before the game?

He and Tribe pitcher Sam McDowell had dinner out with Rose, then they retired to Rose's home for a visit. McDowell had been friends with Rose for several years. Rose met Fosse for the first time that night, and the three players stayed at Rose's home until 1:00 A.M. Then Rose drove McDowell and Fosse back to their Cincinnati hotel.

And the next day, Rose pulverized Fosse.

He did it scoring from second base on a single by Jim

Hickman. The score was 4–4 in the bottom of the 12th inning. Before Fosse could catch a throw from outfielder Amos Otis, Rose "knocked him ears over teakettle," according to Milton Richman of United Press International.

Fosse went to the hospital, where it was believed he had suffered a "bad bruise" of the right shoulder.

Rose scored the winning run, then had to tell writers this was not a cheap shot on Fosse.

"He was about two feet in front of the plate," Rose said. "If I slid in there, I could have broken both legs. If I slid head first, I could have broken my neck."

So he simply went through Fosse.

"I never got hit like that before," Fosse said later, adding he didn't believe Rose meant to injure him.

Most media members supported Rose.

That was Pete being Pete. That's how he played the game. As New York sportswriter Dick Young wrote, "Pete Rose could have slid around Ray Fosse . . . and Jim Brown could have tried to out-nifty guys instead of running over them. A man must play his way. He doesn't have an instant replay to help him make up his mind."

Before the All-Star Game, Fosse played every day. He was the Iron Mule. Bat fourth. Push the pitchers. Throw out base stealers. Carry the team on his broad shoulders. He shocked everyone by playing two days after the All-Star break. That was in Kansas City, where Royals outfielder Amos Otis asked, "How could he even stand up?" It was Otis who threw the ball to Fosse as Rose was scoring the fateful run. Rose himself missed three games as he nursed a bruised knee from the collision. Fosse played, but his shoulder hurt. It would not heal and he would not take any real time off.

In the first half of the 1970 season, Fosse had 16 homers. He had only two more home runs after the collision in 1970. And in the seven and a half years after the collision, he hit only 43 homers.

Suddenly the Iron Mule was a broken-down burro. Bum knees. Broken fingers. Another year, another serious injury. He had lost his swing, and the Indians lost their Johnny Bench.

When the 1970 season was in the books, the Indians had a 76-86 record. Sam McDowell won 20 games for the first (and last) time in his career. Graig Nettles hit 26 homers and played a graceful third base, but two years later he'd been dealt (yes, another dismal deal) to the Yankees—a deal in which the best player coming the Indians' way was Charlie Spikes.

But when you think about 1970, you think of Tony Horton's breakdown and Ken Harrelson's broken ankle. You think of Steve Dunning's broken dreams. And most all, you think of Ray Fosse and you wonder what could have been.

Then you look at the Indians in 1971.

Their final record? How about 60-102?

So much for the future.

# CHAPTER 17

# Wayne Garland and the Power of Delusion

In 1977, the Indians thought they'd win the pennant.

Stop laughing.

Now we know better. Now we know what a pennant winner looks like and what it takes for a team to get to the World Series. Now we have some experience with the winning business, and now we can look back at 1977 and see just how far the Indians were from the World Series.

Eighteen more years, to be exact.

A pennant-winning team does not have Fred Kendall as its starting catcher. Nor does it have an outfield of Paul Dade, Jim Norris, and Rick Manning. That was a starting outfield that combined to hit 10—go ahead, use both hands to count 'em— that's right, 10 homers. Ten homers from three guys!

But in 1977, the Indians thought they were going to win the pennant because they signed Wayne Garland.

Understand something right now.

The current Indians are flush with cash. They have an

owner willing to pay the price to win, and a general manager who understands the free agent market. Never in the history of this franchise has the team been on such rock-solid financial ground. Nonetheless, these Indians would never look at a young Wayne Garland and make him one of the highest-paid pitchers in baseball—certainly not with a ten-year contract.

But that's what the Indians did back in 1977.

In 1977, the Indians were owned by Ted Bonda and something like fifty partners. There may have been even more than fifty, no one was quite sure. It seemed everyone owned a piece of the Indians, and new owners were being added all the time. If you had an extra fifty bucks, you could be an owner of the Tribe. This was a team that could barely meet its payroll, a team that was near the bottom when it came to spending money on its farm system and scouting.

Yet this team went out and gave Wayne Garland a ten-year, $2.3 million contract. It was $230,000 a year for ten years. It came in the infancy of free agency, when an All-Star was happy to make $100,000. It came from an ownership group that figured they'd spread the cash over ten years so some other owners would have to pay for Garland—because, hey, this team is for sale. Someone else will pay for the contract, namely, the next owner. The 1977 Indians wouldn't agree with that interpretation. The 1977 Indians would say they paid Wayne Garland because they wanted to catch lightning in a bottle.

Instead, they got the shock of their lives.

From 1969 to 1975, Garland pitched mostly in the Baltimore farm system. His combined big league record was 7-11. In 1976, he was struck by lightning; for one year, he was a right-handed Carl Hubbell, using a screwball to win 20 games. He completed 14 of his 25 starts. He was twenty-six years old and made $19,000. He also made scowling into an art form. The man didn't smile for fear it would shatter his lips. In Baltimore while he was winning those 20 games, they called him

"Grumpy." The Indians decided he was the Missing Piece. They were wrong, and not just because Garland blew out his arm. The only things the 1977 Indians were missing were hitting, pitching, and cash. I mean, this team thought it was going to win the pennant with Fred Kendall behind the plate? With Paul Dade and Jim Norris playing in the same positions held by Albert Belle and Manny Ramirez in 1995? Few franchises have ever deceived themselves as much as the Indians since 1960, but even for the team that traded Rocky Colavito for Harvey Kuenn, this was lunacy.

There was nothing wrong with wanting a healthy Wayne Garland on your staff. But you have to understand the times: When Garland went on the free agent market in 1977, he hoped to make about $40,000 annually on a three-year contract. His agent thought he could squeeze $100,000 a year for four or five seasons from some team. The agent asked each team interested in Garland to submit a sealed bid. He was amused even to find an envelope from Cleveland. The Indians? What were they offering, Max Alvis's old jockstrap?

He and Garland opened the envelope.

Then you heard two THUDS.

After both men picked up their jaws off the floor, they stared at the Tribe's offer again.

Ten years. Two million, three hundred thousand dollars. That's $2.3 million!

Or, $230,000 a year—for ten years.

This was the longest, richest contract ever given a pitcher.

All this for Wayne Garland. All this from the Cleveland Indians. All this from a general manager named Phil Seghi who proclaimed, "If you want to dance, you have to pay the fiddler."

It turned out that this fiddler played taps.

"I never expected anything like this," Garland said.

"For that kind of money, I'll play in Siberia," Garland said.

"I never asked for this kind of money. What am I supposed to do, give it back?" Garland said.

The Indians thought Wayne Garland would help them sell tickets. They thought the fans would be excited, thinking, "Hey, the Indians are serious about winning, they signed Wayne Garland."

As usual, the Indians thought wrong.

"Most fans thought it was appalling," said Joe Tait, the team's radio voice (along with Herb Score) in 1977. "Fans kept telling me, 'They threw that kind of money at a guy who had only one good year?' They thought it was obscene."

Frank Robinson was the manager. He liked the signing of Garland. Then again, remember that Robinson was managing the Indians in the 1970s. He was a starving man. A can of Alpo would look like a T-bone steak. Robinson even said, "Now that we've added Garland and [Al] Fitzmorris, we're 20 to 25 games better than last season."

Robinson may as well have resigned the moment those words left his lips. The Indians had a respectable 81-78 record in 1976. Add another 20 victories, and that meant they were going to win 101 games? Usually it's a giddy general manager who makes a fool of himself like that.

If you've been a Tribe fan long enough to remember Johnny Grubb, you know what happened:

Garland injured his arm. Injured it in the first spring training game. Injured it *while warming up.* Yes, they pay this guy $2.3 million. They give him a ten-year contract, and he gets hurt warming up for his first exhibition game.

Only the Indians . . .

In 1977, Garland pitched with pain, and pitched remarkably well given the fact that he was tearing his rotator cuff into spaghetti. It was eerie to watch the grim, walrus-faced Garland trudge to the mound with No. 23 on his back. Yes, he wore No. 23 after he signed that $2.3 million contract. He may as well have had $$ on his jersey. Nonetheless, the man won 13 games. He gritted his teeth through 283 innings and he completed 21 starts. He did it for a typical stinko Tribe team, one with a 71-90 record, so it's not like Garland ruined his career to help the Indians win the pennant.

"It was one of the most determined, gutsy seasons I've ever seen from a player," Tait said. "Garland's arm was killing him all year. He never should have even tried to pitch. But Wayne wanted to prove that he was worth the money, and there was no way anyone could do that."

Garland's final record was 13-19 with a 3.59 ERA. He made three starts at the end of the year, each of which could have meant his 20th loss. He didn't lose any of those games as he was determined not to go from being a 20-game winner to a 20-game loser.

By May 11, 1977, the Indians suddenly looked at their books. Just six weeks into the season where they were supposed to win the pennant, the light of truth shone down upon them:

A. Jim Norris, Paul Dade, Fred Kendall, John Grubb, and Don Hood were always going to be Jim Norris, Paul Dade, Fred Kendall, John Grubb, and Don Hood. A baloney sandwich is a baloney sandwich—now and forever.

B. Wayne Garland had a bad arm, and sooner or later was going to need surgery.

C. Al Fitzmorris, the guy who was going to combine with Garland to help the Indians win 101 games? Well, Fitzmorris had a bum arm, too.

D. They couldn't pay the bills.

So six weeks into the season, the Indians sent their top relief pitcher (Dave LaRoche) to the Angels for Sid Monge, Bruce Bochte—and most importantly, $250,000. If nothing else, they could pay Garland.

The Indians became a joke—again.

They had outrageously overpaid Garland, and now they were selling off their players. They fired Frank Robinson as manager. They had an infielder named Larvell Blanks who was upset that he wasn't playing enough, so he burned his uniform in the clubhouse. The team made him pay for a new one.

And the team that was supposed to win the pennant with Wayne Garland? They weren't 20 games better than in 1976, they were 10 games worse.

Garland had major shoulder surgery at the end of the 1977 season. The doctors reconstructed the rotator cuff and then wished him well, saying no pitcher had ever fully come back from this type of operation.

Neither did Garland.

He tried and tried valiantly. He even attempted to become a knuckleball pitcher. Occasionally, his arm would have some semblance of life and he'd throw a remarkable game. He even had two shutouts after his surgery. But that was just a cruel tease. It made the Indians and Garland start to think, "Maybe he'll beat the odds."

If you know anything about the Indians from 1960 to 1994, it's that they never beat the odds—or much of anyone else, either.

Garland had a 15-29 record in his four years after the surgery. The Indians' last payment to him was in 1986, the year in which Dick Jacobs bought the Tribe.

A new era was coming. Eventually. But first, a lot more misery for the team and its fans.

# CHAPTER 18

# The Baseball Beat

When I became the baseball writer for the Cleveland *Plain Dealer*, I thought my father would be happy.

Shows how little I knew about fathers and sons.

When I look back on it now, I wonder why I couldn't see the obvious. My five years covering the Indians (1980–84) was a time when I grew more distant from my father, not closer. It was a time when I no longer knew what to say to him, and he had little idea how to talk to me.

We became strangers.

Back then, I thought it was simply a matter of my growing up. I was out of his house, out from under his influence. I had lived at home through my college years at Cleveland State. I had part-time jobs. My father had lost his job thanks to heartless corporate downsizing, but not much changed between us. He was the father, I was the son. Nothing had to be said; we both knew our place. A few years later, I chased my journalism dreams from Greensboro, North Carolina, to Savannah, Geor-

gia, to Baltimore and finally back home to Cleveland. My father took up a second career in real estate. He wasn't a licensed
agent, he mostly sat in model homes for a friend who was a
builder. He showed the houses to those who walked through
the door, and then he'd hook them up with the builder if they
were interested. He was good at this job, and I heard from some
of his customers that he was quick to tell them that his son covered the Indians for the morning paper.

But when we were together, we didn't connect.

He still loved baseball. He wanted to talk about baseball,
especially the Indians. He wanted to talk to me as he always
had, father to son. But I was no longer just a son; I thought I
was the expert.

He'd say, "That Manny Trillo sure can play second base."

I'd say, "The guy is a prima donna. He'll never last."

I couldn't even concede that my father was right, that
Trillo was a wonderful second baseman; I had to one-up him. I
had to show him how much I knew. When Trillo became disen-
chanted with the Indians and was traded, I couldn't wait to tell
him, "I told you so . . ."

I did this type of thing over and over again.

I was in my middle twenties. He was in his early sixties. I
had my future staring at me through the front windshield;
most of his life was in the rearview mirror. My father was far
more aware of this than his baseball writer son—and he really
just wanted to talk. He wanted to use the Indians as a safe subject, as something to make him feel good. He wanted to remember when he was a hulking, strong forty-something man
who used to take his little son by the tiny hand down the West
3rd Street Bridge and into the Stadium to watch Sonny Siebert
or Jack Kralick pitch.

My father longed to still go to games with his son. I'd
explain that I had to be in the press box, that I was no longer
a fan—I was working the games. I offered to get him tickets
if he wanted to go with someone else, but my mother wasn't

a baseball fan and my father was not a man with many friends.

All I had to do was say, "Hey, come to the game, I can sit in the stands with you for three or four innings, and then maybe we can get something to eat after the game. After the game, you can even sit in the press box and wait for me to finish my story."

But I never did that. And my father never did see the inside of the press box.

He came to a few games with a friend. I'd stop by his seats and say hello, maybe stay for an inning—then I'd rush back to the press box as if the future of the free world hung in the balance and the republic just might collapse if I spent another fifteen minutes away from my phone. My own sense of self-importance drove us apart.

My father would say, "Bo Diaz looks like a good catcher."

And I'd say, "The guy is rude. He's always unhappy."

The truth was, Diaz was a good catcher—better than I thought. Diaz proved as much when he was traded to Philadelphia; my father had seen Diaz through clearer eyes than his baseball-writer son. That probably was because I'd had a couple of clashes with Diaz over stories I'd written—or at least, what he'd been led to believe I'd written. When he was with the Indians, Diaz's English was limited and he had trouble reading the paper. But it was no problem for him to find a player who'd tell him what I'd said in that day's sports pages—even if it wasn't what I'd written at all. There were some veteran players who knew Diaz was emotional and very proud, and they enjoyed lighting a match under him and watching him explode when the young baseball writer entered the dressing room. When I'd deny writing what he claimed, Diaz's temper boiled over. He'd scream. He'd drop F-bombs. He'd challenge me to a fight. Finally, a veteran player such as Andre Thornton or Duane Kuiper would step in and calm him down. Often, I had no idea what he was yelling about, and it wasn't until after Diaz was shipped to Philadelphia that I figured out both of us had been used for entertainment by some of the older players, although I'm still not sure which ones. All I knew was I couldn't stand Diaz, and I didn't want him to play well.

But how could I explain this to my father?

I didn't want him to know I was being tested, and sometimes intimidated, by the players. I didn't want him to think I was in a situation I couldn't handle. I didn't want my father to know I still had a lot to learn.

Of course, I had it all wrong. My father would have loved to hear that there were days when I hated being a baseball writer, when I loathed walking into the clubhouse, because who knew what firestorm was waiting. There were days when I felt underprepared and overmatched for what I thought was the only job I'd ever wanted. And yes, there were days when I wished I was his son again and we were just going to games. I wanted to tell him that baseball was no longer a game, it was my job—and like all jobs, some days were better than others. If I had just told my father that, we would have been closer than ever. Instead, I'd tell him things that I knew he didn't want to hear. I'd tell him that a player he admired had an enormous drinking problem. I'd tell him about another player who messed around on the road, while passing himself off as a Christian family man. I'd sometimes used the raw language of the clubhouse.

I did this knowing:

A. My father didn't swear and wasn't comfortable around those who did.

B. He didn't drink and didn't want to hear about players who did.

C. The whole subject of sex embarrassed him.

Did I just want to shock my father?

Maybe.

But I also was going through an unhappy period in my life. It was a classic case of getting what you wished for, then wondering why you ever wanted it in the first place. The travel of the baseball beat was grinding. Some of the players with the Tribe in the early 1980s seemed as if they had fallen off the lowest rung of the evolutionary ladder—and landed right on their heads. After covering the classy Baltimore Orioles in 1979, I was shocked by what I found in the uniforms of the team of my youth. This was not to say that most of the 1979 Orioles belonged on church windows, but they were a combination of Martin Luther King, Abe Lincoln, and Tom Hanks compared to many of the Indians in the early 1980s. Most of those players didn't like me, and I didn't like them.

When I was at Benedictine High, I'd go to games with my father and sometimes we'd see the sportswriters walking to and from the press box—men such as the *Plain Dealer*'s Russell Schneider, Bob Sudyk of the *Cleveland Press*, and the tall, white-haired Hal Lebovitz, my father's favorite sportswriter. Lebovitz was the columnist and sports editor of the *Plain Dealer*, and when Lebovitz expressed an opinion about the Indians, it was baseball gospel to us.

I'd see Lebovitz and the others at games and I'd tell my dad, "One day, that's going to be me in the press box."

Sometimes, he just said, "I hope you're right."

Other times, he didn't say a word, he just put his arm around me for a fleeting second. I knew my father had always wanted to play for the Indians. He had that same dream for his older son, Tom, who was an exceptional high school player. But my brother lost the sight in his left eye when he was hit in the face with a thrown baseball. He was a second baseman at Ohio's Ashland College and played well even with vision in only one eye, but his pro dreams ended on a dusty Cleveland diamond when he was a senior in high school. I wasn't half the athlete of my father or brother, but I had figured out my own way of making it to the Tribe: I'd write about them. It was a dream my father and I would share, just as my father relived his own athletic career while his oldest son played.

When I was named baseball writer at the *Plain Dealer*, it

was a big deal to him—and me. He thought baseball writing in the 1980s was the same as in the 1950s. He said he'd heard Lebovitz interviewed on the radio about covering the Indians, and it sounded like an adventure, one of the best times of his life.

I thought of that recently, my father's recollection of Lebovitz's days on the Tribe beat. I wanted to know if it was true, so I asked Hal about it. He began to tell stories, the kind of stories my father wished I could have told him.

Lebovitz worked for a paper called the *Cleveland News*. It was an afternoon paper, one of three in Cleveland. Today, only the *Plain Dealer* remains.

"The *Plain Dealer* was the morning paper," Lebovitz said. "We didn't worry too much about them. Their writer seldom went into the clubhouse after a game. The real competition was between the *Cleveland News* and the *Cleveland Press* because we were both afternoon papers."

Lebovitz wrote about the Indians in the late 1940s, doing player features and some game stories. But he didn't become the full-time baseball writer until 1950.

"The Indians were training in Tucson," he said. "A lot of people don't know it, but Bill Veeck moved the team's spring training base to Arizona [from Clearwater, Florida] because he owned a ranch near Tucson."

For his first spring training, Lebovitz traveled from Cleveland to Tucson by train. It took nearly three days. The initial leg of the trip went from Cleveland to Chicago, and then he caught a Southern Pacific train from Chicago to Tucson.

"A lot of the players were on that same train with me," he said. "When we got to Tucson, no one was waiting for us. No cabs. No bus. Nothing. Tucson was just a sleepy little town in the desert in 1950. We stayed at the Santa Rita Hotel. So all of us got out of the train, grabbed our bags, and walked the two and a half blocks to the hotel. I can still picture Bob Lemon and

Bob Feller lugging their bags with me as we dragged ourselves into the hotel lobby."

Another writer on the train was Harry Jones, who covered the Indians for the *Plain Dealer*. He later became the TV voice of the team in the 1960s.

"Harry didn't try real hard to break stories," Lebovitz said. "Because he was the only morning paper, he had the score of the game first. Harry stuck to the nuts and bolts of the game. Occasionally, he'd get a story because he liked going out for a few drinks with the players."

But the main opposition for Lebovitz was a fellow named Frank Gibbons, who was a legendary writer and reporter for the old *Cleveland Press*. He knew Lebovitz was worried about being new on the beat and about not being able to compete for stories. He also knew Lebovitz was like most rookie writers, his stomach was constantly churning as he had a feeling he was missing something. In one of their first meetings, Gibbons approached manager Lou Boudreau and whispered something in his ear. Then he went from one player to another player to a third player—each time, whispering.

All the while, Gibbons knew Lebovitz was watching.

"Know what Gibbons told those guys?" asked Lebovitz. "He said, 'Watch Hal and see how long it takes for him to come up and talk to you.' They thought it was a great joke. I did go from the manager to one player and to another, just saying hello and trying to figure out what was going on."

Lebovitz realized there was only one way he could stay competitive with a veteran, well-liked writer such as Gibbons—he had to work twice as hard.

"I waited in the lobby of the hotel until every player went to bed," he said. "There was only one way in and one way out of the Santa Rita, and I saw everyone coming and going. I'd be up each night until two or three in the morning. I was so consumed by the job, that I hate to admit this."

Almost fifty years later, Lebovitz shook his head as he told the story, finding it hard to believe that he really pulled this stunt.

"I had never been away from my wife for any length of time before until that first spring training," he said. "She flew to Tucson, and I was so scared that I'd miss a story, I didn't pick her up at the airport. I told her to take a cab. I've never forgiven myself for that."

One of Lebovitz's first scoops came when he spotted second baseman Bobby Avila walk into the lobby at 3:00 A.M. Spring training had been underway for several days, and Avila supposedly was being detained in his native Mexico "because of visa problems." Latin players have always used "visa problems" as a way to skip the early part of spring training, which they deem unnecessary since they play baseball most of the winter in their native lands. Lebovitz had been tipped off that Avila was late because he was still playing in Mexico, where he was batting .360. Avila didn't want the Tribe front office to know this, because they were paying him far more to play for Cleveland than Avila was earning in the Mexican winter league.

"That's a different Avila, it's my brother Pedro," he told Lebovitz.

With a little checking, it wasn't hard for Lebovitz to discover Pedro and Bobby Avila were even closer than brothers— they were the same guy.

"For a while, every city we went to, they ran my story in their paper," Lebovitz said. "Poor Bobby thought someone was spying on him because that story kept following him around."

Once, Lebovitz saw Bob Lemon stagger in at 2:00 A.M. Manager Al Lopez decided against fining his star pitcher, who was slated to start the next day. Because there was no fine, Lebovitz didn't report it. Lemon pitched a great game and won.

Lebovitz had until 6:00 A.M. to file his stories.

"We used to send it Western Union," he said. "Once, my story was sent to the *Cleveland Press* [by mistake]."

The *Press* ran Lebovitz's story, without his byline for the obvious reason that he worked for the *Cleveland News*. Meanwhile, Lebovitz's bosses were screaming at him, wanting to know where his story was—and not quite believing it when it showed up in the *Press*.

"Most of the players back then were just guys," he said. "They were great athletes, but we really got to know them as people. We traveled with them on trains. We ate with them. Some writers played cards with them. I didn't drink, but I still was around them a lot. I got to know them, and they knew me. Vic Wertz would have a get-together in his room after a game, and he'd invite the writers."

Both parties learned to trust each other.

Lebovitz said he wasn't shocked when he saw an outfielder named Joe Tipton having "a bottle of moonshine" as a companion. Feller hardly drank, but Early Wynn, Joe Gordon, and Lemon were never afraid to close down a bar. Catcher Jim Hegan didn't drink, but hung around in the bars, playing the piano and leading the joint in songs.

"Guys would sing harmonies," Lebovitz said.

He made it sound very quaint and a lot of fun, even though there had to be times when the abstaining Lebovitz could not have enjoyed dealing with some of these guys who were trying to cut their way through an alcoholic haze.

"Gibbons and I were always looking for a different angle on the game because we were writing for afternoon papers," he said. "I remember when Rocky Colavito hit four home runs that night in Baltimore. There was a party for him afterwards, and I was invited. I was there until about 2:00 A.M., then I went back to my room and wrote a story based on the reaction Rocky had from everyone at the party. It was a nice story, something the other guys didn't have."

Lebovitz said an outfielder named Dave Philley once challenged him to a fight. Several players were watching. Lebovitz said he'd fight, but later—outside the Stadium and after the game. A few hours later, tempers had cooled.

"In 1950, Ken Keltner was on his last legs at third base," he said. "The Indians had a kid named Al Rosen in the wings. I was a rookie writer. Rosen is Jewish and I'm Jewish. We were about the same age and sometimes we'd talk. Keltner saw this and assumed I wanted Rosen to take his job. He didn't talk to me for much of that year. Later, he was traded. Rosen did take his job. But when I saw Keltner after that, we suddenly were great friends. It was as if nothing had ever happened."

Which was fine with Lebovitz, who never intended to alienate Keltner.

"Other than that instance, I can't think of anyone not talking to me for any length of time when I was on the beat," he said. "There were times when they didn't like what I wrote, but I was there the next day to face them and we'd hash it out."

Lebovitz said the most he ever made as a baseball writer was $150 a week in 1960. For this, he wrote about fifteen stories a week.

"I worked seven days, no overtime," he said. "But I made a lot of money on the side. I was the official scorer for $50 a game. I wrote for magazines such as *Collier's, Saturday Evening Post, Sport,* and *The Sporting News.* I paid off my mortgage from all my freelance work."

Lebovitz covered the team from 1950 to 1960. It was before sports talk radio. It was the infancy of television. It was the most competitive time in the newspaper business because Lebovitz knew that either his *Cleveland News* or the *Cleveland Press* would not survive forever. The two afternoon papers fought for every story, every reader, and every advertising dollar.

In 1960, the *Cleveland News* folded. It was my father's favorite paper. Lebovitz switched to the *Plain Dealer,* where he was named sports editor and columnist in 1964.

"The only reason I got off the baseball beat was I spent ten years away from my family," he said. "I had two kids, and I wasn't around enough to help my wife raise them. That always bothered me."

But the beat itself?

"I loved it," he said. "I really did."

I wish I could say the same as Lebovitz. I wish the Indians of the late 1970s and early 1980s were the same as the Indians of the 1950s.

But the Tribe team I inherited was owned by F. J. "Steve" O'Neill, an elderly man who had made his money in the trucking business. He was recruited by Gabe Paul, the master of romancing money men and convincing them that what they needed to do was . . . drumbeat, please . . . own the Cleveland Indians! And better yet, Gabe Paul himself would stay around as team president to help the new owner learn the game. What a deal! At least that was Paul's sales pitch for nearly thirty years in Cleveland. The remarkable part of the story was how often it worked. There always was another guy willing to believe that Gabe Paul was just the man to turn the Indians around. Most of these guys didn't have the cash to do it, even if Paul had been the John Hart of his day. At best, Paul was a very ordinary baseball operator with little vision or creativity. Team him with George Steinbrenner in the 1970s, hand Paul a wad of money that was twice as thick as anyone else's in baseball—and yes, Paul would produce a winner.

The man was no idiot, no Frank Lane.

But when I began to cover the Indians in 1980, Steve O'Neill was bearing down on eighty years old. Paul and general manager Phil Seghi were in their seventies. The Indians were twenty-six years away from their last pennant, twenty-one years away from the Rocky Colavito trade and their last legitimate contender. They were light years away from being able to compete in baseball during the free agent era. Paul and Seghi brought in players such as Bake McBride, Manny Trillo, Gorman Thomas, and Ross Grimsley. They were all at the end of their careers. The last place they wanted to be was that old, drafty, damp Cleveland Stadium. For the most part, they were as much fun to be around as a cemetery on a rainy day.

Paul and Seghi were desperate. They knew the owner was old, and probably dying. They knew time was running out for them. They knew the rest of baseball looked at them as two old men whom the game had passed by. They desperately wanted to put together one last contender in Cleveland, to prove everyone wrong. This led to one plan after another. In 1979, they had a team based on power bats with the likes of Bobby Bonds, Cliff Johnson, Andre Thornton, and Toby Harrah in the lineup. By 1981, it was a pitching team—Len Barker, John Denny, Bert Blyleven, and Rick Waits forming one of the better rotations in baseball. But that was the strike year. Also, the Indians didn't hit. So the pitchers were traded for hitters.

It was like that, year after year. Pitchers traded for hitters, then hitters traded for pitchers. One year, it was a veteran team. The next year, the veteran players were traded for kids.

There were so many plans, there was no plan.

When I tried to explain this to my father, he'd grow silent, a bit sullen. He didn't want to hear this. He was still a fan. He wasn't foolish enough to wake up every February and believe the Indians were finally going to win the American League pennant, but he liked to think they *might* improve, that they just *might* be fun to watch.

My father always wanted to go to Tucson for spring training. I remember sitting in the car with him when I was a kid, listening to Herb Score; from those Arizona outposts such as Yuma, it sounded as if Score were calling the game while sitting in a garbage can. Score's voice sort of echoed. He was never sure who was on the field with all the players being changed nearly every inning. Nor was he sure where some of the games were being played. Was he in Scottsdale or Tempe or was it Sun City?

No matter, my father wanted to be there. Just once in his life, he wanted to go to spring training.

I knew this. I could have made it happen.

For five spring trainings, I went to Tucson with the Indians. I was there for six weeks. I lived in an apartment where there was plenty of room for him. All I had to say was, "Dad, fly down here for a week or so, I'd love to have you."

He'd say he didn't have the money for a ticket. For $300 I could have made it happen, and I did have the $300 to spare. But I didn't say a thing.

I didn't want him around. Not that I was ashamed of my father; I guess I didn't want to feel like his kid anymore. I was too proud, too self-centered to understand what that trip would have meant to him. To me, Tucson in March meant having to watch Jack "Stubby Fingers" Perconte kick one ground ball after another at second base. But for him, it would have been a chance to walk the same streets where Bob Feller and Bob Lemon lugged their bags to the Santa Rita Hotel. It would have been a chance for him to see the Santa Rita, or at least what was left of it. Finally, it would have been a chance for him to page back through his own Tribe family album, to soak up the desert sunshine and to think about the Indians teams of the late 1940s and 1950s, teams that meant so much to him. If I had taken some time to think about it, I might have realized that was what he wanted. Instead, I ignored the few times he mentioned going to Arizona. I said, "Maybe some day . . . ' "

Then I never brought it up again.

Here I thought I was being an adult, but I now realize that when I was covering the Indians, I was still a kid—and not a very smart one.

# CHAPTER 19

# The Pennant

THE FIRST YEAR my generation's Indians won the American League pennant was the time when my father and I truly came to a sense of peace with each other, at least in my adult life. The year was 1995. My father was two years into his stroke and beginning to come to terms with what it had done to his body, and yes, to his mind. I was two years into a new life that saw me travel to Florida for a few days every month to see him.

Along came the 1995 Indians, and all the joy the team brought him. I realized how he felt taking me to games when I was a kid, how just being at the Stadium made us happy, no matter how the Indians played. Even though my father lived in Sarasota, he had a chance to see several Tribe games a month on TV; ESPN had discovered the Indians and the fact that there were Tribe fans all over the country who couldn't get enough of their team. So ESPN carried the Indians a lot, and my father never missed a game.

What he saw was remarkable:

A team that would win 40 games in their last at bat.

A team with three superstars—Kenny Lofton, Albert Belle, and Carlos Baerga.

A team with three venerable veterans in Dennis Martinez, Eddie Murray, and Orel Hershiser.

A team that won the Central Division by a major league record 30 games.

Never in my lifetime did I expect to find an Indians team capable of attracting players with the baseball pedigrees of Martinez, Murray, and Hershiser. Never did I believe the Indians would have enough money to pay them. And even if the Tribe did, never did I think Cleveland would be the place where veterans such as these would want to play. Hey, these guys are at the end of their careers. They'd want to play for a winner, right? That would leave out Cleveland. And they'd want to play for a team in a city that embraces its baseball team. That wasn't the Cleveland of my youth.

But so much had changed, and nothing was more symbolic of the rebirth of this franchise than the move to glorious Jacobs Field. The ballpark was a magnet for the fans and the players. I almost passed out in utter shock when I heard Hershiser say, "I know the Indians haven't been to the World Series in over forty years, and the team that makes it to the World Series will be remembered in Cleveland forever. I want to be a part of that team." Orel Hershiser actually believed the Indians would win the pennant! Orel Hershiser, who was Mr. October, at least when it came to pitchers. Orel Hershiser had that much confidence in the Indians?

Okay, everything seemed to be coming together. I could see that. Dick Jacobs took over as owner in 1987. He muscled the city into finally building a new ballpark. That was crucial. It brought the Indians into contention during this era when the difference between baseball's haves and have nots often is a state-of-the-art stadium capable of producing revenue from luxury boxes and club seats.

Jacobs also hired Hank Peters as the team's president. It was Peters who traded Joe Carter for Sandy Alomar, Jr., and Carlos Baerga—for once getting great young talent instead of giving it away. It was Peters who took the bullets when he slashed the major league payroll in order to spend more on scouts and the farm system. And it was Peters who hired Mike Hargrove as manager and John Hart as general manager. It was Hart who traded Eddie Taubensee for Kenny Lofton, Hart who signed Martinez, Murray, and Hershiser, and Hart who became recognized as one of the most astute general managers in all of baseball. And it was Hargrove who became the Indians' best manager since Al Lopez.

Even early in 1995, the longtime Indian fan residing deep in my baseball soul kept whispering, "Something will screw it up."

Just two years before, in 1993, the Indians had lost three pitchers in a spring boating accident. Tim Crews and Steve Olin were killed, while Bobby Ojeda was seriously injured and pitched only briefly after that.

Then came 1994.

The Indians were a contender for the first time since 1959. On August 10, 1994, the Indians beat the Blue Jays, 5–3, in the Toronto Skydome.

Jason Grimsley won his last game with the Indians (Okay, he won only eight for the Tribe, so it's not like we're talking about Bob Feller). But give Grimsley credit: He pitched well on August 10, 1994, which also happened to be Rocky Colavito's sixty-first birthday. But the Curse of Rocky Colavito still had some spunk. That's because August 10, 1994, was the last day the Indians played baseball that season. The next day, baseball went on strike. It went on strike with the Indians only one game out of first place in the Central Division. It went on strike with the Indians in prime position to secure a wildcard playoff spot and appear in the postseason for the first time since 1954. It went on strike and stayed on strike, wiping out the World Series for the first time in baseball history.

Here the Indians had their best team in my lifetime, and this was the one year—*the only year*—a strike erased the World Series.

Not long after the strike began, I visited my father in Sarasota. He was sitting in his favorite chair, the TV remote in his hand. He was surfing from channel to channel, looking for a baseball game.

I reminded him there were no games—the strike, remember?

He shook his head sadly, "Oh, Man."

He put out his good hand, his left hand, with the palm faced up. It was his way of asking, "Why?"

I knew what he meant, and the question had nothing to do with revenue sharing, pension plans, or anything else that was stuck on the bargaining table. The question wasn't "Why is there a strike?" but rather, "How can they do this to us?" It was asked on behalf of all the people such as he, shut-ins who had spent their lives loving baseball, for whom the game on TV that night was the focal point of their day. I remember reading stories about how some people said the strike was a good thing, because now they could read, walk in the park, or go to Little League games instead of watching the big leaguers on TV. Well, my father and millions like him couldn't read, couldn't walk, and couldn't leave the house for very long. Maybe baseball shouldn't be that important to them, but it was. They had so little else. When the strike came, it was devastating. It seemed like one more lousy, rotten trick in the final days of their lives.

Then came 1995.

Then came the 1995 Indians.

But even in 1995, the Curse hung on for a few more weeks. Spring training and eighteen regular season games were cancelled by the seemingly never-ending, stupid, pointless, cement-headed, galling strike.

Finally, a judge issued a restraining order.

At last, the best Indians team in forty-some years was allowed to play ball. And baseball was back on TV for shut-ins such as my father. Yes, a lot of fans stayed away from the ballparks, but my dad was thrilled to have the games on TV. And the 1995 Indians grabbed baseball by the scruff of the neck and brought it kicking and screaming out of the strike. It was a team that played in front of sellout crowds at home. It was a team that played in a city once declared dead, but which now was vibrant. It was a team for every Tribe fan who could remember Duke Sims, Alan Ashby, or Andy Allanson. It was a team for every Tribe fan who remembered the Clapper, who sat behind home plate at the old Stadium and fiercely pounded his hands together before every pitch. That's right, every pitch— maybe a dozen claps before every pitch, all night, for all nine innings. And he was there for almost every game. It was a team for the Drummer, who had pounded away on his drum for all those dismal decades at the Stadium. The Drummer sat in the bleachers at the old Stadium, maybe seventeen miles from home plate. It was a team for fathers and sons, mothers and daughters . . . or any combination of mothers, fathers, sons, and daughters . . . anyone who really grew up with the Indians.

After his stroke, the summer of 1995 was probably the best time for my father. Yes, his right arm never did much more than hang down, helpless and lost. Yes, despite four different speech teachers, he never was able to find any new words. But his paralyzed right leg began to show some life because he simply willed it to. He relentlessly worked at therapy, in sessions where he was placed on a table for two hours three times a week and turned into a pretzel. A therapist would work on his legs, his hips, his ankles, his toes—every muscle and every tendon was pushed and stretched and brought alive. He reached the point where he could take his good left hand, grip the walker hard, and then sort of fling himself across his house for maybe thirty steps.

To the rest of us, this was the same as running thirty miles.

After his stroke, two doctors said he would never be able to walk at all, not a single step. They said he'd never he able to live anywhere but a rest home. They may as well have said, "Just bury him, he's worthless." At this point, my brother, Tom, stepped up like a cleanup hitter and changed the doctors, finding a couple more who were willing to work with my father, to give him a chance. Then my brother found a therapist named Aaron Mattes, whose staff was willing to treat my father as if he were Jim Thome coming back from an injury. By 1995, my brother's connections in Sarasota had paid off to make my father's life so much better.

In the first months after the stroke, I wondered if my father would ever be able to do much of anything besides sit in bed. But his therapists kept telling me that my father "was a tough guy." They kept telling me that they loved to work with him. They said, "I'm not sure exactly how much he will be able to walk, but he will walk. It will take a long time, but he'll walk." Just as the Indians were rolling through the American League in 1995, my father was making huge strides. He was so proud to be able to make the twenty steps from his favorite chair to the bathroom. He still needed someone to pull down his pants and ease him down on the toilet, but he was walking. As the Indians were wrapping up the pennant in September, my father had reached the point where he only used the wheelchair when he left the house. To him, that was as much a victory as the Tribe's pennant.

He still had terrible, depressing days where he'd look at my mother's picture and begin to cry. Even though she had been dead for eleven years and their marriage was sometimes rocky, he missed her terribly. He had dreams where he was a younger man, a man who never had a stroke. Then he'd wake up and find himself wearing diapers, trapped in a body that seemed to be nothing more than a broken-down old Buick. He'd cry out at night. I'd see him in bed, eyes wide; he'd point to his right side, the arm that wouldn't work, the leg that refused to listen to his commands.

It would take a while, but finally I'd figure out he was dreaming. I'd tell him that.

"Man . . . MAN . . . MAN!" he'd say, a few tears in his eyes.

I'd ask questions, figure out he'd dreamed that he was healthy, and he wanted to know what had happened to him. In essence, he had forgotten he'd suffered a stroke.

So I'd tell him that he'd had a stroke. I'd remind him what the stroke had done to his body. I'd tell him how hard he had worked to come back, to be at home in his own bed—and how the doctors never thought that would happen.

I'd hold his good left hand. I'd stare into those sad blue eyes. I'd tell him how proud I was to be his son. I'd tell him that he was brave. I'd pray as I was speaking so God would give me the right words to calm him. After a while, he'd remember. The stroke. The diapers. The pain. Who knows what else. He really couldn't tell me all of it, but I'd see it coming back to him. He'd reach out and touch my cheek, his way of telling me that he loved me. I'd tell him to try and get some rest, that there was a baseball game on TV tomorrow. I'd tell him that we'd go to his favorite restaurant, Der Dutchman, and he could get his favorite meal—pork chops, sweet potato fries, and fruit Jell-O. In fact, it was the only meal he'd order, even if we went there three straight days. I'd tell him that the Indians were going to win the pennant, and I'd tell him anything else that would come to mind.

And usually it worked, as he'd relax and go back to sleep.

The 1995 Indians were so important to us.

The chip was off my shoulder. I no longer had anything to

prove to him when it came to baseball. We could just watch the games on TV, talk like a couple of fans. I didn't feel compelled to tell him how truly aggravating Albert Belle could be; I just said the guy was no bargain to be around, but he just may be the best power hitter the franchise had ever seen.

I'd tell him how Dennis Martinez was my favorite pitcher. I told him about a story I wrote about Martinez in 1979. I was a rookie baseball writer in Baltimore, and Martinez was a young pitcher with the Orioles. He was from Nicaragua, and his English was limited. I wrote a story where I quoted him exactly, in very broken English. I thought I was being funny.

The next day, a veteran Baltimore sportswriter named Phil Jackman asked me, "I read your story about Dennis. I was just wondering, how is your Spanish?"

"What do you mean?" I asked.

"Your Spanish," Jackman said. "Wonder how you'd do if you were interviewed in Spanish."

I said I had taken two years in high school, and I remembered about twenty words. But I also had gotten Jackman's point and I was feeling about two inches tall.

"Look, cut these Latin guys a break," he said. "They come over here at sixteen years old. They don't know any English. They give you time for an interview, and you . . ."

"I know, I know . . ." I said.

"Listen, just help the guy," Jackman said. "I'm not saying make him sound like Abe Lincoln, but you know what he's trying to say—don't embarrass him."

My father liked that story, probably because it's the kind of advice he'd have given me if he had been in Baltimore that year with me.

In 1995, my father was glued to ESPN. He loved to watch the news clips from Jacobs Field, where the stands were jammed and it seemed every day another player was being showered with a standing ovation. I knew he'd have loved to be at the games, but he showed no bitterness; he was content to follow the team from Florida, to hear me tell him about the Indians during my monthly visits.

The summer of 1995 was my father's longest stretch out of the hospital. For about six months, he had no setbacks, no scares. He seemed to keep getting stronger and more confident, just like the Indians. I'm not naive enough to say the Indians were the reason that he had his best post-stroke summer, I'm just saying it happened. And I'm saying the Indians were fun for him, and that the baseball team brought us even closer together.

"This must be what it was like for Indians fans in 1948," I said to him more than once.

"Yes!" he'd say.

It was remarkable how once in a while, a different word would come to him. You could put a gun to his head and demand that he say the word Yes, but he couldn't do it on command. He'd just say, "Man . . . MAN . . . MAN!"

But as a quick answer to something that moved him—something like the 1995 Indians—well, YES, he could say it.

We'd see Omar Vizquel make a great play at shortstop, and I'd ask him if Omar was as good as Lou Boudreau—and my father would say, "Yes! Man . . . MAN . . . MAN!"

When my father came to baseball in the 1920s, there never would have been a shortstop like Vizquel—at least not a shortstop from Venezuela. The major league baseball of my father's youth was played only by white men from America. But my father was like most fans of his generation. When it came to baseball, they had only one question: "Can the guy play?" It was the owners more than the fans who had racial hangups and fears. That's why my father could watch Vizquel play a few games and immediately think of Lou Boudreau. White? Latino? One guy played in the 1940s and 1950s, the other in the 1990s? Doesn't matter. If my father had been able to speak with all the words he had possessed before his stroke, he'd have said, "Both guys are the kind of shortstops that take a team to the World Series."

Why is that?

"Because they make great plays, but they don't make errors," my father would have said.

You may think I'm taking some literary license. You may believe it's presumptuous of me to be so sure of what my father would say comparing Vizquel to Boudreau. On this point, you'd be wrong. On this point, my father's words are branded into my brain. "A great fielder doesn't make a lot of errors," he told me over and over.

When it came to shortstops, my father believed steady hands that gobble up grounders are more important than great range. An accurate arm matters more than a man with a bazooka who had lousy aim. Boudreau's arm was not especially strong, and the same is true for Vizquel. Boudreau had a knack of getting the ball to the first baseman just in time. Sometimes, it seemed as if his throws had a bit of an arc in them as they leisurely made their way across the diamond. But he'd shock you with the ability to make long throws from deep in the hole, the kind of throw that seemed to leave a vapor trail, the kind of throw that had you saying, "I didn't think he had such a strong arm."

That also is the case with Vizquel.

Hal Lebovitz has insisted Vizquel is the superior shortstop because of his range.

"Both make all the routine plays," he said. "But Vizquel is more spectacular. He makes more great plays than Boudreau did. I have seen every Indians shortstop since the 1920s, and no one is better than Omar. And I've talked to people who saw the shortstops before that, and I'm confident that none of them played the position better than Omar."

When men such as my father and Lebovitz not only rave about Vizquel, but put him on such a lofty historical perch, then indeed he is special. If fans were ever forced to be truly honest, they'd admit that the players they love the best are usually the players whom they first saw when they discovered the game. That is why the baseball of our youth tends to look better than the game of today. Yes, it may indeed have been just that there were fewer teams, therefore the talent wasn't as diluted as today. But it's far more than rational. It's emotional. It's nostalgic. It's viewing the game through more innocent eyes, because we were more innocent. Vizquel seems like a player from another age, from a time when baseball was played like poetry, when it could be set to classical music.

Graceful.

That was Boudreau, and that is Vizquel at shortstop.

Boudreau was the more productive hitter, Vizquel the more acrobatic and athletic fielder.

It still goes back to grace, a word that's been applied to both players. Grace is why so many elderly fans quickly adopted Vizquel after he was traded to the Indians prior to the 1994 season. Grace also shows up in Vizquel in his willingness to sign autographs, do interviews, and take time for the little things. He is one of the Indians players who finds time to call children in hospitals and to visit with special-needs kids brought to the park. The front office considers Vizquel its "go-to guy" when the subject is public service, and Vizquel has received several national honors for his work in the Cleveland area, especially with the mentally retarded.

Allen Davis is the Indians director of community relations. He also works closely with the Latino players, because Davis was born in Puerto Rico and speaks fluent Spanish. One day, he walked into the Tribe dressing room and saw Vizquel working with Enrique Wilson, a young Tribe infielder from the Dominican Republic.

"Now, write the word—*socks,*" said Vizquel.

Wilson took a pen and slowly wrote s-o-c-k-s.

"Good," said Vizquel.

Wilson smiled.

"Now, try *pants*," Vizquel said.

Wilson tried to write the word, but made a mistake.

Vizquel corrected him, then had Wilson write it again.

P-a-n-t-s, Wilson wrote

"That's good," said Vizquel.

"I never saw one player take the time to teach another English like Omar was doing with Wilson on that day," said Davis.

That's because Vizquel remembers what it was like to sign with the Seattle Mariners at the age of sixteen. He had learned his baseball in Caracas, Venezuela, which is the New York City of Venezuela. He learned his baseball on small diamonds with no grass—just clay, dirt, and rocks. He learned his baseball from his father, Omar Sr., who had been an excellent amateur shortstop and later became an electrician. He learned the game with a little salsa, almost fielding to a lively Latin beat. He learned to catch ground balls with his bare hands, compensating for the crazy bounces off the wildly unkempt fields. That is why, to this day, Vizquel comes roaring in from his shortstop position, fields a roller with his barehand and throws all in one motion—much like a third baseman. Occasionally, he even has grabbed a high-hopper with that bare hand to save a fraction of a second in order to throw out a runner at first base.

"People ask me how I can do that," he said. "It's how I grew up learning to play the game."

"And the amazing thing is Omar never drops the ball on those plays," Manager Mike Hargrove said. "It used to scare the hell out of me. I've never seen a shortstop make as many barehanded plays as Omar. With someone else, you'd tell them, 'Don't even think about it.' But if Omar wants to try it, I've learned that he can do it. I'm awestruck by how he plays. I don't know if anyone in the history of baseball has ever played shortstop like him."

Vizquel learned to assume that every bounce will be bad. He learned that every throw was important, and that most first baseman like a soft toss about chest high—so he doesn't cut loose just to show off his arm. He learned that your feet are just as important as your hands when you play shortstop, because good balance and the ability to move sideways quickly determines how you'll handle those difficult plays deep in the hole or those times when you need to charge in to gobble up a slow roller. So Vizquel played soccer, not just because he liked the game but because it helped his footwork in baseball.

Even today, Vizquel will have someone throw an easy grounder to him, and he'll kick the ball straight up in the air so he can snatch it with his glove. Occasionally, he'll do this during warm-ups between innings of a game. The feet. The hands. The glove. The ball.

"It all comes together," he said. "It's all one."

That was something his father preached to him on those rutted dirt diamonds in Caracas.

"I always wanted to be a shortstop because of my father," Vizquel said. "When I was five years old, I got my first glove. My father told me that I had to take care of it. He didn't have enough money to buy me a new glove every year. It had to last at least three years."

To break in his new glove, Vizquel put a baseball in its pocket. Then he took a sock and tied the glove closed. Then he went to bed, hugging the glove close to his heart like a favorite teddy bear. He learned to massage the glove with baby oil. He carried the glove with him constantly.

"Sometimes, I took a nap and used it for a pillow," he said.

As a big leaguer, Vizquel uses only one glove per season, even though he has an unlimited supply. He says it's because he only needs one glove, but it probably goes back to his father and that Christmas present when he was five years old. It goes back to knowing a glove is precious, and "if you take care of it, it will take care of you," as the old baseball men preached.

Vizquel had just turned seventeen when he signed his first pro contract. The Seattle Mariners shipped him to Butte, Montana, where he learned to eat chicken and eggs while breaking into pro ball in the Pioneer League. Every day, it was chicken or eggs. That's all he knew how to order at a restaurant. Those were the first words of English he learned.

"But I also figured out that I had to learn English real fast," he said.

So Vizquel talked to some of his American teammates. He watched a lot of TV. As his handle on the language became steadier, he forced himself to read the English newspapers. Rather than fight his new language, he embraced it—and he promised himself that he'd help other young Latin players to do the same. That was why he worked with Wilson, even though Wilson was the best shortstop in the Tribe's minor league system. Vizquel didn't feel threatened, he felt fatherly.

It took Vizquel seven years in the minors before he became a regular big league shortstop. The problem was his balsa bat, so soft he had to learn how to be a switch-hitter at the Class AA level, which can be very scary. What if the experiment failed? What if all he'd ever be was a good-field, no-hit shortstop? But Vizquel almost willed himself to learn to swing from the left side of the plate, even though it felt about as natural as trying to run with his shoelaces tied together. Slowly, he developed into a fair hitter. He had little power, but he could steal a few bases—and no one played shortstop with his flair or sure-handedness. But he played in Seattle in the early 1990s, where few people outside the Puget Sound noticed.

On December 20, 1993, Tribe General Manager John Hart made a deal that would become one of the most important in the history of the franchise, but few realized it at the time. The Indians were coming off a 76-86 season. They were moving into Jacobs Field, but fans didn't realize what a new ballpark would mean to the franchise. As for trading Felix Fermin and Reggie Jefferson to Seattle for Vizquel, few fans even bothered to discuss it on the local radio talk shows. To them, Vizquel was much like Fermin, another light-hitting, steady-fielding shortstop—probably not much better than Tom Veryzer.

And three weeks after he joined the Indians, Vizquel committed three errors in a game. This from a guy who was supposed to be a Gold Glove shortstop? The impressive sidelight to that dismal day at Jacobs Field was Vizquel standing up in front of the unrelenting glare of the TV cameras, staring straight into the microphones and notepads, and saying simply, "It is my fault. I messed up the game. My three errors cost us seven runs. No excuses."

Vizquel later said he'd never made three errors in a game, "And I won't ever again, I promise."

The next day, the newspapers were full of stories not just of Vizquel's errors, but of his mature handling of the situation, of his willingness to take the blame. A few days later, other players revealed Vizquel played that day with a fever and the flu, and that he was offered a chance to skip the game—but he insisted that he play. And Vizquel himself never mentioned he was sick.

In 1994, he made only three more errors in the remaining games of that strike-shortened season. He won his second Gold Glove. Then he won a third. A fourth. Heading into the 1999 season, he'd won six consecutive Gold Gloves. He'd turned himself into a guy who hits around .280 and steals 30-some bases per season. His passion for the game and good-natured personality have led to the fans embracing him much as they had Boudreau.

In 1995, my father watched Vizquel a lot on TV. Even though he lived in Florida, the Tribe was a regular on either ESPN or another network. My father built his days around watching those games, and it was a wonderful time for him, a release from the bars and chains that the stroke had become to his body.

Then came the postseason.
Then came something called the baseball network.
My father couldn't wait for the playoffs to begin. ESPN had been advertising them, as did one of the networks.

Then came the games.

Only there were no Tribe games on TV, at least not for my father or anyone else in Florida. ESPN would tell him that the Indians were facing Boston that night and stay tuned, but all he'd have on his TV would be the Braves game. Once in a while, there would be the Indians, but only if Atlanta wasn't playing. I'd be on the phone with Karen Cochran, his primary caretaker. She'd tell me how he couldn't find the Indians game on TV. I was utterly confused and angry. I didn't know what to tell her. I had no idea when—or if—the game would be televised.

How was my father supposed to figure out the schedule and reasoning for the baseball network when baseball itself couldn't quite explain it? All he knew was that every playoff game was on national TV before 1995, and when the Indians finally were in playoffs, all the games weren't being broadcast. That made him so mad one night, he turned off the Braves games, watched bowling for a while, and went to bed early.

"Dad, just hang in there, when the Indians make the World Series, you'll get to see all the games," I'd tell him from the Jacobs Field press box.

"Man . . . MAN . . . MAN!" he'd say.

"I know, it doesn't make much sense," I'd say.

I wanted to say something else, but what? What was there to say? Like so many fans of so many teams who didn't happen to live in the city where their favorite teams played, he just wanted to watch his team play in the postseason. Who could blame him?

Thank God, my father did see the best Indians game of 1995.

That was Game 6 of the American League Championship Series. The Indians had a 3–2 lead over the Seattle Mariners in the best-of-seven series to decide who would go to the World Series. That sounded pretty commanding, until you looked a little closer. Games 6 and 7 were to be played in Seattle. In Game 6, the Indians had to face Randy Johnson. In 1995, the

Indians never beat Randy Johnson. No one beat Randy Johnson, especially not in the Kingdome. And if the Indians didn't beat Randy Johnson?

"Charlie Nagy was pitching Game 7, and Charlie, he never likes those domes."

Those words were spoken by Dennis Martinez, the man pitching for the Tribe in Game 6. He said that to *Akron Beacon Journal* baseball writer Sheldon Ocker and myself about five hours before he was to pitch. Martinez was sitting in the hotel lobby, as nervous as a cat in a room full of bulldogs. His eyes darted from one end of the room to the other; his voice never stopped for long. He wanted to talk . . . to anyone.

Ocker and I just happened to come along at the right time.

"I hope these guys are ready," he said. "I hope they aren't thinking that they'll wait until tomorrow just because they gotta face Randy Johnson."

Martinez paused.

"We lose today, we could be in big trouble tomorrow," he said. "Game 7. In the Kingdome? Charlie pitching? You tell me . . ."

Before we could tell Martinez anything, he launched into a long discussion of the managing in the series. Basically, he didn't think much of the job done by either manager. He brought up situations, pitching changes that were made at the wrong times, pinch hitters that should have been used. It seemed to comfort Martinez, dissecting the managers.

Then he said, "I hope I'm not out there by myself."

"What do you mean?" I asked.

"I feel the weight of the world on my shoulders," he said. "And right now, I'm wasted physically."

His elbow hurt. His knee hurt. His whole body hurt.

"I hurt my knee first," he said. "Then I hurt my elbow because I pitched with a bad knee. You know, the knee bone is connected to the elbow bone, the elbow bone is connected to the shoulder bone . . ."

Martinez laughed.

"A mess, that's what I am," he said. "And they're sending me into the lion's den against Randy Johnson."

If you didn't know Martinez, you'd have been ready to bet your last dime on Seattle. But Martinez did this before every big game. He turned it into David and Goliath, only he was David with an empty slingshot. He relished being the underdog, putting the pressure on the other guy. And he *always* had to face the opponent's top pitcher

"You notice, I'm supposed to be an old man, but it's *always* me," he said. "They don't send some young guy against Randy Johnson."

On this October afternoon, Martinez was forty-one years old. He had won 231 major league games. He had made the 1995 All-Star team. His two-year record with the Tribe was 23-11. Martinez first wore a big league uniform with Baltimore in 1976; the Seattle Mariners franchise wasn't born until 1977, so you could argue he had more experience than the entire team he was facing.

Yet Martinez wanted you to believe he was Frank Funk.

Then Martinez grabbed his slingshot. He trudged into the mouth of the lion. He used every cliché in the baseball book. And he beat Randy Johnson, 4–0. He beat the man who was considered the most intimidating pitcher in baseball, a totem pole of a man with a perpetual scowl, seaweed for hair, and a flamethrower for an arm. He matched this man pitch for pitch until one of them blinked—and it was Johnson. The Indians scored the game's first run in the fifth on an RBI single by Kenny Lofton. The game remained 1–0 in favor of the Tribe until the top of the eighth, when the Indians broke through with three more runs.

They were headed to the World Series for the first time since 1954.

I told my father the story about Martinez in the lobby of the hotel. I told him that our conversation with the pitcher ended when Bob Feller showed up. Martinez has a sense of baseball history. He knows Feller is in the Hall of Fame. He also knows Feller never won a World Series game. And before that night in Seattle, Martinez had never won a postseason game.

Feller hugged Martinez. I stared at the two men as they embraced and realized they had nearly 500 big league victories between them. Feller then whispered something in Martinez's ear. They both laughed. Feller handed him "a lucky buckeye." Martinez put it in his pocket.

Thinking about this now, I realize this was the kind of moment that made it so special to be a sportswriter, the kind of moment Hal Lebovitz had so many times when he rode the trains with the Tribe in the 1950s. It was the kind of moment that brought a wonderful smile to my father's face when I told him the story. It was even more meaningful to him because that crucial game in Seattle was finally televised in Florida for him to see.

In the end, it didn't matter that the Indians lost to Atlanta in the World Series. It really didn't.

They finally had gotten there.

That's what counted to me, to my father, to any Tribe fan with a sense of history that predated Albert Belle. I was content to cover the games, just to see what happened. My father was thrilled just to watch them from his favorite chair in Florida. And while we were so many miles apart, during those games we felt as if we were together.

# CHAPTER 20

# Nineteen Ninety-seven

THIS WAS a year that was a shock to Tribe fans. The team lost Albert Belle to the Chicago White Sox via free agency. It traded Kenny Lofton to Atlanta due to a contract dispute. Carlos Baerga had been traded in the middle of the 1996 season because of weight problems as well as a bat that had turned to balsa.

No Belle, Lofton, and Baerga . . .

Yet the Tribe went to the World Series—their second World Series in three years.

What the Indians did was nothing short of remarkable. It demonstrated that owner Dick Jacobs, General Manager John Hart, and Manager Mike Hargrove had found a way to build a long-term contender in the ever-changing free-agency-driven baseball world of the 1990s. It was a true revelation to realize the Indians actually had a great front office, capable of fielding a contender every year!

As this was happening, my father was failing.

Sometimes, I wondered what happened—how did *he* end up being so old, so frail? How did it ever come about that I was in charge? What should I do to make him feel better, to give him a little comfort? In the summer of 1997, I saw my father still working as hard as ever at his rehabilitation, but the progress stopped and he just seemed so tired. He sometimes couldn't take even ten steps with his walker—not without his heart racing, his left hand shaking as he tried to hang on to the walker. I'd stare at his frightened blue eyes, at the sweat beading up on top of his bald head. I'd close my eyes and pray because I knew he was on borrowed time, that he was just too worn out and too beat up to fight back much longer. Sometimes he'd grow so tired, he'd sit in his wheelchair, holding his toothbrush and acting as if he had no idea how it ended up in his hand or what he was supposed to do with it.

Thank God for the Indians—especially their run in the playoffs to the seventh game in 1997. Those games made my father feel alive. They brought us even closer. We really did know what the other was thinking without speaking a word. We had seen enough together to know that if the Indians ever made it to the seventh game of the World Series, something awful just had to happen. We dreamed about it, longed for it, were sure we could handle whatever came about—but still, it was enough to make a grown man cry.

This team has spent most of my lifetime doing things like trading Pedro Guerrero for Bruce Ellingsen. It went from 1960 to 1994—that's thirty-four years—without playing one meaningful game in the month of September. Don't tell me about Boston Red Sox angst or the long-suffering Cubs fans; a veteran Tribe fan will match his misery against anyone's. For thirty-four years, the Indians just stunk. For thirty-four years, they never were in contention. For most of those thirty-four years, Herb Score called those games on the radio, saying things like, "There's a two-hopper to Duane Kuiper, who catches it on the first bounce." A ball goes through Bill

Buckner's legs and you think that's tragedy? Try losing two pitchers in a spring boating accident.

They almost had to pick me up off the floor when the Indians won 100 games and went to the 1995 World Series. They lost, but so what? They'd win it the next year.

And in 1996, the Indians won 99 games—and then were upset by Baltimore in the first round of the playoffs. Roberto Alomar beat them with a homer. Man spits on an umpire, slides on the suspension, then slaps the faces of Tribe fans everywhere.

That's more like the Indians we knew so well.

When the core of that 1995 team (Albert Belle, Carlos Baerga, and Kenny Lofton) was all gone by opening day of 1997, a lot of Tribe fans expected the worst. When the team struggled to win the lame Central Division with only 86 wins, we expected another early exit.

Then came the playoffs, and this team made you fall in love with them.

The 1997 Indians were not as talented or as powerful as the 1995 or even the 1996 model. But it was a team of good guys, a team that played with dignity and respect for the game. It was a team that made you proud.

But still you cry.

You'll remember how your team had this World Series won, was only two outs away from its first World Series championship since 1948. Then they let it get away. They lost, 3–2 in the bottom of the 11th when Florida's Edgar Renteria singled with the bases loaded just past the glove of losing pitcher Charles Nagy.

You'll remember how Jaret Wright gave you shades of Bob Feller in this, the biggest game of his life—the biggest game of anyone's life.

You'll remember how manager Mike Hargrove said his team had no reason to feel sorry for themselves, how they overachieved in the playoffs just to force a seventh game. All of that was true. But it wasn't enough.

You'll remember how Tony Fernandez drove in both runs

to put the Indians in position to win this game in the ninth inning—and how his error in the 11th helped give it away.

You'll remember how Jose Mesa couldn't hold a 2–1 lead
in the bottom of the ninth. You'll remember how Charles Nagy
(of all people) was on the mound in the bottom of the 11th inning. You'll remember the chills you felt when Nagy came into
the game, the utter fear. You just knew they'd lose it the moment Charles Nagy came in from the bullpen. This was not
Charles Nagy's month; this wasn't even supposed to be his
game, as Hargrove wisely chose to start Wright instead. Yet
Nagy ended up back on the mound because there was no one
else . . . because it was fated to happen . . . because these are the
Cleveland Indians. You can spend months, even years, perform-
ing an autopsy on this last game, just as you can dig through
the bones of those old Tribe teams—it won't change a thing. It's
like looking at pictures of a bunch of old relatives and remembering the awful stories about them.

Super Joe Charboneau.

The first man in baseball history to be American League
Rookie of the Year one season, then back in the minors the
next. Heck, he drifted all the way down to Class AA. Yet, when
the Indians were in the World Series, there was Charboneau
doing reports for a local TV station—almost like a ghost of
scary Indian Summers Past.

Herb Score.

There he was in the radio booth. Score came to the Indians
as a left-handed pitcher in 1955, the year after the 1954 World
Series collapse. Talk about curse or coincidence, he was Rocky
Colavito's roommate and best friend in baseball. Score was like
Jaret Wright, only he threw even harder. In 1956, he was a 20-
game winner. Early in 1957, he was hit in the eye by a line
drive off the bat of Gil McDougald. He was never the same.
Score had spent the last thirty-four years as a Tribe broadcaster,
inspiring one of his former radio partners, Joe Tait, to say, "No
one in the history of the game has seen more bad baseball than
Herb Score."

Between his time as a player and a broadcaster, Score was around for approximately 5,000 Tribe games before retiring at the end of the 1997 World Series.

You'd think the man would be allowed to call a World Series win in his last game. You'd think there would be some justice for Herb Score, if no one else. No wonder Score was a bit dumbfounded during those final games. One night, he had rightfielder Manny Ramirez playing second base (instead of Tony Fernandez). Another night, Andre Thornton was pitching, and Thornton is a former Tribe first baseman who retired in 1987.

My father would remind you that being a Tribe fan means watching bad things happen to good people. So, go ahead, shake your head remembering how that ground ball in the 11th inning went right under the glove of second baseman Fernandez—but don't be surprised. Yes, the guy was a Gold Glove shortstop. Yes, he played a solid second base for the Tribe. Yes, he made one clutch play after another in this playoff drive, hitting .471 in the World Series and sweeping up grounder after grounder hit to the right side of the infield.

And yes, the ball he missed wasn't even a difficult play.

He just missed it, to use his own words. Fernandez said he didn't know how he missed the ball—he just did.

But Tribe fans should be used to that, guys missing balls at absolutely the worst time. Yes, the Indians reached the seventh game partly because of their tight infield defense. And yet, an error cost them the game.

Before you drown in your own tears, ask yourself, "If someone told you twenty-five years ago, or even five years ago, that the Indians would lose in the seventh game of the World Series, would you take it?"

Of course.

You'd just want a taste, and you'd welcome the heartbreak. After all, you've waited for the seventh game all of your baseball life.

Then it happens.

They come so close . . . they lose like this . . . and you feel as if your best friend just died. You tell yourself that baseball shouldn't be this important. You tell yourself it's just a game. You remind yourself of all those awful years—make that decades—of bad baseball. You remind yourself how exhilarating it is to have a contender in town.

That is what my father would say.

And yet . . . And yet . . .

It took a long time, but my father reached a point when not even the Cleveland Indians mattered much to him. It was only a few months after the 1997 World Series, the same World Series that made him as happy as he had been in years. He didn't care that the Indians lost. It was fun to watch them play throughout the month of October, to see them win one clutch game after another, to stay up until the wee hours of the morning watching baseball and munching popcorn while sitting back in his favorite reclining chair.

If he could talk to me, I know my father would have said, "Now that was a baseball season."

He loved the wild card, the extra layer of playoffs. It meant more Tribe games on TV, more games to watch at his home in Sarasota. But a few months after the World Series, his right leg turned black. His leg had turned strange colors before, but this time it was scary. Before, it would turn a bluish black, but within a couple of hours it would clear up. We'd see the leg looking a little black, take him to the doctor's—and by the time he was examined, the leg was fine.

The leg that turned colors was on his paralyzed, right side. Despite four years of therapy, it was getting weaker instead of stronger. Despite the best doctors and the best exercises administered by the best therapists, the leg was turning to Silly Putty—and turning colors.

Now the color was black—and it stayed black.

When blood stops flowing, Black Death happens—a blood clot. And when your leg is black as the sky at 2:00 A.M., doctors shake their heads. Doctors worry. Doctors use words like "gangrene." Especially when there is a wound on the foot that refuses to heal, as was the case with my father.

Then the doctors used words such as "amputation."

I could not believe it.

They were going to chop off his leg?

It wasn't enough that he couldn't talk, that he couldn't walk, and that he wore diapers. It wasn't enough that, for whatever crazy reason, his nose would run whenever he ate hot food. It wasn't enough that the running nose embarrassed him as it just dripped right down, sometimes into his food, and he wasn't aware of it until it was too late. The right nostril was part of the right side of his body, which also was paralyzed.

And it wasn't enough that he couldn't drive, he couldn't talk on the phone, and he hated to leave his house because his home was the only place he felt truly safe.

Now, gangrene.

Now, amputation.

The doctors came up with the idea of leg surgery, sort of a bypass in the veins much like they do with hearts. I didn't want to approve the surgery. My father didn't want the surgery. I sensed that for the first time in his life, he just wanted to sit in his favorite chair, close his eyes, and die. There was no more baseball on TV to watch. There were so few foods he enjoyed because, for whatever reason, not much of anything tasted good to him. His right, paralyzed arm hurt. His right leg hurt. His gums hurt, although he wasn't sure why.

And yes, his heart hurt.

I thought he was in congestive heart failure. Doctors said that's "premature," whatever that was supposed to mean. I felt it made no sense to put him through surgery when it was obvious he had so little time to live. It's hard to stand there, telling a doctor that your father is dying. I knew it. My father knew it. The doctor knew it. But the doctors said gangrene was no way to die, that the pain was excruciating.

So I agreed to the surgery.

Remarkably, it worked. At least that was what the doctors said. The circulation in the leg improved. It was no longer black. He was out of the hospital in three days.

But it didn't last long.

Within a few weeks, he was back in the hospital. His leg was fine, but he had begun to bleed from the rectal area. First, they said it was ulcers. Then it wasn't ulcers. The doctors had the ulcers under control, but his heart was failing. He spent eleven days in the hospital for no apparent reason. He was not getting any better. There was little the doctors could do for him. They just didn't want to let him go home, probably because they were afraid he'd die.

I told them that was precisely why he should go home: He wanted to die at home. If he had to die, I wanted it to be at home. I'd take him. He had been the responsibility of my brother and me since he'd had the stroke, and I saw no reason for that to change—so I brought him home. He was tired. He was a little depressed. He knew what was happening. He was also scared.

I knew I had to do something. Feeding him, changing him, giving him medicine, and watching TV with him wasn't enough. He was looking at me with those wide blue eyes for something. He had raised me in the Roman Catholic faith, and until his stroke he went to church every Sunday. So did I. But we never really prayed together—not until his final days.

Like many men of his generation, my father kept things inside. He had bitterness in his heart toward some people who had been close to him. He clung to that, gnawing on it like a bone. For two days, we prayed about this. Then I connected him by phone with a friend who was pastor back in Ohio, a man named Fred Perkins. My father knew Fred Perkins and respected him because he was a Vietnam veteran and owned a meat business in addition to pastoring a small church. He was willing to listen as Fred talked about guilt and anger and letting it go, putting it at the foot of the cross. My father wept and said, "Oh, man . . . Man . . . MAN . . . MAN!!!"

When the converstion was over, he was exhausted.

The next day, he felt a real sense of peace. He was kinder to me, my brother, and his caretakers than he had ever been before. He sensed death was near, but so was salvation.

Eight days later, he passed away.

When people like my father die, you never read about it on the front page.

They never made a million dollars.

They never broke a contract or demanded to be traded.

They never embarrassed themselves or their families.

They never did anything that ends up in headlines.

That's the shame of it.

Being a good father is taken for granted. Being a loyal husband is shrugged off. Working at the same miserable job for too many years to support a family is considered rather antiquated. People such as my father were born during the Depression. They served their country in World War II. They sent their kids to college. They saved and bought houses and cars—and hated credit cards.

They believed in God and country.

They didn't rock the boat.

They made this country work.

For that, most of them have been ridiculed or—even worse—ignored. They lived, they raised families, they died. A couple of paragraphs on the obituary page serves as the final words. Those words don't tell you that these people are the reason so many of us are teachers, coaches, lawyers, doctors, and writers. They paid a big part of the bill for us; they demanded that our lives be better than theirs.

They seem to die as they lived—quietly and with little fuss.

My mother and father had two children. My brother and I have both graduated from college, and they made sure that happened, even though they were only high school graduates. Watching my father work so hard for so long at a job he loathed was one of the reasons I became a sportswriter. His advice always was, "Don't worry so much about the money; get a job you love."

This came from a man who was often obsessive about money, partly because he lived through the Depression. But I still got the message.

Now I find myself thinking about his life, and mine. He never was very good at expressing his feelings; he sometimes had a real knack for saying the wrong thing at the wrong time to me—or so I thought. Now I know better. Now I feel closer to him than ever because of all we shared after his stroke. We had no choice; we had to pull together. After he couldn't talk, I thought so much about what he'd once said. He spent a lot of time reminding his family, "Anyone can end up in the poorhouse." I heard a lot about the Depression and the poorhouse from my father.

I heard a lot about FDR and World War II and gas rationing.

I heard a lot about a hard life I'll probably never know.

Then I saw what those lessons meant to my father, how they helped him carry himself through the stroke's aftermath. I can still see this proud man, once a strapping minor league first baseman, feeling helpless in diapers. But I also see this strong man who took me to ballgames, who used to pick me up, put me on his shoulders, and carry me around the house—making me really feel like king of the hill.

I'll always remember our games of catch, his potbelly hanging low and the cigarette dangling out of his mouth as we tossed a ball back and forth in the driveway.

I'll remember him taking me to ballgames when he'd rather just take a nap. I'll remember him telling me to get a job I enjoyed, so I wouldn't have to endure the same grind that he faced day after day—and decade after decade.

I'll remember my father in his final years, how he struggled to take just a few steps with his walker. I'll remember how proud he was to be able to take off his own shirt. I'll remember how he had to brush his dentures, comb his hair, and use his electric razor in the same way, the same order—every day.

I'll remember how he loved to play the card game he called Greek Rummy—and play it hour after hour.

I'll remember his final happy moments, when the Indians made their glorious run through the American League play-offs. I'll remember knowing he was sitting in his favorite reclining chair, feet up and eating popcorn while watching those games—the same games I was writing about from the press box. I'll always be grateful that baseball could make him happy when he had little else to smile about.

I'll remember how he wanted to die at home, how he clutched my left hand, looked at me with wide, questioning blue eyes. I'll remember the bleeding ulcers, the blood clots that turned his leg black, and the suffering that seemed like it would never end.

I'll remember how he died at home, in his sleep, on his seventy-eighth birthday.

Eight months after my father's death, I sat in Yankee Stadium watching the Indians play New York in the American League Championship Series. He never saw a game here; he never went to New York City in his life. He never saw Boston or Fenway Park either, he'd have loved watching the Indians win their first-round matchup there.

Suddenly, I missed him so much—more than at any time since his death. I thought of the agony that was the last six months of his life. I thought of the relief we felt when he finally passed away—not just my brother and myself, but I know my father felt it, too. He was just sick and tired of being sick and tired. So while I've missed my father, the ordeal of his last years has kept me from wishing that he were still alive.

But on that day in Yankee Stadium, I did. I knew if he

were still alive, he'd have awakened that morning with one thing in mind—the Indians were playing the Yankees tonight. He'd build his day around waiting for the game, watching ESPN and other all-sports stations for their reports from Yankee Stadium. He was like a lot of shut-ins and elderly people who can't get out to the ballpark: Their world is reduced to their house or rest home, their sports come solely from the TV set, but the thought of a big game that night makes breakfast taste better, the sun shine brighter, the chair feel softer, and the people who take care of them a little nicer.

When I write stories, I think of men and women such as him reading them. I think about what they'd want to know. I try to talk to them as if they were sitting right next to me in the press box. I worked at my father's food warehouse for parts of six years while I was in school; I remember the breaks that came at 10:15 and 2:15, with lunch from 12:15 to 12:45. I remember sitting on the floor of the men's room with the guys who were smoking—the men's room was the only place that was allowed. I never smoked, but I wanted to be with them. And I remember them taking out the sports pages and talking about the stories, about what the Indians were doing. That was when I began to dream of being someone who'd write the stories those guys would argue about in the men's room as they sucked on Camels and Kools. There would be something very honorable about that.

I still think so.

I think of so many people like my father who can't get to the games, who rely on newspapers, radio, and television to tell them about the Indians. I wish they could have sat next to me in the press box when Charles Nagy pitched the game of his life at Fenway Park, beating the Red Sox in Game 3 of the Division Series. I wish they could have seen David Justice's double rattle around the nooks and crannies of center field in Game 4 at Fenway. I know my father would have enjoyed being at Jacobs Field when Tribe manager Mike Hargrove went nose-to-nose with umpire Joe Brinkman, sparking the Indians to come back to win Game 2 against the Red Sox.

A man named Bill Dannemiller wrote, "I had the privilege of going to Game 2 of the Boston series with my father. It was so routine going to games with my dad that it usually wasn't a big deal. That day had a different feeling. It was a beautiful fall day, and I began to think how truly special this was. I began to think of all the games I'd been to with my dad, and we were going to an Indians playoff game in October! A game that was rare in my lifetime . . . I'll never forget it. The shoddy umpiring, the ejection of Hargrove and Dwight Gooden, and the energy from those events that sparked the fans . . . I'm just grateful that the last game I saw with my dad was that one. I felt like I was sharing a great moment with Dad, and I was conscious of it while it was happening. That day was a gift from God. . . . My dad passed away about the same time the Indians were being eliminated by the Yankees. He had a stroke. . . . I'm sad because I'll no longer be able to spend time with him, but I'm happy for all the memories—especially that last game."

My father's last game came a year earlier, but I know how Bill felt.

When it came time for my father's funeral, we had to pick clothes in which he was to be buried. We thought about the usual shirt, tie, and sport coat—but my father hated wearing a suit. For a while, he had to wear a tie and jacket on his job; the moment he stepped out of the warehouse door, the coat came off . . . then the tie . . . then the collar was unbuttoned. By the time he reached his car, he had it all off.

I would not send him off in a shirt and tie.

I thought about what he loved to wear, especially in the final years of his life. Whenever it was a little chilly, he wore his bright red Tribe jacket and Chief Wahoo cap. When I was a kid, I loved to dress up in my Indians stuff—and at the end of his life, my father was the same way.

So that was how we buried him.

Tribe jacket.

Tribe sweatpants.

A Tribe cap at his right hand, a copy of *The Curse of Rocky Colavito* in his left.

# Sources

Back copies of the Cleveland *Plain Dealer*.
Back copies of the *Cleveland Press*.
Back copies of the *Cleveland News*.
Back copies of *The Sporting News*.
*The Cleveland Indians* by Franklin Lewis.
*Cleveland Indians Encyclopedia* by Russell Schneider.
*Roger Maris: A Title to Fame* by Harvey Rosenfeld.
*Roger Maris: A man for All Seasons* by Maury Allen.
*Shoeless Joe and Ragtime Baseball* by Harvey Frommer.
*Veeck As in Wreck* by Bill Veeck and Ed Linn.
*The Curse of Rocky Colavito* by Terry Pluto.
*Burying the Curse* by Terry Pluto.

# Index

# About the Author

Terry Pluto is the author of seventeen books and a sports columnist for the *Akron Beacon Journal.* He twice has been honored by the Associated Press Sports Editors as the nation's top sports columnist for medium-sized newspapers. He is a four-time winner of the Ohio Sports Writer of the Year and has been nominated for a Pulitzer Prize for commentary.